EUROPEAN JOURNEY

MORET
12th May
E. Sanders

MORET

EUROPEAN JOURNEY

By PHILIP GIBBS

Being the Narrative of a Journey in FRANCE,
SWITZERLAND, ITALY, AUSTRIA, HUNGARY,
GERMANY, *and the* SAAR, *in the Spring and
Summer of 1934. With an Authentic Record
of the Ideas, Hopes, and Fears Moving in the
Minds of Common Folk and Expressed
in Wayside Conversations.*

Illustrations by E. LANDER

DOUBLEDAY, DORAN & COMPANY, INC.
Garden City 1934 *New York*

CONTENTS

v

CONTENTS

ILLUSTRATIONS

vii

ILLUSTRATIONS

EUROPEAN JOURNEY

Introduction

THE IDEA OF THIS BOOK was to make a journey through Central Europe twenty years after the beginning of a war whose consequences are still unsettled and unpaid. My mission was not to interview statesmen and politicians, or the new rulers of the human tribes—one knows in advance what they will say —but to get into touch with the common folk whose lives are unrecorded and whose ideas are unexpressed. What are they thinking now, twenty years after that war which scarred the bodies and souls of those who survived? Do they ever think back to those days, or have they forgotten? How do they like these dictatorships which have put them under a new discipline? What hopes have they for the future? What kind of life is theirs, at a time when almost every nation is in the trough of a depression which is called "a crisis" but is, perhaps, the end of a system by which civilised peoples have, for a thousand years, carried on their life and industry? All that would be interesting. I was to take things as I found them, not writing a political discourse or getting answers to leading questions. It was to be a journey descriptive of things seen and heard in this Europe of 1934, including any beauty I might find, or any little adventure by the wayside. I might see places which do not find their way into the guide books. I might give a picture of Europe not written by special correspondents despatching political news from the capitals, or accounts of crime and disaster.

Villages might give me more than capitals, and peasants more than politicians. My material would be the minds of men and women in fields, and factories, small shops, and modest inns— the ordinary working folk who know nothing of secret diplomacy or high finance but try to get a living somehow, at a time when mysterious forces are at work, robbing them of the fruits of their labour and altering the values of work and wages. I might hear new points of view—the unknown philosophy of the ordinary man—by chance talks over café tables, and get a glimpse of truth below the surface of this bewilderment of life, in this time of transition between a past which is dying and a future which is unshaped. I might even get a clue to what is happening in the minds of young men who wear different-coloured shirts and march about with strange devices on their way to new adventure.

The idea of such a book appealed to me, though I saw its difficulties. I should want a lot of luck to get into the minds of such people. They are not glib talkers, as a rule. In England they are inarticulate. Abroad they might not reveal themselves easily to a stranger speaking their languages badly. Could I be sure of getting good results if I sat down at a café table and tried to make conversation with an intelligent-looking fellow, ab- sorbed in an illustrated paper, or watching the girls go by? The journey might lead to nothing but guide-book stuff, boring to my readers and failing to carry out the essential idea. But the risk was worth taking, and looking back at my journey now, before I begin to write about it, I am astonished at the way in which a number of men and women did talk to me, with a frankness and sincerity which was sometimes dangerous to them, and which was often illuminating. And I marvel at the intelligence of these people of humble class whom I met on the wayside or in the market places. They looked out on life with shrewd eyes. They were realists. They had summed things up. They were able to express their ideas, their fears, their bitter- ness—some of them were bitter—with remarkable clarity and gift of speech. That is a quality which we do not find so often in this country. These foreigners are good talkers. Their ideas jump into their words. I heard some unforgettable phrases, terribly ironical, as outside the new Palace of the League of Nations at Geneva, where some labourers told me things which made my hair stand up

But there will be nothing sensational in this book for readers in search of that. It is a journey book in Europe today, with word pictures of life in villages, cities, inns, and market places. I was not exclusively interested in political ideas or economic facts. If a man talked to me about art, or the making of a horse-shoe, I was as much interested as when another man talked to me about the political situation bearing down upon his life and liberties. But what I do hope will be found here is a true picture of this Europe—certain countries of it—as I have seen it in recent months, with a desire to keep my eyes clear of political bias and all prejudice.

Just before making this special journey for the purpose of this book, I had visited five capitals in Europe, and part of this experience finds a place here. It was a time of seething passion below a troubled peace. In France troops or police had opened fire on a vast crowd in the Place de la Concorde, stirred to indignation and fury by the corruption of politicians, revealed by the scandals of the Stavisky case. Something was stirring below the surface of French life, and many groups were forming and arming, I was told, with rival policies for a change in the structure of government. In Austria there had been the Fascist attack on the Social Democrats of Vienna, and a new dictatorship had been set up after a bombardment of the work-men's dwellings. Germany was threatening to force a Nazi union with their Austrian sympathisers. A kind of ultimatum had been sent to the Dolfuss government. Italy was behind the Austrian Heimwehr—the Fascists—backing the independence of Austria against union with Germany. There was an ominous tension in Europe, as I found in those capital cities, and after-wards in the minds of villagers and small folk whose lives and business were involved in these political issues. It was, from the point of view of human interest, a good time for such a journey, though a bad time in the history of these peoples.

For the purpose of this book I decided that motoring was the only way of travel. Walking would have been better, as Hilaire

Belloc went along the path to Rome, but to walk through
Europe would have taken a long time, and the beginning would
have been ancient history at the end of the walk, if I had gone
far. A horse would have been good, but I am no horseman, and
that animal is slow-going also for a hurrying age. A motorcar
has great advantages. One can stop where one likes. It has
room for companionship, and I am a fellow who detests loneliness, especially when journeying, though I have made many
travels alone in this Europe which I was setting out to see again.
My companions will be met in this book, now and then, as the
Chorus of my wanderings. One of them I call the artist, because
he happens to be one, though no one would suspect it by his
face if they look for æstheticism and soulfulness. He has a humorous face which might belong to the skipper of a tramp steamer
with a suitable vocabulary for stevedores, though it might also
belong to an archdeacon with sporting instincts and a taste for
old prints and old brandy. As an artist he used to draw with his
left hand, as I knew when thirty years ago he and I went on
many expeditions together to feed the maw of Fleet Street, he
with his pencil and I with my pen. During the war, when, as a
good officer of Fusiliers, his discipline was softened by a sense
of humour which kept his battalion laughing at very odd times,
a bit of steel smashed his left arm—just like the war, which was
utterly without consideration for the fine arts!—and he had to
learn to draw all over again with his right hand, and learnt very
well. He is known by the name of Uncle in many cities as far
away as Delhi, having a host of honorary nephews and nieces
who have painted with him and laughed with him.

My other companion I call the novelist. He is in appearance
a strange and attractive combination of Lord Robert Cecil as
a young man and that great genius Grock in his noble moods.
Temperamental, excitable and nervy, he has a childlike quality
of responding to every new impression. He is well known as a
novelist, critic and poet, and I inflicted great agonies upon him
by claiming the literary copyright of all things seen and heard
on this journey we were to make together. There were moments
when he found this condition intolerable. His fingers itched
to record his impressions. The scenes through which we passed

incited him to prose and poetry. The sight of a piece of blank paper was a temptation he found hard to resist. Looking back on the journey I have a sense of guiltiness in having thwarted his genius. But it was my job. We joined him in Paris and dragged him down from the society of French dukes and other aristocrats to our social level, which was strictly limited to second-class hostelries and ordinary folk.

After Paris, where all good journeys start, we had another companion. He was the driver of a hired car and went by the name of "Gaston," because he had once known a barber of that name in St. Petersburg, when he was the captain of a cruiser in the Russian Imperial Navy, before Revolution came, destroying all caste, and turning Russian nobles, if they escaped with their lives, into Parisian taxi drivers, or sword dancers in cabarets, or waiters in restaurants. Gaston, as we called him (until the last day, when he took off his chauffeur's cap and parted with us on level terms), was a fine driver and a good companion. There were moments, as in the crossing of high mountains, when a little habit he had of taking both hands off the wheel to describe one of his adventures in the Russo-Japanese War, or to expound his philosophy of life as the driver of a hired car, was slightly disconcerting to a nervous man like myself. But confidence was quickly restored, and need never have been lost, because Gaston has the most tender regard for his passengers' lives and has a record with American matrons and English spinsters unbroken by any accident. There was a competition to sit by his side, because of his dramatic narratives, his knowledge of life, his inexhaustible supply of amusing anecdotes. We suspected for a time that when we put up at second-class inns our Gaston was doing himself proud in the best hotel. We slunk round corners for cheap lunches of bread and cheese and beer, believing that our driver was regaling himself at a more expensive restaurant. Those suspicions were unfounded, though he needed a good lunch, having driven hard on certain days. But always in the evenings, when we three sat at some cheap café talking to a chance acquaintance, we saw our Gaston emerge to take in life as it might exist in a small provincial town. He was no longer in his chauffeur's cap, but set forth with a felt hat at a fine angle and the swinging stride of a naval officer.

Later, for a week or so, we were joined by a lady. That was not part of the programme, and was a lamentable affair, as I shall tell.

The Way to Paris

I AM NOT AIRMINDED, having no confidence as yet in that way of travel, and we went to Paris by train and boat. It is the way most people go, and I want to begin this journey in the ordinary way among ordinary people. They were very typical that morning on the platform of Victoria Station. In spite of the world "crisis" and the weakness of English money on foreign exchanges, there was the usual scurry of passengers. Among them was a group of gay lads in yellow and blue pull-overs, with neat-looking girls in tailor-made frocks. Somehow this class still contrives to exist in a world which is slipping beneath their feet. A young German and his wife sat in our carriage, busy with their accounts after an English holiday. Opposite me sat a Japanese gentleman, anxious about a box studded with brass nails. Unlike most of his countrymen, he was tall and thin, with skin drawn tightly over his high cheek bones. A Japanese business man, I thought, going to undersell every market in Europe with cheap goods made by sweated labour on depreciated yen. I was wrong there: he was a naval officer, as afterwards I learnt.

My artist friend sloped down the platform to buy himself a tin of tobacco.

"Remember the customs," I warned him. "You'll get into trouble."

"Not a chance!" he answered. "I always say *blessé dans la*

guerre,' and they let me through without a murmur. It's a great asset in France—this war wound."

He was reminiscent on the boat. We both remembered cross-channel passages when these boats were crammed with troops, mostly sick in foul weather, all wearing life belts because of German submarines. They were keen to get out to France, having trained until they were stale in English camps.

"Nearly twenty years ago, old lad, and now a dream!" said the artist. "It seems like yesterday, all the same."

One of the stewards talked about that ancient history.

He had been soldier and seaman too, having served at the Dogger Bank and in the Dardanelles and then with the West Kents in France before he got a "packet" in his leg.

"The Froggies are not very happy with themselves just now," he said, looking towards the coast of France. "I wouldn't be surprised if there's a lot of trouble. Queer world, ain't it? People don't seem to settle down."

Another man looked towards the coast of France, now very near after an hour's run. It was a man I knew slightly, very rich, and very prominent in the philanthropic world.

"Those are the people who are making all the trouble," he said with his gaze on France.

He saw the query in my eyes and hastened to hedge.

"Of course, one understands their fear. Twice invaded, and with Germany growing strong again! One has to sympathise with their nervousness. All the same——"

He sighed heavily, smiled, raised his hand in a farewell salute as passengers began to get busy with their bags.

"Good old Calais!" said my artist friend, "and no temporary gentleman with a megaphone to direct all officers to the A.M.L.O. and the R.T.O., and other mystical potentates who directed the destiny of our little heroes and told them where to go and die."

It was a mistake, perhaps, to harp like that on old memories of a forgotten war. It was a sign that we two were getting old. Nobody else gave a thought to that ancient history—nearly twenty years ago—as they went down the gangway and touched the soil of France. We scrambled through the customs and were

duly passed, but my artist friend was startled when two sinister-looking men demanded to know what he had in his pockets. That *"blessé dans la guerre"* didn't work this time. But the thing which bulged in his pocket was a fair-sized sketch-book with which, later, he was to record many old buildings and charming scenes.

"Strange!" he murmured. "Not even my honest-looking mug disarmed their nasty suspicions. Gave me quite a shock!"

2

The Japanese naval officer was our opposite companion in the train to Paris. In the corner, facing him, was one of those hearty ladies of uncertain years who carry the spirit of Surrey and Sussex to the uttermost parts of the world, where their husbands still govern a far-flung Empire in which something seems to be slipping. She refused the lure of the luncheon bell. She was well provided with sandwiches. Having eaten most of them, she looked over to the Japanese gentleman and thrust the remnants at him in a paper bag, like poking a bun to a bear.

"Have a bit!" she said cheerily.

The Japanese naval officer—a man of immense reserve and dignity—was startled. For a moment his ivory skin flushed slightly, as though he felt himself insulted. Then he understood. This was an English lady. He had met them before. She meant to be kind.

He raised one of his thin hands and smiled.

"You are very obliging. But I am not hungry."

There were three other ladies in the carriage, one with dark and rather sad eyes, another sleepy in her corner, and the third more elderly but with the complexion of an English rose. The artist opened conversation with them. They were on their way to Singapore, and my friend was envious of such luck. He had always wanted to get out to that part of the world.

"You wouldn't be so keen," said the more elderly of the ladies, "if you had made twenty-five journeys out there, as I have."

The dark lady with the sad eyes—until they were lit up now

and then by laughter—had left a small child at school in England. Perhaps that accounted for the sadness. She was the
mother of a Wee Willie Winkie, and I thought of other mothers
I knew who have this wrench at the heart when they go back to
husbands in Malaya and India. Truly this trainload of people
on the way to Paris was typical of any train that goes from
England, and no other nation would despatch such passengers.
The Empire counts for something still as an outlet for the
Mother Country, although the Dominions have shut down for a
time on immigration, and have declared their independence.
It would be harder for public-school men to find some job of
work—it is getting harder every year—unless there were still
places out East wanting managers, engineers, administrators
and traders. If ever the Empire cuts away—if India goes more
than it has gone—we shall be a little middle-class island overcrowded with place hunters, shabby-genteel if not poverty-
stricken. Aren't we getting like that, as far as those who used
to be called the Upper Classes are concerned?

3

The restaurant car was fairly full as we passed Etaples.
None turned from the food to look at the cemetery there in the
sand dunes. Forgotten all that, and perhaps it's just as well,
twenty years after. I was one who remembered, having a
morbid kind of mind. I remembered a hot day early in the
war when a military band was playing the marvellous song of
death, which is Chopin's Funeral March, and when lines of
men in khaki reversed arms as a coffin was carried past on a gun
carriage, with the body of a man who had been a very cheery
soul before he had a headache and knew that he had only one
chance of escape in—I have forgotten how many chances—
from a disease called cerebro-spinal meningitis, in which he
was an expert. He was one of the heroes of the war, and around
him in the sand dunes lie a crowd who were brought down from
the battlefields on their way home.

"*Vin rouge ou blanc, monsieur?*"

"*Encore du pain, s'il vous plaît.*"

Amiens came after a heavy lunch—damnably expensive when one reckons the English exchange—and a doze in the corner seat. Amiens! It meant nothing to a young man in a blue pull-over, smoking a cigarette in the corridor and very bored with this train journey. He was in his nursery when crowds of muddy men walked down the Rue des Trois Cailloux, looking through the plate-glass windows of the shops, after living in wet trenches under shell fire, to which in due course they would return. Round the corner of the cathedral was Charlie's bar, until it was blown into splinters. A jolly good spot for young officers—English, Scottish, Canadian, Australian —who drank three eggnogs before dinner at the Godebert and slept at the Hôtel du Rhin, the last sleep they might have between sheets. There was a waiter at the Hôtel du Rhin, a Gascon type of fellow, boastful and amusing. I met him after the war. "France," he said, "was the steel shield between England and Germany. France saved England, and there is no gratitude, because, after all, England is a nation of shopkeepers and with a few exceptions, monsieur, without a soul." It was only a year or so after a million of our men, mostly boys, had fallen in French fields.

Creil. . . . Yes, I remembered Creil. It was Sir John French's headquarters for a night or two on the retreat from Mons. There were many stragglers with bandaged limbs. "The Germans came on like lice," they said. . . .

There was a team of English football players on the train. They talked with a northern burr, and looked forward to a good time in Paris. Their manager, as I think he must have been, was a little fellow, four feet six in his socks, who had drunk too much at lunch and was still drinking after tea but became more humorous as the hours passed. The young German whom I had noticed in the train at Victoria thought him priceless as a joke, and abandoned his wife to laugh at him. A little Italian also was vastly entertained. They sat in the restaurant car drinking whisky. The Scot paid, and when the waiter brought him his change, in French silver, he scattered it on the floor with a noble gesture of disdain. He saluted the young German—a handsome and merry fellow—by raising his right arm and shouting, "*Heil Hitler!*" He had moments of great gravity when he told the Italian that Mussolini was "a good lad," and when he assured the young German that if ever he came north he would find some good Scotch whisky waiting for him. "I fought the Germans," he said, "and I like them. A fine people. To hell with all enmity!"

The German laughed heartily and presented his card.

"I have a little villa in the Mediterranean," he said. "You must be my guest."

"You're a bonny wee lad!" said the Scot, putting his arm round the neck of the Italian, who screamed with laughter.

The waiter pretended not to hear his call for more whisky.

The Scot thrust his hand into his pocket and pulled out a handful of silver which he scattered over the floor again.

"Trash!" he cried. "Trash! Bring me whisky, boy. *Heil Hitler!*"

There was no time for more whisky. We were getting into Paris, past the boxlike factories, past the allotments and shacks, past workmen's tenements with washing hung from strings across the windows. There was the Sacré Cœur, white on the hills of Montmartre.

Paris!

III

The Spirit of Paris

I ALWAYS GET A THRILL of excitement on arriving in Paris and plunging through the tumult of its traffic in a taxi driven by an acrobat like a trick cyclist, making astonishing swerves, and avoiding collisions with half an inch to spare. There seems to be no order in this chase. It seems to be go-as-you-please in a wild whirligig, but really there is some mysterious law governing this moving tide racing to the boulevards. Somehow—with luck—one escapes death.

But it is not this traffic which excites me. It is the spirit of Paris and a thousand memories of all that Paris means in my own life and in human drama. I can hardly guess what this city means to those who see it for the first time, and especially to those who have no knowledge of its history and people, like English trippers who nudge each other on cross-channel boats and look forward to a week-end in "Gay Paree," with night life and naughty ladies. The hideous vulgarity of this tradition —exasperating to the French—still lurks in English minds of a certain class. To me Paris is still the city of Danton and Camille Desmoulins—I see their ghosts in the Palais Royal—and of Victor Hugo and his Misérables, and of Alexandre Dumas and all the pageant of historical romance. To me, as to many others, its old houses—they are pulling them down ruthlessly—are haunted by the lives of poets, and scholars, and poverty-stricken fellows, who had some little flame in their souls to keep them warm, though there was no carpet on the floor and Mimi hung

13

her petticoat across the window against the draught. The *Vie de Bohème* still goes on. Thirty years ago I wandered, and lingered, by the bookstalls along the quays. They are still there, though so much has changed. One can still get cheap wine and good conversation in the restaurants on the Left Bank. Genius is not dead in Paris, nor wit, nor the audacity of youth, though the Parisian has lost some of his gaiety under pressure of anxious times. I have had many adventures in this city and made many friends. I go back to it always with pleasure—and a little sadness because one grows older and things change.

We put up at a modest hotel behind the Madeleine, and after dinner strolled out to breathe the air and get into the heart of Paris. It was not long after the shooting in the Place de la Concorde. We drank a vermouth at the Weber in the Rue Royale, and one of the waiters told me of what had happened there on the fatal night.

"This restaurant was a field dressing station. The wounded were carried in constantly. It was a tragic affair, and the politicians—those dirty dogs!—will have to pay for it. It was a massacre of honest folk—the *anciens combattants de guerre*—who were protesting against corruption. You have heard of the Stavisky scandal?"

Yes, I had heard—who has not? Every newspaper in France was crammed with details of its sinister ramifications implicating many famous names in France, if one could believe these newspaper accusations. Stavisky, one of the greatest swindlers of the world—most nations have produced one or two—had, it was said, bribed politicians, ex-ministers, even judges, for years after they knew that he was a forger of bonds sub-scribed to by middle-class folk out of their small savings.

L'Action Française, the Royalist paper edited by Léon Daudet, had abandoned all restraint and was using every name in the vocabulary of abuse against the suspected personages, calling upon the youth of France to overthrow a government steeped in corruption and degrading public morality. Murderers and assassins were the mildest names applied to those who had given the order to fire on the crowd in the Place de la Concorde. It had been a middle-class crowd made up of ex-soldiers, clerks, business men, and boys of Royalist views belonging to L'Action Française and the Croix de Feu. They had marched down from the boulevards, smashing newspaper kiosks, and tearing up the railings round the trees as weapons of offence or defence. The Chamber of Deputies was their objective—that talking shop of politicians with whom they were furiously indignant. The police has been overwhelmed. The Gardes Mobiles had been unseated from their horses and badly mauled. Somebody had given the order to fire. Thirty people had been killed and a thousand wounded, including a little maidservant watching the scene from a window of the Hôtel Crillon. This shooting had aroused a storm of fury in public opinion. The French government under Daladier had yielded to this demonstration of rage and indignation and to the panic of the deputies, some of whom were chased like rats when they dared to show themselves. A brave old man—M. Doumergue—formerly President of the Republic—had been summoned to form a national government. He had made an eloquent appeal to the patriotism of the French people, promising a full inquiry into all scandals and the punishment of all who might be implicated. It had done something to appease passion, but when I arrived in Paris I was told that this government could not hold the situation very long and that there were all the symptoms of revolution in the mind and temper of the people. Young men belonging to many political groups of the Right and Left were buying cheap revolvers. Underneath the surface of French life there was, said my friends, a smouldering fire.

There was no sign of that when the artist and I walked across the Place de la Concorde after dark. It was a scene of peace and astonishing beauty. It seemed as though Paris were illuminated for a day of triumph, though it was not so. It was lit with lamps which flooded the public buildings. The statues of the cities were touched by these fingers of light, dazzling white in that great empty space where few people passed at this hour. We stood looking into the Tuileries gardens. The grass was turned to a vivid emerald, and down the vista towards the Petit Caroussel and the darkness of the Louvre a fountain was lit by a light which made its water like leaping crystal.

"Magic!" said my artist friend.

But the most magical was what we saw from the bridge leading to the Chamber of Deputies, guarded now by armed police. It was Notre Dame, flood-lit and perfectly white, with its tall towers and spire and pinnacles and gargoyles clear-cut against a velvet sky. It was dreamlike in its beauty—a cathedral of light in a city of enchantment.

We walked up the Champs-Elysées to the Arc de Triomphe. The business world has moved that way in Paris, away from the Boulevards where the best shops used to be. Under the Arc built to commemorate Napoleon's victories a little flame was leaping, seeming to go out now and then, and then rising again from some hidden fire. It is the Flame of Remembrance for those millions of young Frenchmen who fell in the World War. The traffic surged round it unceasingly, and it was too rash an adventure to walk across the wide space, through that circling tide of motorcars and taxis, to get near the shrine. We stood watching it from afar. No hat was lifted, as far as we could see, because of that leaping flame and its message of the dead. The taxis hooted. Humanity went on its way to drink its vermouth or meet its women. Even the flame was dimmed by brighter lights down the Champs-Elysées advertising automobiles de luxe.

2

I became friendly with a man of early middle age in the hotel behind the Madeleine. He was a handsome man, with the warm complexion of a southern Frenchman, and very bright vivid eyes in which an inner fire shone. We had a talk in a salon furnished in the style of Louis Quinze, with faded tapestries and gilt-backed chairs, a little tarnished. In the same room a young man was talking earnestly to his mother-in-law who seemed to be annoyed with him, as I overheard. My new acquaintance with the vivid eyes was anxious to tell me about the political situation in France, but dropped his voice and looked round watchfully now and then across his shoulder.

"Monsieur," he said, "you must understand that what happened on February the sixth in the Place de la Concorde was due to the indignation of respectable people with the disgusting immorality of a government which is entirely composed of assassins, thieves and charlatans. They have betrayed those who fell in the war, and those, like myself, who have survived the war. They are essentially corrupt. They sell France to forgers and robbers like Stavisky. They weaken France so that Germany becomes arrogant again. They paralyse all government by political intrigues for personal gain. The situation, monsieur, is intolerable. It must be changed. There are young men in France, and men not so young, like myself, who intend to change it."

"In what way?" I asked. "What is the alternative?"

His vivid eyes looked straight into mine, and I saw the fire of fanaticism in them—a dangerous fire always, and one which alarms me.

"Nothing can save France but the return of the Monarchy," he told me. "I am a Royalist, as I am proud to affirm. I was in the Place de la Concorde with the Camelots du Roi, who are all Royalists, as you know. With us were the young men of the Croix de Feu, not Royalist but strongly on the Right. Our movement is spreading rapidly. Everyone who believes in the ancient traditions of France, in its need of discipline, in the vital necessity of cleansing up this gang of ruffians who are now in power, is advancing towards the monarchical idea."

"In the provinces?" I asked.

That question checked him for a moment. He thought within himself before answering.

"The provinces remain aloof," he admitted. "They are tainted by a tradition of so-called democracy. They are more interested in beetroots and turnips and the market price of pigs. But it is Paris that counts. It is Paris which has always led the way. In Paris we make the revolutions which the provinces accept, as history tells. They will accept a king when he is crowned in Notre Dame."

"The Duc de Guise?"

"Certainly! He is the legitimate King of France. We acknowledge him."

He glanced over his shoulder again at that young man who was having earnest conversation with his mother-in-law.

"All this is a little dangerous," he whispered. "Excuse me."

He bowed to me politely and departed with his Royalist faith and hopes, leaving me much interested by his conversation but convinced that he exaggerated the Royalist feeling in France and the number of its adherents. Everything he had said was a paraphrase of leading articles in *L'Action Française*, which I read in my little bedroom, with the noise of traffic surging like an endless tide below my window. I did not believe then, and I do not believe now, after talking with many citizens of France, that the Duc de Guise will ever be crowned in Notre Dame.

3

It was outside Notre Dame that my artist friend made his first sketch, with a *demi-blonde* at his elbow, on the table of the terrasse at a corner café. I watched the faces of the passers by, these types of Paris, going on their business—students from the Latin Quarter, shabby and ill-shaved; neat little shop girls with high heels tapping on the pavement; huge-shouldered fellows from the meat market; sallow clerks; young soldiers in *horizon bleu; agents de police;* old men stooping to pick up cigarette ends; and an endless stream of middle-class folk of no special costume or character which might fix them in any category. All their faces, I thought, looked anxious and strained, without gaiety, unless my imagination was falsely at work because of that tragedy in the Place de la Concorde. Paris was not amused just then with political, private, or world affairs. Business was bad, I was told a score of times. Once the most cosmopolitan city in the world, getting great wealth from its visitors, it was now without a tourist traffic. The artist and I had walked the whole length of the Rue de Rivoli—once crowded with our race —without meeting a single man who was obviously English or a single woman whom we could tell as our own. Amazing that! Gone were the boys who used to wear plus fours in the capital of civilisation, as though it were a golf course. Gone were the harassed patrons of cheap tours. The seller of unpleasant post-

Paris
May 1934

PARIS

cards edged near to us with his well-known leer, but slunk off at the scowl of an artist who is one of our bulldog breed. Business was bad for such exploiters of vice and the purveyors of meretricious pleasure. Night life in Montmartre had died.

The cabarets were empty. An occasional American, keen to see the sights, sat alone listening to jazz music, wailed at him by a starving orchestra. All other kind of business was languishing. The jewellers' shops in the Rue de la Paix saw only the noses of people who gazed at their glitter through plate-glass windows. Nobody was buying jewels, real or artificial. The modistes were bringing down their prices but not doing well. The middle-class Parisian was groaning under taxation, direct and indirect, which skinned him. He took no comfort in the fact—denied it indeed —that taxation is heavier in England. *"La vie coûte cher,"* he answered to any inquiry about the cost of living. *"C'est effroyable."* And things had gone wrong in the government of his country, more wrong than ever perhaps since 1870. The Stavisky scandal had been a dreadful revelation. It was a profound shock to every honest Frenchman. It hurt his pride. It was the cause of fear. They had had no idea that things were as bad as all that. Then happened that shooting in the Place de la Concorde. A horrible crime! A new sensation was the murder of a judge named Prince—certainly a murder connected with the Stavisky crimes to hush up evidence against high personages. Every edition of every newspaper caused another shudder in the soul of Paris. I don't think I was wrong in thinking that the faces of these Parisians, passing the corner café opposite Notre Dame, looked anxious and strained.

I went into the Cathedral. It was cold and quiet there. All these transitory troubles, these passing anxieties, assumed a different value inside that old shrine of history. It is strangely bare of memorials, unlike our Westminster Abbey, overcrowded with statues, and monuments, and tablets. It is stark in its austerity. But it is thronged with ghosts for those who remember history—the ghosts of all French life since the beginning of its glory. How many tears have been shed here by women whose names are like a lovely litany in the pages of French history books! How many crimes have passed through the brains of men standing here before the altars! How many cries for pity, for pardon, for the help of God, have been uttered here in aching hearts when France was unfortunate in war, when enemies were at her gates—no more than twenty years ago—when many sons of France lay dead on many fields! All the characters of Dumas came here—the Valois, princesses of Burgundy, and Henri IV, to whom Paris was worth a Mass. Ronsard stood here behind a pillar and watched the fair necks of pretty women. Victor Hugo stared up the high nave and peopled it with strange company. Marie Antoinette prayed here, knowing that Terror was creeping close. A host of genius, loveliness, gallantry, villainy, has passed between these aisles into the ghost world. . . . Outside the doors beyond this quietude there seemed to be trouble brewing again in this city, where human passion has fought so often behind barricades.

But there is always intelligence at work in single minds that stand aloof from the conflict. Paris has many philosophers in all her classes. One of them was down there below the Pont Neuf with a long fishing rod. *L'Action Française* might use up the language of vituperation, boys might march against the Chamber of Deputies and get shot on the way, but it is fine to fish in the Seine and to think of the folly of men. So I saw Frenchmen fishing during time of war when the Germans were very near Paris, and again, in Arras, when they were no more than four and a half yards away from the Maison Rouge which was held by the French, who received me politely, in a drawing room with plush-covered furniture, and let me look through the sand bags at the windows. The French are great fishermen.

4

I came in touch with French intelligence along the quays where the artist, having finished his sketch of Notre Dame, lingered over old books and old prints. He had found many a good thing at these bookstalls in the long ago—original sketches by Forain and Steinlen, sold for a few francs and now priceless.

I spoke to one of these book vendors who was arranging his stall.

"Did you see anything of what happened on February the sixth?"

Yes, he had seen most of what happened. It was not amusing.

He was an *ancien combattant*. He had hoped never to hear another shot, especially between his own people.

He was a middle-aged man, with a face tanned to the tint of old leather by this open-air life along the quays. He had a straight look in his eyes, and the nose of a Norman ancestor. When I asked him about the feeling in Paris and the spirit of the young men he took time for thought. One cannot sum up the spirit of a people or of a city without a moment's reflection, and perhaps not then.

"Ninety-nine per cent of the French people are moderate," he said. "That is my opinion. That is my experience. The danger comes from the two extremes who are in a small minority but make a lot of trouble. But France, in my judgment, will stay a long time in the middle. People talk more than they mean. Words are cheap. Socialism in France is not fanatical. It is not revolutionary. It represents the liberal-mindedness of the great majority, a little to the Left, but not too much to the Left. The Communists exist. In Paris there are numbers of them, but they too talk words which, mostly, are meaningless."

"What about Fascism?" I asked him. "I am told that many young men in Paris are really Fascists, though they call themselves by different names, such as Royalists and Young Patriots."

He dusted one of his books and placed it back carefully.

"Youth wants to take charge," he said. "It wants to wrest power from older men. It's impatient. Can you wonder? It's a hard time for youth nowadays. There is much unemployment. The high cost of living keeps them poor, without much margin for amusement. They have many anxieties and sometimes a sense of anger. Over there—" he pointed to the Latin Quarter —"there are many young men who have to study hard without much hope. They do not always eat enough. I know. I talk to them."

He told me that business was bad for books. Many stared at

his store and dogs-eared them, but did not buy. His American customers had disappeared.

"One day they will come back," he said hopefully.

He was silent for a few minutes, moving to arrange another pile of books. Presently he came back as though he wanted to say something else.

"The problem of life is always difficult, monsieur! In every age, no doubt. There is always change, and it makes trouble. It is hard to adapt oneself to change. Things get broken. Hearts too, sometimes. But life does not remain stationary. One must have change, unless there is death. Youth moves on to new ways. We older men don't like it. We are afraid, perhaps. We suffer. But that is life, is it not? So in France now there will be changes. Youth will insist. There will be more trouble. But I assure you we are a moderate-minded people. We desire peace and order. We are not fanatical. Good-day, monsieur."

I set down his talk exactly as he spoke. It seemed to me very wise and very true. He stood, down there by the Seine, for the common sense of France in middle age and in middle-class Paris. I respected him.

5

"*La vie coûte cher*," say the French housewife and the French hotel keeper and the French peasant. That is true, especially to an Englishman who has exchanged his money into francs at a heavy discount.

That hotel behind the Madeleine was quite expensive for a small place. At least, a pound a day is not too cheap. And one could not lunch or dine, I found, at a place like the Cheval Pie or the Restaurant de Père Louis—one of those Normandy kitchens which are very popular in Paris now—under twenty-five francs, which amounts to six shillings or thereabouts. But one can still feed cheaply in Paris, if one looks about on the Left Bank for a place where students ease their hunger of body, if not of soul. The artist and I found such a place in the Rue St. Jacques. It was called La Belle Etoile—an attractive name—and it advertised, very plainly for passers-by to see, that *déjeuner*, of three courses including wine, was 5.75 francs.

"One and fourpence halfpenny. Not beyond our means!" said the artist, who was all for doing things cheap and leading the simple life.

A party of students sat at the next table outside this restaurant. The girls were hungry and studied the menu with care to find how much they could eat for five francs seventy-five. So did we. It seemed to be an admirable menu, of ample nourishment. But there was a snag somewhere. From the students' table we heard an ominous word uttered at intervals by a good-natured waiter with a not-too-white apron to protect his black suit.

"*Supplément, mademoiselle!*"

"*Mais, comment donc! Qu'est-ce-que vous voulez dire avec ce sacré supplément?*"

We met that snag early and often. My friend ordered *petits pois*, for which he has a passion.

"*Supplément, monsieur*," said the waiter.

It was a *supplément* of twopence-halfpenny for *petits pois*. The same for *choux-fleurs*. The same again for *pommes frites*.

"To hell with all *suppléments!*" said my friend who has the soul, but not the face, of an artist. "I'm going to feed for five francs seventy-five."

We stuck closely to the *carte du jour*, and with admirable results. It was a satisfying meal, including a quarter of wine for each of us, which, I swear, tasted like wine. It was as good a meal as afterwards, in reckless mood, we had at an expensive restaurant which nearly wrecked our financial programme. And we had excellent conversation with the waiter, who was a man of wit, good-humour, and sound ideas. When called upon to cut up the meat for my friend because of that smashed arm, he was quick with sympathy and consideration.

"You were then wounded in the war, monsieur? I also, but more lightly. It was not very amusing, that war!"

"Oh, I don't know," said an artist who was also a soldier. "It had its moments. Not a bad war! Any chance of another?"

He spoke in English, having the theory that any foreigner can understand his way of speech. The waiter laughed heartily, suspecting a joke from the humorous eyes of his customer. I interpreted the question, and it excited our little waiter and made him eloquent, to the annoyance of a student waiting for the *blanquette de veau.*

"Another war, messieurs? Do not think so! There will be no war if France is asked. Let me tell you what I believe and know. I tell you not only as a waiter in a restaurant but as an *ancien combattant de guerre* with many comrades. If a vote were taken—what is called a plebiscite—the whole of the French working class would be against war, for any reason, I wish you to understand. I say *for any reason.* There would be revolution first. . . . Excuse me, gentlemen, a moment."

He was being hailed by the young man impatient for his *blanquette de veau.* One of the women students consulted him on an item in the menu, to which he answered with a familiar phrase.

"*Supplément, mademoiselle.*"

He came back, smoothing down his not-too-white apron, and I asked him whether there was much Communism in Paris among the working classes and the factory hands. There had been Communist riots following the shooting in the Place de la Concorde.

"Negligible!" he answered. "French Communism is not dangerous. It is on the lips only. Naturally, a few groups have scuffles with the police now and then and loot a few shops. That is their way of amusement, like your English football. All Frenchmen are, of course, critics of the government. It is our privilege. It is a tradition. I am myself a talker and a critic of the government. We read too many newspapers. That is a bad habit because the newspapers exaggerate everything. Those journalists, messieurs! *Sacré Nom!* Those journalists who make up lies and stir up hatreds and create false views of life! They are the cause of much evil in the world. Without them we should not hear so much about a war which they do their best to bring about."

The artist was in cordial agreement with the waiter. He was in favour of shooting quite a number of journalists in every country *pour encourager les autres.*

Our waiter talked largely on life. And life passed down the Rue St. Jacques as we sat at the little table of the Belle Etoile.

A loud speaker was giving forth noise—the shriek of a soprano singer—an evil innovation of Parisian life. Some nuns were escorting a procession of young girls dressed in white for their first Communion. I noticed how many coloured men were loping past our tables. Every minute or two one of these darkies went by. France has broken down the colour line, and North Africa is invading Paris—to the horror of the Germans who believe in Nordic blood for Europe. . . .

We ended a pleasant meal—*sans supplément*. It was worth one and fourpence halfpenny.

6

That afternoon we took the Métro to the Buttes de Chaumont, a place unknown to English tourists but interesting. It lies on the outskirts of Belleville and La Villette, the working-class quarters. The Butte de Chaumont is a small park in which there are several little conical hills from which one has a view over Paris. In the old days Forain and Steinlen, those great artists, used to come here to get their types of working folk and the squalid comedy of the poorest quarter. In their sketches frowsy women nurse their babies at the breast, and the children of poverty play about among grotesque types of ragged humanity. Under the bushes young sluts from the stalls in La Villette fondled their lovers from the meat markets and flea-infested tenements. My friend has some of these sketches, as I have said, and he looked round for the same types. They had gone. Some change had happened. Something had lifted from the life of the French working quarter—its squalid ugliness, its filthy poverty. The people in the Butte de Chaumont were like those one sees in Battersea Park. There were no ragged children. The mothers with their babes were neatly dressed, with stockings of artificial silk. Forain would not have known them.

We walked through Belleville. It was not always safe to walk through Belleville in the old days before the war. It was the home town of the apache. Now it is as safe and respectable as the Rue de Rivoli. Great gaps were being torn out of old

streets, and new houses were going up. Here and there did I
see bits of old Belleville as it existed before the war—seventeenth-
century houses with blackened walls, courtyards overgrown
with weeds or littered with refuse, wooden staircases, broken
and unsafe, leading to rooms with dirty mattresses bulging
through their windows for an airing. In the Rue de Belleville
some of the old shops still stand. Jews were selling second-hand
clothes. But the working classes in Paris, as well as in London,
have reached a higher standard of life, in spite of the world
"crisis," and unemployment, and the cost of living.

7

We paid a surprise visit to Mr. and Mrs. Yellowboots and
little Malvina, their daughter. Yellowboots, who has another
and Russian name, was so called because he appeared, after
frightful adventures in a war and revolution, in a pair of boots
of that striking and attractive colour, and a suit of clothes
hanging loosely about his body, which had shrunk in times of
privation and peril without destroying his gift of laughter or
the soul of an artist in him. He is one of those thousands of
Russian refugees who have found a home and some kind of
work in Paris, which has been kind to them. His wife, who is
also an artist of great talent, was pleased to see us. Little Malvina gazed at us with wonderment and listened to our talk
with big eyes in which a smile lurked. Yellowboots appeared
later, having heard on the telephone of our arrival. He had a
bottle of wine under his arm for our entertainment, but he
nearly smashed it when he embraced my friend with cries of
delight and kissed him a score of times on both cheeks.

"No more of that fondling!" cried my friend, pretending to
be embarrassed, but inwardly delighted by this loving welcome.

We drank the wine, after raising our glasses and calling
down blessings. We went on our hands and knees to look at
the latest masterpieces by Yellowboots, who designs the most
exquisite patterns for silk and other fabrics. At frequent intervals Yellowboots desired to kiss my friend's bulldog face. We
laughed for no reason at all, except this reunion of friendship.

And then, later in the night, Yellowboots became serious and talked of the state of things in France—his adopted country. He was anxious. He didn't like the look of things. That tragic happening in the Place de la Concorde had been a great shock. There were forces at work which were moving towards conflict. He had been through one revolution. . . .

8

I called on a French friend, who is famous for many books written with exquisite style and careful scholarship, to which he adds wit and irony. I had already notified my visit by telephone and had frightened him by asking him to tell me his views on the situation in France. He admitted his alarm when he held out his very thin and delicate hand.

"I am not a politician!" he said. "I know nothing about politics!"

I reassured him and glanced round his room, which is elegant.

"You are a philosopher," I told him. "You know what is happening in the minds of men and women. Tell me what is happening in the French mind."

He made a little grimace of amusement and then sighed.

"There are many minds," he answered. "None of them thinks alike. One cannot say France thinks this—France thinks that."

He handed me a cigarette and curled himself up in a deep leather chair, with one hand, so thin and delicate, over the arm.

"It is true," he said presently, "that things are happening in the minds of France and especially in the younger minds. It's inevitable that the younger men should become impatient with the Parliamentary system. They are touched by the same impatience which has led to some form of Fascism in other countries. They don't like what is happening in Germany under Hitler, or in Italy under Mussolini, but they are inclined, here in Paris, to adopt the same methods of action, and to use sticks instead of votes to obtain decisive results in cleaning up the political situation. Everybody admits that it wants a lot of cleaning up!"

I gave him time to think things out. He went deep down in his leather chair. I almost lost sight of him.

"Paris has always been tempted towards dictatorship," he said after that silence. "You remember the affair of General Boulanger? The present time is opportune for dictatorship—but no one exists. There is a great lack of leadership in France, due, no doubt, to the losses in the war. It's the same in England, isn't it?"

He explained the causes of contempt into which the French Chamber had fallen. The group system with its political bargainings to support or overthrow a government led to constant crises and unstable policy. The deputy had too much power, he thought. It put temptation in his way, and being ill-paid, he yielded.

"The power of the Executive will have to be increased," he said, "in order to limit the independence and political corruption of the deputies. It's the system which is at fault. It is the cause of corruption."

He put one long leg over the arm of his chair.

"It's not that French deputies are necessarily more corrupt than English members of Parliament," he said. "But as Parliament cannot be dissolved in the English way they can't be unseated and have a certain tenure of office. They have also more patronage in their hands. A provincial deputy is subject to constant pressure for jobs and influence. He's hail-fellow-well-met in local society. He's surrounded by sycophants eager for a place for their sons, their nephews, or their business friends. The patron of the café where he takes his apéritif shakes him by the left hand—nearest to the heart!—and whispers into his ear. Women surround him with flattery on behalf of their husbands, sons, or lovers. His patronage reaches down to the smallest provincial posts, and he likes to please the people who support him. Owing to the centralization of Paris the provincial deputy is the liaison officer between the provinces and the capital, so that rural France believes in Parliamentarism and feels itself in touch with the central government when a deputy returns to report on what he has done, or is pretending to do. for local interests."

"Is there any real importance in the Royalist movement?"
I asked.

My friend smiled from the depths of his chair.

"Royalism without a king, perhaps," he answered.

Undoubtedly, he thought, there was a movement to the
Right among young middle-class men, especially in Paris.
They were disgusted with so many revelations of corruption
in high places. The Stavisky affair had brought that to a head.
They had been scornful of the Parliamentary system before
then—like so many young men in Europe. They could not
bring themselves to adopt the Fascist system or phraseology,
but they were joining groups—La Jeunesse Patriote, La Croix
de Feu, and so on, which called on them to rally in defence of
discipline and order against the disintegration of the national
spirit.

"The situation is undoubtedly serious," said my friend.
"There is an exasperation and bewilderment at the moment
in the French mind. Some change will have to be made."

9

On the last night in Paris, before we went motoring through
France and countries beyond, the artist and I went up to the
Dôme, where we had a rendezvous with Yellowboots and his
wife Malvina. The novelist who was going to join us on the
motor journey was also there with some of his friends. The
Dôme at Montparnasse was an old haunt of my companion.
He had known Kiki and many other models who, poor dears,
had drunk too much absinthe there and had been too easy in
their loves. He had known many members of his craft, who had
come here in pre-war days with large portfolios holding the
fruits of genius, which went begging in the market place until
death brought dealers and many dollars. He had exchanged
drinks with English and American art students who had called
him "Uncle," and laughed very loudly when he said, "Be your
age, kid!" at some folly on their lips, or some confession of
despair. He had watched with savage irony the antics of would-
be artists, who posed for the public with long hair and La

Vallière ties and dirty fingernails; and he had grinned at the
simple tourists who came here to see the *Vie de Bohème* and
thought these charlatans were marvellous. I also knew the
crowd at the Dôme before the war, and afterwards, and must
confess that I have seen the most poisonous collection of de-
generates around the tables whom one might find in any city.

It was a fair evening, warm and light. Spring had come, and
there were leaves on the plane trees, and a touch of ecstasy in
the air of Paris, the most enchanting city except one, which
is Rome, when spring comes. The traffic surged up the Boule-
vard Raspail, and from the direction of the Boul' Mich'.
Many tables were taken outside the Dôme. But I was quick
to notice certain changes. Most of the people here were speaking French instead of American. It is very noticeable now
in Paris that one hears people talking French. And the charlatans—those poseurs with long hair—had gone, swept away,
poor wretches, by the brutal force of an economic crisis. Most of
them perhaps had starved to death or had taken jobs in the
Galeries Lafayette—serving out socks, instead of atrocities
called Art. It was possible that they had cut their hair and
cleaned their fingernails. There was no small boy selling dolls
with limp legs and arms, for the cushions of American ladies
who could afford to pay five dollars for one of these spineless
creatures. The waiters had time to breathe, and there were
empty chairs for late comers.

The novelist arrived, pleasantly excited by the thought of
the journey ahead. He and the artist exchanged glances, like
the touch of swords to try each other's steel. Yellowboots and
his wife were introduced, and I found my hand grasped by
one of the novelist's friends, a young Frenchman whom I knew
already. He has a passion for England. He loves English people
and English gardens and English weather—a proof that he is
a very exceptional kind of Frenchman. The novelist raised his
hand and smiled across the table, and I could see the glint of
adventure in his eyes. He had another friend, whom he presented across a Grand Marnier. He was English, as I saw at
a glance, with a good athletic figure and steel-blue eyes in a
clean-cut face. I had heard of him. He controls a big organisa-

tion in Paris. He is a war-time flying officer who still pilots his own machine.

I sat between him and Yellowboots. Around us there was a buzz of talk and the clink of glasses and the traffic of Paris. Coloured lights gleamed across the pavement. Taxis circled round each other in the wild whirlpool. Somewhere a loud-speaker was blaring out jazz. Presently, of course, there was a street row. One can hardly sit for half an hour at any terrasse outside any café in Paris without seeing a street row. The crowd rushes out to see what happens. It interferes in any good quarrel. Complete outsiders argue fiercely on the merits of the case and sometimes fight it out. This was an arrest: some drunken fellow had been making a nuisance of himself and abusing an *agent*. He was resisting half a dozen *agents*. Some of the crowd were on his side. At least, that is what I guessed, without enough evidence to swear to facts. All very amusing! It is sad that one can't sit down in London outside a café and watch life go by. In Paris there is no need of other amusement than to stare at faces as they pass; faces which are sometimes grotesque like a sketch by Forain, and sometimes very attractive, like a young man who went by the Dôme that evening. He was smiling to himself. A street lamp touched his profile. He had a little black moustache and Gascon-looking eyes. I knew him. It was D'Artagnan, back in Paris. A priest passed in his long soutane, not giving a glance at this crowd of ours. A Negro, with a long loose stride. Two lovers, with their arms round each other's waists—a shop boy and his girl—as though they wandered in Arcady, though it was Paris by night with the hooting of the taxis. A body of young men in blue shirts—members of La Solidarité Française—marched along whistling. So they passed, old and young, sad and gay, haggard and anxious, ugly, commonplace, or good-looking—the faces of Paris.

Yellowboots was talking to me. We talked until it was time for bed. He was saying things worth attention. Before sleeping under a yellow silk counterpane in a small hotel with faded tapestries and gilt-backed chairs, I jotted them down.

"The French are obsessed by fear," he said, in French, which

is his adopted language. "That explains all their political
actions. They are afraid of a new war which they believe is
creeping close. It fills them with terror, that thought. They are
the most pacifist people of any country in the world, but with
this terrible fear in their minds they do the wrong things. It is
like marriage. If there is no confidence between husband and
wife nothing can be done but quarrel and make things worse.
It poisons all their relationship. It's the same between France
and Germany, who ought to get on together. There is really
no cause of quarrel between them. The Germans have given
up Alsace-Lorraine. The Saar is bound to go to Germany.
But it's a paradox—a tragedy—that France will not believe in
the possibility of peace with that neighbour and is helping to
make war certain. It is not because they are militarists. There
is no spirit of militarism in France. You will never see French
children playing at soldiers or war games. Their parents forbid
it. Anybody who was in the war is seized with horror at the
thought of another. But they have this terrible obsession. They
see Germany growing strong again, dynamic, more forceful
than France. It is better organised. It is growing in numbers.
One day, as every Frenchman believes in his heart, Germany
will be ready to attack again. Meanwhile France is weakened
by internal troubles. The French political parties—fiercely
hostile—are becoming stronger. The younger men are recruiting. All the young men on the Right are arming against the
Socialists and Communists, who are well organised and preparing for a fight. If it comes to a revolution it will be a bloody
one. There will be barricades in Paris again."

Somebody offered me a Cointreau. A group of students
was getting noisy at neighbouring tables. A taxicab escaped a
collision by a hairsbreadth. The artist was having an amusing
time with Mrs. Yellowboots. The young Frenchman raised his
glass and smiled into my eyes.

The Englishman on my right gave me his view of things.
He had heard nothing of what Yellowboots had been saying.

"Unemployment is getting bad in France," he told me.
"They admit to over a million. It's due to deflation, of course,
exactly as it was in England before we went off the gold stand-

ard. They ought to bring the franc down to a hundred and ninety-four. With all their gold they could do it easily, with full control, so that it would not get out of hand. That would stimulate trade again and bring back the tourist traffic, without which they are going bankrupt in the big hotels and shops."

I told him about my experience in the Butte de Chaumont, and he agreed that the standard of life among the working classes was now much higher.

"They resist any attempt to bring it down," he said. "That's going to lead to trouble."

Without knowing what Yellowboots had said, he confirmed some of the views I had heard from that friend. Paris was in a state of nervous tension. Young men were buying cheap revolvers. Anything might happen if Doumergue lost his grip.

"They're afraid of war," he said. "They believe it's coming."

"Do you?" I asked.

He was thoughtful and answered after a pause.

"I don't believe the Germans want war. I believe Hitler is sincere when he talks peace and offers friendship to France. That is the strong impression I brought back from Germany. But one young Nazi told me that they would fight for an ideal —equality, for instance—though not for possession. Of course, it would be easy to switch over to war, if something happened which they believed intolerable to their pride and race. An accident may happen."

He had a theory new to me.

"The next war would be fought in the air, if it came, and for that reason I believe it's impossible for Germany."

He saw my raised eyebrows.

"They haven't got the oil to fight a modern war in the air. They make it from coal, but that's not enough."

He hedged a little after that statement.

"Of course, it might be a quick business. Nobody knows what could be done by a swift, deadly knockout blow. A big attack on Paris would demoralise the whole city. They might not be able to stand the strain. They might scream for peace.

So might we! The air is an incalculable factor."

My artist friend grabbed my arm.

"Time for bed! An early start tomorrow!"

The novelist promised to be outside our hotel at nine o'clock.

Yellowboots kissed the artist on both cheeks. They laughed with great amusement and affection on the curbstone beyond the Dôme.

"*Bon voyage!*" cried Mrs. Yellowboots.

The artist and I walked back part of the way to our hotel behind the Madeleine. The streets on the Left Bank were quiet. Paris had gone to bed in that quarter, except here and there where a lamp gleamed behind the blinds in some attic where a student read late.

I thought back to that conversation at the Dôme and to many things I had heard in Paris. It was obsessed with fear, they told me. Young men were arming. There was trouble ahead. The soul of this city was anxious, strained, restless, and divided by passion. There was no sign of all that as we walked through the quiet streets.

IV

Provincial France

I T WAS PLEASANT to leave Paris on a May morning for the open country, with a long journey ahead which would lead us to many places of beauty and ancient history, and across many frontiers, if we had luck on the roads. Our car was driven by a middle-aged man of great dignity who had been an officer in the French army. It was before the time of Gaston who appeared later, as I shall tell. We travelled light, with two bags apiece. On the rack was the artist's sketchbook, with blank pages awaiting his pencil. The novelist excited the astonishment and admiration of France as we went on our way by a remarkable cap which he had bought in Italy. It was a white cap with a yellow peak of transparent celluloid, making him look like a yachtsman who had lost his yacht. I wore a béret which gave me a French touch, I thought, though nobody else did. The artist was determinedly English in a mustard-coloured suit crossed by brown lines at distant intervals in a chessboard pattern. We were in good spirits at the prospect of our future wanderings. We still had some English tobacco. All was well.

We left by the Porte d'Italie, after driving down the Rue des Gobelins. The old ramparts defending Paris had been demolished in 1922, useless as a defence against modern gunfire; but the city still ends abruptly where they stood, and beyond there is only a straggling line of wooden huts and sheds and the untidiness of rubbish heaps before the road stretches out to the fields and farmsteads. It was one of the long straight roads of France, built first by the Roman legions marching through Gaul. It was bordered by tall poplars, and away to our left the Seine made its way through the valley, with gentle hills in the distant haze.

We passed La Belle Epine, where there is an old coaching house at which the postchaises changed horses before the days of motorcars. The kings of France stopped here also, for the same reason, on the way from Versailles to Fontainebleau, with their mistresses and their favourites and their concourse of courtiers. There was a great blowing of horns and jangling of bits and spurs and swords. There was a kaleidoscope of colour, as gentlemen of France in silks and velvets swept off their feathered hats to ladies of great loveliness and easy laughter, who might whisper a word on their behalf to the bored-looking man who fondled them if he liked their allurement. All gone now!—kings and coaches and courtiers and pretty ladies. Our car sped by down a lonely road.

At Orly there is a big aviation camp, military and civil, with an immense hangar which was built for a Zeppelin captured from the Germans. At Ris-Orangis—queer name!—there used to be a post for diligences. Now there is a home for old and broken actors, at a time when so many theatres are half empty in Paris, partly perhaps because of four tall masts we passed beyond the village of Juvisy—the most powerful broadcasting station in France. At Essones the fields were strewn with gold, and in the cottage gardens lilac trees were in bloom, drenching the air with a sweet scent. At Plessis-Chenet the chestnut trees had lit their candles. Peasants were bending over the earth—those French peasants who are forever working from dawn to dusk, scraping, weeding, ploughing, reaping. We were in rural France beyond the restlessness and roar of the great city.

We were in no hurry. We were not going to rush through France like speed maniacs. We halted often by the wayside, and the artist would pull out his sketchbook and get busy, while I wandered round to talk to any human being who might be in sight, or now and then attempted a sketch of my

own under the guidance of a master who could teach a man
without hands to draw with his feet and make something of it.
The novelist was not to be beaten. Later on his journey he
bought materials—sketchbook, chalks and pencils—watched
how the trick was done, became absorbed in this pursuit, and
produced some very creditable efforts, startled into excited
laughter at his own success. They were good hours. What more
does a man want than to sit in a field of France with larks
singing a silver anthem incessantly in a cloudless sky, with the
air perfumed by a myriad flowers, and a little talk now and
then on art and life? Now and then we wanted something more!
A long drink of cold French beer—that was easy to get in any
village—or something to stay the pangs of hunger. Bread and
cheese were good enough, and often we ate it on the wayside.

We halted in a field outside Barbizon. It was the field where
Millet painted his Angelus. The scene has hardly altered.
There was his background almost as he saw it—here and there
a new roof or two—beyond those two bowed figures, so simply
and truly seen, without a touch of mawkish sentiment in their
ugliness and beauty. But it was the novelist who first saw a
signboard which spoilt the picture.

"Isn't that too ghastly!" he exclaimed. "An outrage!"

The ghastly thing was an American advertisement for a
roadside restaurant.

TUMBLE INN
AT ALF GRAND'S
OPEN AIR RETREAT
Real Food.
Mint Julep.

It was a relic of the days before 1929, when Paris was still the
paradise of Americans, and the road to Barbizon was crowded
with their cars. Now they too had gone, like the coaches and
courtiers of the French kings. We were alone on the road to
Barbizon.

We walked through the village with its old cottages and inns and flower gardens. Not much changed since Millet and Rousseau and Corot and other painters came to live here in dire poverty but fired by the flame of genius. Not much changed, except for a few restaurants for tourists, exploiting the fame of men who were paid beggarly prices for their work until they died, according to the rules in those days, and sometimes now.

We went into the studio of Rousseau—the painter and not the philosopher!—who died in 1867. It is next door to a little church with a wooden belfry and remains just as when he dropped his brush to die. On the wall was a charcoal sketch by Corot of a scene in the forest of Fontainebleau, and the well-known picture by Aimé Perret of the Return of the Harvesters. In this studio, I was told, that strange, alarming woman, George Sand, whose ugly face allured every man of genius who came under her spell of passion, first met Alfred de Musset, who became her slave and victim.

The artist was interested in the pictures, which I confess left me without enthusiasm because they seemed rather drab and dull. I had an interesting talk with the guardian, who was an Englishman in exile.

"Barbizon is in a bad way," he told me with a laugh. "It is no time for art. Most of our artists are starving. They can hardly afford to buy their paints. The cost of a frame is beyond their means. Who is going to buy their pictures at a time when most people are having to economise on clothes and food? Why, even the peasants round here are all in debt and hardly able to carry on. They haven't sold their last year's grain. And there is no tourist traffic to keep up the inns and restaurants. It's a treat to see you three gentlemen. Quite a crowd, it seems, after so much loneliness!"

He laughed as though he might be exaggerating the situation somewhat. Then he became grave again.

"France is having an anxious time. I hear a lot about it from my friends. But it's the same everywhere in Europe, as far as I can make out. What's going to happen? Something must be done, or we shall all be ruined. How's little old England?"

I told him that little old England seemed to be doing rather better. We had come through our troubles rather well. There might be others ahead, of course—even worse.

I was sorry to hear sad things in the village of Barbizon. They spoilt its charm a little, and took the colour for a moment out of the wistaria which spilt its purple down whitewashed walls. It's very rough on artists if they can't afford to buy their paints! I wondered what I should do if I couldn't afford to buy the paper on which I write so many words. "Starving," said the guardian of Rousseau's studio. Well, that no doubt was the language of exaggeration. I did not see any gaunt or hungry figures down the village street, and artists know how to feed cheap. Millet and his friend Rousseau lived on two francs fifty a day—equal to about two shillings in modern value. That included wine and lodging. I daresay they did very well and were not stinted in their wine. Money values have changed since then—and the prices of pictures, if they are done by dead men. Daumier, who painted here in Barbizon, was poor, like all his friends. Six years ago a collection of his paintings was sold for eight million six hundred thousand francs.

We went to Millet's house and met a man of enthusiasm and hero worship, who did not seem to be worried about the cost of living or modern artists who are underfed. I doubt whether he thinks very much of modern art or would grieve excessively if most modern artists died of starvation. He was interested only in Millet, in the genius of Millet, in the noble spirit of Millet, in which he found his happiness and consolation. He was the curator of the house—an elderly man like the portrait of a Frenchman in the time of François Ier, with a little beard and full wine-coloured cheeks and luminous eyes. He heard that one of my friends was an artist. He heard that the other was a writer. It delighted him to show us the works of Millet, the letters of Millet, and many of his relics. He brought out big books and made me read certain letters in which Millet had rebuked his critics when they accused him of betraying art by his realism and by painting nature without a sense of beauty.

"Read his answer!" said our new friend. "What nobility of language! What dignity of reproach! What courage of truth! Is not that magnificent when he tells these critics that he is a humble worshipper of nature, and that in his paintings he tries only to depict the very truth of nature which, if it is true, cannot be ugly, because all that is natural is beautiful!"

This enthusiastic old gentleman had an assistant who was a pretty young woman speaking English with the accent of Chicago, in which she had lived a while, but he would not give her much chance with us, and insisted upon our being under his own direction, so that we should see the pictures at the best angle and learn all he had to tell us.

"Look at that unfinished picture!" he cried. "There is nothing in it and everything in it. Close to it looks like vague smudges. Now, come away! See how those masses are revealed as peasants and animals and trees. Astonishing, is it not? What genius!"

He was pleased by our interest and enthusiasm. He would not accept money for tickets or catalogues. Were we not artists and writers? We understood genius. We had a reverence for art at a time, and in a vulgar age, when genius is despised and art goes begging, unless the dealers rig the market.

"Gentlemen," he said, "you have given me great pleasure. I delight in talking with intelligent men. There are so many who are not intelligent. I wish you a very good journey."

We went away with some emotion. There was no insincerity in this welcome we had had. That old gentleman would not take our money. And it was rare and splendid to see such worship of art, at a time when most men were talking politics, and counting the cost of living, and getting worried about next year's income tax. In Barbizon there was one man who was happy in a shrine of art.

The novelist was studying a tablet on the wall of an old hostelry. It bore the name of Robert Louis Stevenson, who had stayed there.

"A queer creature!" said the novelist and critic. "I must admit I don't read him now with vast admiration. Overrated, in my opinion."

The artist would not hear of it. He had read all Stevenson with profound pleasure. He spoke of *The Wrecker* as one of the great novels. And what about *The Master of Ballantrae* and *Treasure Island?* Who could deny their genius?

We discussed the quality of the Barbizon school and the poverty of its painters over a lunch in a pleasant garden. It was a very good lunch, but the bill made us shudder. We were caught in a tourist trap.

"No more of this kind of thing," said the artist. "In future we lunch on a ham sandwich by the side of some babbling brook."

The novelist, who was treasurer, made some notes in a small book and looked for a moment like Grock when he has fallen down the lid of the piano and is patient in affliction.

"O Barbizon!" he murmured reproachfully.

Before leaving the village I went into the little church with the wooden belfry. Over the altar, before which flowers had been placed, there was a picture of the Crucifixion, painted by Hubert de la Fochefoucauld in 1927 as a memorial to the men of Barbizon who had fallen in the war. The sun streamed through the windows. Birds were singing outside. Somewhere a blacksmith was hammering on his anvil. The lilies before the altar sent up their sweet incense.

2

We drove through the forest of Fontainebleau. It was cool and calm down the glades where the tall trunks were criss-crossed by bars of sunlight; and it was very quiet there. No hunting horn sounded, as when Louis XV went with his caval-cade in chase of the wild deer, leaving the hunt sometimes to follow a pretty wood nymph in green velvet and cocked hat. The forest cleared. There was the great château where the kings of France had their pleasant home outside Paris and away from its stench and dangers. (One could smell Paris forty miles away in the good old days, they say.) Our car stopped before the great gates.

"No rubbernecking for me!" said the artist. "I'm not a tourist."

The novelist and I decided to go in and look round, much to the scorn of our friend.

"Guide-book stuff, eh? Very well, you two babes go and amuse yourselves. I shall stay here and make a sketch."

He didn't make a sketch. He fell fast asleep after that lunch in Barbizon.

We had to wait in the courtyard of the Château until our guide was ready. A few visitors had arrived—less than a dozen where, five years ago, before the downfall of the world's money, there would have been hundreds. Not a single English tourist was there, not a single American. Two of the visitors were Germans, I guessed, though never once did they open their mouths. The others were middle-class folk from the provinces, who followed the guide round without comment or any apparent gleam of interest.

Truly such places seem dead. Life has gone out of them. These tapestries, these painted ceilings, these pieces of old furniture, belonging to every period, seem no more than show pieces in a museum like South Kensington where the very vastness and richness of the exhibits tire one. And yet here, at Fontainebleau, these things had been lived with by many kings and queens of France. François Ier himself—Old Tup, as his courtiers called him behind his back—the leader of the Renaissance, crowded these rooms with artists and craftsmen from Italy and Flanders, and sat under the gilded ceiling which he had had put into an older and grimmer chamber. He had sat in the very chairs beneath it with his women, among whom was Diane de Poitiers. Behind these tapestries there had been the whispering of courtiers and courtesans. Like rats they had scuttled along the corridors when a king was angry or lay dying. Mazarin passed through some of these rooms with Marie de'Medici. Richelieu's robes swept these polished boards when he came to tell his king that more of France belonged to him, or that La Rochelle had been captured from the English Duke of Buckingham. At the doorways the King's bodyguard of musketeers had been on duty—among them such men as Athos and Aramis, and the stout Porthos, and such a man as D'Artagnan. The Scottish archers came here. Henry of Navarre had known these passages before he fell on the Pont Neuf, killed by an assassin who waited for him. In these beds had been born the little dauphins of France, the little princesses. In one of these rooms Le Roi Soleil had sat in his wig, his embroidered waistcoat, his satin coat, his silk breeches, listening to reports of great victories—until later he listened to news of unpleasant defeats, in Canada, in India, and on the seas swept by English men-of-war. In other chairs and other rooms Louis XV toyed with his women's hair, yawned at their kisses, pushed the cards away when they were against him, smiled as he heard the whisperings of intrigue behind the tapestry, said, *"Après moi, le Déluge."* Madame de Pompadour looked out of these windows. She rested her fair arms upon the window ledges as for a moment she watched the return of the hunt down there in the courtyard, with men running to help the King out of his saddle, with horns blowing and hounds baying, with the clatter of hoofs on the cobblestones, with laughter and chatter of great nobles and ladies who soon, in a few minutes, would be paying their court to the Pompadour herself, in whom was all power and patronage. And later, that red-headed slut Dubarry would come to the Château of Fontainebleau to amuse a jaded man by the wit of the Paris streets and her own shrewd humour and vulgarity and courage and vivacity. It was before crowds had swarmed into the Place de la Bastille; before a guillotine was set up in the Place de la Révolution, which is now the Place de la Concorde. It was before a little stout man, with an Italian complexion and an Italian name, came here to sit where the Valois and the Bourbons had sat, to use their beds and chairs, to pace these long rooms with one hand thrust into his waistcoat, to sleep on a short hard bed under a canopy which is there still, at odd hours of the day and night, before starting up to dictate more despatches, and those innumerable letters in which his genius and character are best revealed, to send his generals hither and thither across Europe, to arrange for a new campaign in which he would win fresh victories. Josephine was there with him once. Afterwards Marie Louise and a small boy who was called the King of Rome. Napoleon was here when his eagles were carried through Europe in triumph, and when a hundred courts were swept away by a stroke of his pen, following the thunder of his guns. And one day he was here after a hard campaign which had not gone well, knowing that the end had come, or almost the end. His enemies had risen and combined against him. He had made that fatal mistake of the Russian campaign. He had used up his men too recklessly. He had fought his way back to Fontainebleau, and now, at this table, on this very bit of wood before us, he signed his abdication. Out in the courtyard there on the flight of steps, he stood facing his Old Guard. He had to take farewell of them. It was his moment of agony. His words still remain in the memory of France.

"Soldiers of my Old Guard, I bid you farewell. For twenty years I have marched with you on the road to honour and glory . . ."

He went down the ranks of these grizzled men in whose eyes there were tears. In his own eyes there were tears.

"I embrace you all in the person of your general. Adieu, my soldiers. Do not forget me!"

From the ranks of the Old Guard who had been with him at Austerlitz and on all his days of victory there came the last shout:

"*Vive l'Empereur!*" . . .

The little group of sightseers followed the guide round. They did not seem to hear these words or to feel the vibrations of many centuries of French history. Fontainebleau seemed dead in these rooms. All that life was dead. This was a museum and a mausoleum.

We escaped before our time by the courtesy of the guide. Outside the gates our artist friend roused himself.

"Well, rubberneckers! Had a good time?"

He had slept soundly in the car.

3

We spent a pleasant time in the little old town of Moret, beloved by French painters because it still holds the spirit of mediæval France and builds up into a picture which calls for paint and canvas from the low-lying fields by the river Loing. It's a broad fast-running river spanned by a fine old bridge where, close by, there is an ancient mill used for the tanneries of Moret far back in history, and still turning with a rush of water through its wheel. Above old roofs with brown tiles rises the ancient keep, where many kings of France from the sixth Louis came for protection when Burgundy was up in arms. There is something more than a legend that the tax collector and treasurer Fouquet was held here as a prisoner under the guard of a famous musketeer whose name was D'Artagnan.

Higher still is the tower of a church which took four centuries in building, and was first dedicated to the service of God by a certain Archbishop of Canterbury living in exile at Sens, not far away, because he had quarrelled with his king. His name was Thomas à Becket. Two old gates, like the towers to an ogre's castle, still keep guard on each side of the town, and one can still walk round the ramparts which defended its huddled houses.

The artist sat him down in the meadow below the bridge which was good to draw. From the town came the sounds of life, the music of an anvil, the whir of a sawmill, the rush of water, girls singing as they washed their linen on flat stones by the water's edge.

> *"A genoux contre la rivière*
> *Regardez cette lavandière*
> *Qui fait sa prière*
> *Aux poissons."*

I left the river's bank to walk through the narrow streets of the town, and stood, now and then, to look up at a bit of sculpture over a stone archway, or at a grotesque figure carved in wood, or an ancient doorway through which six centuries ago men and women passed into quiet courtyards and timbered houses which have defied the tooth of time. In a wooden shed a man was sawing some planks and standing in a heap of shavings and sawdust. He was humming a tune to himself, and looked up with a smile, seeing me watching him at the doorway.

"Bon jour, monsieur!"

I wished him good day and said something about the charm and interest of Moret.

His dark eyes were amused. He brushed some sawdust off a brown arm.

"You find it interesting? It is not exciting, this town, for those who live in it!"

"Do you like excitement?"

He shrugged his shoulders and laughed.

"I am not discontented. I earn a living wage. That is something these days. I am a carpenter, as you see. I know something about wood. You are an Englishman."

"Yes. I have come from Paris. I am on my way through France."

He repeated the word *Paris* and laughed.

"Paris! . . . A city in which one does not live in tranquillity! The people of Paris get excited with their politics. They read too many newspapers. They are always making trouble for themselves and the rest of France. I have no use for those Parisians. Here in Moret we don't agitate ourselves about the political situation. Life goes on very calmly here. It is, perhaps, because it is a very old town, as you perceive, and we keep to our own affairs, with an ancient tradition of staying behind our ramparts, shut up in ourselves."

"There are no politicians in Moret?"

He laughed again and shrugged his shoulders.

"Some of my friends talk great nonsense. Some of them pretend to be Royalists. Others have an idea that Communism will come to France and make all men equal. I listen and do not say much. I'm a carpenter. I'm earning wages which are not too bad. I have no belief in revolution."

He went on with his sawing after a civil "*Bon jour, monsieur.*"

I looked into a bookshop and had a talk with a man who sold me a small guide to Moret and some picture postcards. He deplored the lack of visitors. Many tourists used to come and look at the old town. Now he was selling very few postcards. He too spoke of the tension in Paris.

"Things are not too good. The newspapers fill me with apprehension. Here in Moret we know nothing but what we read. That Stavisky case is a lamentable revelation of corruption. Something must be done to cleanse the political system. It is, perhaps, fortunate that in Moret we are removed from the centre of political excitement which agitates the younger minds in Paris. Here we live quietly."

They lived slumberously, it seemed, behind their ramparts.

There was a spirit of peace in Moret, perhaps because the sun was warm that day and the only sounds one heard down by the river were the flowing of water past the mill wheel, and the clink of an anvil, and some girls singing as they washed white linen. Some children were making daisy chains in a field below the bridge. An old man slept on a wooden bench. Larks were singing high overhead.

I read a passage in the guide book which I had bought and found it amusing:

This ancient town of Moret is a jewel placed daintily in the lovely frame which surrounds it. In this favoured countryside everything unites to please and tranquillise the mind of man tired by the agitations of modern life. Innumerable years have passed without destroying its beauty. It is a fact that generations born here always have a passionate love for this place. And passers-by, those who only make a short pilgrimage to Moret, cannot resist the delicate and familiar aspect of the place, nor defend themselves against a sense of emotion in the presence of its crystal stream, its old gates and ramparts and towers. And how can they not be inspired by the fine and simple poetry which rises from all these things?

It is a little old town set on a hill. There are grander towns in France. But a true thing was said by that amazing, ugly woman, whom men of genius loved, and whose spirit has passed in Barbizon. "What does the size of things matter?" wrote George Sand. "It is harmony of colour and proportion of form which make up beauty."

I met the novelist on the bridge. He had been hunting picture postcards to add to his collection of ten thousand.

"An exquisite old place!" he cried.

The artist had done a good drawing.

"I like this Moret," he told me. "I could be happy here for three months or so in a nice little pub."

The impression of its charm stays with us.

4

We motored along the way of a lovely river which we crossed many times on our way through France. It is the Yonne, and

often it made me think of the Thames by Cliveden woods, because it flows through the same kind of countryside, gentle and
tranquil. But the fields of France were without hedges, and the
horizon seems farther away. An old woman was leading the
horses while her husband, an old man with gnarled hands and
skin like leather, was guiding the plough. A picture, I thought,
for Millet, had he been alive to paint it. For how many years
had this husband and wife ploughed their land together? How
long ago was it since they had made the first furrow across this
strip of earth? They were old and weathered now, and alone
together.

We came into Sens, much larger than Moret and on a nobler
scale, very old and very important among the ancient towns of
France. Here is the oldest Gothic cathedral in the land, it is
said, and its streets are rich in ancient houses going back to the
time of Henri IV.

We put up at an old inn called L'Ecu de France, the écu
being a gold coin minted in the old days when gold was used for
buying things, instead of lying in the vaults of banks, and when
gentlemen of France made it ring on the tables of such a hostelry
as this. Mine host who came to greet us in his courtyard startled
us by the excellence of his English. Upon inquiry we found that
he had been in the service of the R.A.C. in London for two years
or so, and had been at several hotels in England before the war.
His cuisine was good. His wine was good; and there was something very pleasant in the atmosphere of this old place. Its spirit
reeked of ancient days when coaches stopped here, and travellers from Paris put up for the night to give their horses a rest.
For many centuries this courtyard had resounded to the clatter
of hooves, and the rubbing down of horses by whistling ostlers,
and the distant notes of coach horns announcing new arrivals.
Men who had ridden hard with news for Richelieu had flung
themselves down on benches in this courtyard and called for
wine. In the bedrooms where we slept there had been many
dreams. In the darkness between the walls men had sat up,
trembling, and listening to voices below, at a time when it was
not safe to be a nobleman of France, and the red cap of liberty
was the only fashion. Out in the courtyard one day sat a group

of men in top boots and grey coats. One of them was a short man with an olive-skinned face, who sat with his arms folded and his head bent deep in thought, while his companions watched him uneasily. Because of his visit a tablet hangs on the wall of the Ecu de France:

> A la fin de la
> Campagne de France
> le 20 Mars, 1814,
> Napoléon Ier
> accompagné
> du Maréchal Bertier
> et du Général Gougaud
> a arrêté et déjeûné
> à
> L'Hôtel de L'Ecu de France.

We explored the streets of the city. There is a marvellous old timbered house at the corner of the Rue Jean Cousin, richly and elaborately carved, and in many other streets there are fine doorways and stately courtyards, which recall the times belonging to many periods of French architecture from the twelfth century onwards. But Sens is older than the twelfth century. It was ten centuries old then. The Romans had made a great place of it. They had built temples, theatres, baths and villas here. Spades and picks still strike against their foundations. Bits of Roman wall still stand. Mosaic pavements, rich in colour, have been found beneath the fields around. The Roman gods and memorials of their emperors and captains have been unearthed where foundations have been dug for new buildings. The city of Sens stands above the relics of another great city, which crumbled into dust after centuries of splendour, when the legions marched down the long straight roads and Romanised the Gauls.

It was dusk when we went into the cathedral, and stood

silently looking up the long highway of the nave, with its vista of tall columns and painted arches, so tall, so simple, and so noble.

"Somehow it makes me think of Canterbury," I said.

It was curious that I said that. I did not know until afterwards that it was a man from Sens, a great craftsman and builder—Guillaume de Sens—who had been chosen among all competitors to rebuild Canterbury Cathedral after its destruction by fire in 1175, leaving those parts which the fire had not destroyed. There was another connection with Canterbury which I have already told. The tall ascetic figure of Thomas à Becket, once the worldly favourite of Henry II of England before his priesthood, and afterwards the cause of that cry, "Who will rid me of this turbulent monk?" came here in exile and stayed here until his return to Canterbury, where he died, above a flight of steps when they ran their swords through him.

The cleaners were busy in the cathedral. I noticed that flowers had been placed before the statue of Jeanne d'Arc. A friendly voice spoke to me in French.

"Would you like to see the Treasure?"

It was the sacristan, and I answered doubtfully.

"Isn't it too late? And aren't you too busy?"

He insisted on showing us the Treasury, though it was late, and he had to pull aside the curtains which had been carefully drawn across the windows for the night. There was light enough in those rooms for us to see wonderful things. Some people might think them dull and uninteresting, but I confess I had a thrill when I was shown the very robes worn by Thomas à Becket himself when he was here at Sens. His heart, in exile from England, had beat against them. His thin hands had touched them. They had clothed his living body before it bled from many wounds. They brought back the brave spirit of the man—if one had any sense of history, any sensibility to vibrations which bring the past to the present—this ghostliness of life in which we also pass quickly, leaving something of ourselves, perhaps. There were other treasures, though I will not bore my readers with guide-book stuff. There were, for instance, the belt and mitre and sandals of another Englishman and martyr who came from Canterbury, St. Edmund, whose body lies at Pontigny, and a chasuble made of Byzantine silk, belonging to the very beginning of French history, when Charles the Hammer of France put to flight the Saracens who had ravaged the valleys of the Yonne down which we had passed that day.

I don't know how it was that I fell into conversation with the sacristan about the present state of France, and the troubles in Paris, and the tension all over Europe. In the Treasury of the cathedral the light was fading. We stood in the dusk among the old tapestries—some of them had belonged to Cardinal Wolsey —and cloth of gold, and ivories marvellously carved, brought back from the Crusades by Saint Louis of France and his knights.

"It is terrible," he said, "this talk of a new war with Germany. It is inconceivable that such a horror should come again. The newspapers fill me with despair. Are we all mad? Have our statesmen no sanity—and our young men—and those politicians in Paris? No, I cannot think that it will happen. We are not unreasonable. The French people have an instinctive intelligence and common sense. We must make an arrangement with Germany. Why can't we live in peace with those people—who are Europeans like ourselves? There is no reason for a new conflict between us. The Saar will certainly go back to Germany. They are German folk there. That is undeniable. After that, what do they want from us? We must make an arrangement to live on terms of peace. It is necessary for the future of civilisation. Nobody wants war—none of the working people who remember the last. The next war, if it happened, would destroy everything that is meant by civilisation. Think of these treasures here, this shrine of history! Isn't that a heritage of civilisation? Must not Europe defend itself from anarchy and ruin and death? I am certain that everybody in France is against another war. We are the greatest pacifists in the world, because of our losses twenty years ago. If only we could get rid of fear between ourselves and Germany! Hitler says he wants peace with us. He has said it several times. I want to believe that he means it."

We spoke together for twenty minutes or more. The man was very thoughtful and earnest. I liked his type. He had a reverence for all this treasure in his charge. He loved the history of France.

He was a simple man with great sincerity. We parted good friends.

In the cathedral, twilight had come, and the colours had faded out of the painted windows. A little man came up to me and grabbed my arm.

"Don't go yet," he whispered. "There are many things to see!"

I could not wait to see them, as I was keeping friends from dinner. But the little man became excited.

"I will tell you something that will interest you. I believe I can give you a very great pleasure!"

There was a kind of laughing excitement in his eyes which twinkled at me in the gloom of the cathedral.

"In an hour's time," he said, "I am going to ring the great *bourdon!* It is a big fellow. We have many great bells in this cathedral. One of them weighs sixteen thousand kilos! That is something, eh? There is another of fourteen thousand. Not a little chap! In the belfry there is a very old bell called Marie. She was made in 1375. But I am going to sound the big old *bourdon*, the giant! You could come up with me. It is an experience. It is not unamusing when the reverberations go through every part of the cathedral and travel out into the world! It makes one's soul quiver. It is tremendous. It would give me a very great pleasure to take you up."

I regret now that I did not accept his offer because of dinner at the Ecu de France. This little man was a great character. He was an enthusiast of bell-ringing. It was a great event in his life to hear the giant *bourdon* sending its vibrations over the city.

When I offered to pay for a guide book of the cathedral he refused the money.

"I have not told you all this for the sake of money," he said, "but because I wish to show you my friendship."

I shook hands with him and he patted my hand as another sign of friendly feeling towards a stranger who had come to see his cathedral.

"Listen for the voice of the old giant!" he said.

At dinner in the Ecu de France I heard a deep note which made the room quiver and then filled it with a vibration, long and lasting. The note came again, sonorous, deep, majestic, and very solemn. The vibrations merged. They were loud over the city of Sens. They travelled away across the quiet countryside. More than six hundred years ago they sounded over Sens, and in the ears of its citizens on feast days, and days of victory, and days of mourning. No doubt its rope was pulled by a bell-ringer up there in the tower when the flower of France fell on the field of Agincourt, and on other days of destiny in France.

5

There was a wedding party that night in the Ecu de France. They dined in a big room separate from the ordinary *salle-à-manger*, and several times I went to have a look at them. The bridegroom was a young man with his hair well greased and a nosegay in his buttonhole. The bride was a pretty dark creature with timid eyes. The guests were in their Sunday blacks and belonged to the *petite bourgeoisie* of the city. They were in gay spirits and dined to the music of a gramophone which, I am sorry to say, played American jazz tunes. I would rather have heard the old songs of France. Every now and then came bursts of cheering. Glasses were raised to the health of the bride. Glasses were raised again to the health of the bridegroom. His back was slapped until it must have hurt, by enthusiastic friends. There were shouts for speeches. There was loud and prolonged laughter when the bridegroom forgot all the things he had meant to say and broke down hopelessly and said, "I am no orator, my friends!" Waiting-maids of the Ecu de France were kept busy feeding this company and bringing in more bottles of wine. All the young men and women were well behaved, except for the boisterous spirit of youth. There was no drunkenness, as far as I saw. The dance that followed dinner was decorous and even formal. But I can't give evidence as to what happened some hours afterwards when I was in bed but not asleep. It was difficult to sleep with that wedding party just below my floor boards. The laughter came up through the cracks in the floor. The cheers were louder and more frequent. There was the noise of dancing feet and that gramophone music beating out the rhythm of American fox trots. Now and then

the gay company below burst into song and cheered themselves
again for the success of this melody. The laughter of the girls was
shrill. Other sounds came into my room as I tried to sleep. Bells
were ringing. Clocks chimed the hours, the half hours, and the
quarters. There was the hooting of motor horns as some of the
wedding guests departed in ramshackle cars. Then I fell asleep
and awakened after too short a night to hear other sounds—a
swishing of water in the courtyard, a conversation between two
chauffeurs of whom one was our own driver, Auguste, that man
of gravity who had been a French officer in time of war. The
bells of Sens began to ring in a new day. There were the mooing
of cattle and the bleating of sheep. A siren gave a long shriek, no
doubt from one of the factories where they make fur from rab-
bits, or from one of the flour mills on the outskirts of the city.

The artist had not slept much and was an early riser. He was
sitting in the courtyard making a sketch of the cathedral tower
as seen above old roofs. I joined him and ordered a *café complet*
in the open air on one of the wooden tables. The novelist was
shaving himself at his bedroom window. He greeted us cheerily
with a wave of his safety razor and a soapy smile.

"What a night! I never heard such noise. I'll be down as soon
as the coffee comes."

There were two cars in the yard—one of them ours, the other
a big touring Delage. Our Auguste was in earnest conversation
with a tall, clean-shaven, fresh-complexioned man whom afterwards we knew as "Gaston," ex-officer of the Russian Imperial
navy.

It was Auguste who announced news which he regarded as a
tragedy.

"I have been working all night at the car, but the affair is
serious. I shall have to return to Paris. It is abominable."

For a moment I was dejected.

"How are we going to continue our journey, then? Must we
wait until the car is repaired?"

"Another car has already arrived," said Auguste. "It is there.
I telephoned to Paris."

Great are the powers of Thomas Cook and Son. Noble is
their tradition of service.

E. Lauder
SENS
13 May

SENS

"This," said Auguste, "is your new driver."

An ex-officer of the Russian Imperial navy raised his cap and bowed politely with a humorous smile.

"It is very sad for Auguste," he said. "But these little things happen now and then. I shall be glad to drive you. My garage friends call me 'Gaston.' It is not my name but it does very well."

He had travelled all night in answer to a telephone call from Paris. He denied that he was in the very least degree tired. He was ready to start at any moment we desired.

We were not in a hurry to start. It was pleasant in the Ecu de France and the city of Sens on a May morning when one drank the air like sparkling wine and when the sun gleamed upon the pinnacles and carvings of the cathedral which rose above the old roofs beyond the yard. Its great mass was in shadow against the morning sun.

"Topping, isn't it?" said the artist, who was enjoying himself.

The novelist had a moment's consternation at the news of the breakdown. After much dialogue, hot coffee, and an admiring glance at the artist's drawing—"I can't think how you do it!" —he set off in search of adventure and picture postcards.

I read a book lent to me by the proprietor of the inn. It was a book called *Master Humphrey's Clock* and recorded a visit to the Ecu de France by a very humorous man with vivid eyes which saw everything at a glance. He signed his name as Charles Dickens. It is getting on for a hundred years ago now since he slept a night in that old hostelry, and I was vastly interested in his description. He travelled with four horses and a postilion with a very long whip and immense jack boots. There were ninety-six bells on the horses—twenty-four apiece, and the noise of these chimes on a jolting coach aroused excitement in the Ecu de France which was then called the Ecu d'Or.

The landlady of the Hôtel de l'Ecu d'Or is here: and the landlord of the Hôtel de l'Ecu d'Or is here: and the femme de chambre of the Hôtel de l'Ecu d'Or is here: and a gentleman with a red beard like a bosom friend who is staying at the Hôtel de l'Ecu d'Or is here: and Monsieur le Curé is walking up and down in a corner of the yard by himself, with a shovel hat upon his head, and a black gown on his back, and a book in one hand, and an umbrella in the other hand. Everybody, except Monsieur le Curé, is open-mouthed and open-eyed for the opening of the carriage door. The landlord of the Hôtel de l'Ecu d'Or dotes to that extent upon the courier that he can hardly wait for his coming down from the box, but embraces his very legs and bootheels as he descends. 'My courier! My brave courier! My friend! My brother!' The landlady loves him, the femme de chambre blesses him, the garçon worships him. The courier asks if his letter has been received? It has! It has! Are the rooms prepared? They are! They are! The best rooms for my noble courier. The rooms of state for my gallant courier; the whole house is at the service of my best of friends. . . .

Dinner is announced. There is very thin soup; there are very large loaves—one apiece; a fish; four dishes afterwards; some poultry afterwards; and no lack of wine. There is not much in the dishes but they are very good, and always ready instantly. When it's nearly dark, the brave courier, having eaten two cucumbers, sliced up in the contents of a pretty large decanter of oil, and another of vinegar, emerges from the retreat below, and proposes a visit to the cathedral whose massive tower frowns down upon the courtyard of the inn. Off we go; and very solemn and grand it is, in the dim light—so dim at last that the polite old lantern-jawed sacristan has a forlorn little bit of candle in his hand to grope among the tombs with, and looks among the grim columns very like a lost ghost who is searching for his own.

Underneath the balcony when we return the inferior servants of the inn are supping in the open air, at a great table; the dish, a stewed meat and vegetables, smoking hot, and served in the iron cauldron it was boiled in. They have a pitcher of thin wine and are very merry; merrier than the gentleman with the red beard, who is playing billiards in the light room on the left of the yard, where shadows with cues in their hands, and cigars in their mouths, cross and recross the window constantly. Still the thin Curé walks up and down alone with his book and umbrella. And there he walks, and there the billiard balls rattle, long after we are fast asleep.

Times have changed. There are no coaches arriving at the Ecu de France with four horses and ninety-six bells. But apart from that life goes on much the same in Sens, at least outwardly.

I saw a thin curé pacing slowly up a street with a book in his hand. The wedding guests who kept me awake were the grand-children of the people whom Dickens met in Sens as he went about with his vivid eyes, laughing at a thousand little things which he found unusual. I could see him there in the courtyard where we sat for breakfast. He would have known the place again.

But the minds of men have changed even in Sens. There are new anxieties in them, new passions, new theories of life. I had a talk with a man who knew his city well. It was an old shop-keeper who peered at me through his glasses and was ready to talk. He talked about the political state of France and the unrest in Paris.

"It is this youth which plays the fool. Young men often think they know better than their fathers. They want to push us out of the way and take charge of things. That is absurd. It will lead to great disaster if it happens. I have no patience with these Jeunesses Patriotes and these associations of hot-headed boys who want to change the Constitution and overthrow the Re-public. Of what value is the opinion of a boy of eighteen? What does he know of history or government? Does he imagine that he could govern France with more wisdom than M. Doumergue? It is the conceit of youth! On the other side are the young Com-munists. We have them here in Sens, in the fur factories and the flour mills. They hold meetings at the factory gates. They are not to be taken seriously. They don't know what Communism means. It is just a catchword. It is just a pretext for getting up against the police and buying cheap revolvers which they don't know how to fire. All the same, I don't like the look of things in France. I'm afraid a clash will come. Some madness seems to be getting into the brains of youth all over the world. It is, I sup-pose, impatience with the old system, which is creaking and cracking. One cannot look into the future. Perhaps that is as well. I am an old-fashioned Frenchman. I believe in tradition. I am out of date!"

He smiled at me through his glasses, and we talked for some time in his shop.

6

On leaving Sens I took the seat next to our new driver, who spoke excellent French, and started that series of anecdotes, and serial story of philosophy applied to life, with which he entertained us by turns through France, and Switzerland, and Italy, and Austria, and Germany and all our journey—a most cheery and humorous fellow, in spite of having been dragged down to poverty by revolution and having gone through tragic adventures which would have left most men—but few Russians— embittered. He had had a fine time as a naval officer. He had enjoyed social life during the days of Czardom in St. Petersburg and Moscow. He had sailed to many ports in the Far East and had had gay adventures of youth in China and Japan. He had landed in Constantinople, after the retreat of the White armies, with thirty francs for himself and his wife. Part of that story was left untold, and he skipped it until he related his experience as a taxi driver in Paris, and then as the owner of his own car, until *la Crise* came and threatened to thrust him down again.

We drove along the valley of the Yonne again, that beautiful river which wanders through Burgundy, with innumerable twists and turns. It led us through the arched gateways of Villeneuve-sur-Yonne, one going in and one going out; and then through villages, with names like French songs, on the road to Joigny with its fine bridge over a broad reach of the river. On each side of us were noble woods and gentle hills, and fields where peasants were toiling. The roads were lined with trees, like all good roads in France, and many of the fields were a tapestry of flowers—the flowers of which Ronsard sang in his lyrics to fair women. It seemed as though all the gold in the Bank of France—that gold which should make France the richest country in Europe, if gold were real wealth—had been spilt on these fields. And in others it seemed as though all the silver of the Orient had been melted and poured out on this earth, though it was the silver of flower petals.

We had a good time in the old city of Auxerre, where life is still very busy after two thousand years of history round its market place. It was Sunday morning, and the citizens were

AVALON
1934
E. Bouda...

AVALLON

streaming out from High Mass in the cathedral. All the shops
were open, and there was a fair in one of the squares. The
pompiers seemed to be assembling for a church parade, or something of the kind. They were in gay schoolboy spirits and
chased each other and scuffled together. Down a side street a
battle was in progress between two young men and two young
women. They pelted each other with bits of paper. Some nuns
passed by with a group of children in white frocks, and following
them was a French officer in full uniform with many medals.
We wandered around, losing ourselves in narrow streets with
timbered houses which we should call Elizabethan. Many of
them were finely carved, and I noticed an old tavern above
which was a carving of a man seated at a bench with wine
flagons. At the very entrance of the town is a big golden boot
hung outside a shop called "La Botte d'Or." At every step
there was some bit of carving, some old doorway, some little
statue, some touch of art and craftsmanship belonging to the
character of mediæval France. When we were there the streets
were *pavoisé* with flags, in honour, we were told, of Jeanne d'Arc,
whose feast day was at hand.

The *pompiers* of Auxerre were getting down to serious business.
They had lined up and were sounding their trumpets. But we
went out of the streets for a while and entered the Abbaye of
St. Germain.

No one else was there, and it was in the silence of a tomb
that we went down into the eighth-century crypt, with its
vaulted roof and rough pillars, built when there were Saxon
kings in England and Frankish chiefs in France. The beginning
of Christianity in France saw these stones built. The first altars
were here. Saints and martyrs who died for their faith were
buried in these niches. Outside in the country places people
still clung to pagan gods and superstitions. Charlemagne was
the successor of the Cæsars. At Cologne and Aachen, and all
along the Rhine, his craftsmen were building great churches in
the Roman style—Romanesque, as we call it. France was still
a land of fighters and half-civilised men with fierce passions and
strong lusts and cruelties. In their midst were these sanctuaries
of peace and learning, where monks illuminated their manu-

scripts as the first artists and the first scholars, trying to tame the wild beast in the heart of man to some sweetness in the spirit of Christ. We spoke in hushed voices in that old crypt. The novelist was excited and awed. He explored dark little passages and climbed down flights of steps, worn a thousand years ago by the feet of the first ancestors of France. He touched old stones to get their vibrations from the past.

Then we came into the light again and paid a visit to the cathedral of Auxerre, which is the glory of its town, with its tall tower—Norman, as we should call it—and an old red-tiled roof weathered by the centuries over its nave and transepts. The shadows between its flying buttresses were black beyond the sunlight. The great tower rose into a blue sky, and all around were houses of sixteenth-century France, red-roofed also, like the cathedral in their midst.

We stood a while in the nave, looking up to its high roof and the lovely tracery of its pointed arches of twelfth-century style. Some nuns with beautiful grave faces were busy round the statue of Jeanne d'Arc, placing fresh flowers before that peasant girl in armour beneath the flag on which were the lilies of France. I thought of how the French had been inspired to a new devotion during the war to the Maid of Orléans. Had she not been miraculously aided to clear France of its enemies—who were then the English?—Perhaps if they prayed hard enough she might bring aid to young soldiers of France—their sons—fighting a harder war against another enemy. There were always candles burning round her statue in little churches and great cathedrals, within sound of gunfire. Now the incense of flowers was rising at her feet. Consciously, or unconsciously, French people are thinking of Joan of Arc again, because of that chill of fear creeping into their hearts at the thought of a new war.

As we left the cathedral the artist became eloquent.

"It's pretty marvellous when one thinks of all the labour which went to the making of these cathedrals! I suppose the very names of the builders are unknown. But they were good craftsmen all right. And they took a pride in their job and dug their character into it. They had real fun in carving some old gargoyle. They spent years—perhaps all their lifetime—up the scaffolding, and didn't think the time wasted. It was loving toil. We don't do that kind of thing nowadays."

The novelist had found a choice collection of postcards depicting the beauties of Auxerre. I think it must have been here —or perhaps it was in Autun—that he bought his materials for sketching, to which afterwards he was devoted with a new-born passion, sitting up half the night over one of his drawings, sketched in outline by the wayside. He has all the talents, and can write poetry more easily than I can get down a bit of prose. A materialistic age, they say, but the spirit of art still claims its victims and its martyrs, who are mostly starving, or at least very hard up. The amateur who has some kind of job, more paying, has all the luck, as well as all the thrill, whatever his results may be. Perhaps art will be left to the amateur.

7

After Auxerre we came to Avallon, a pleasant little town with a lovely name, approached by a long avenue of noble chestnut trees, very tall and spreading, leading to a Roman gate through which Cæsar was carried in his litter. Bells were ringing from an old belfry, and we were aware, by seeing groups of sightseers gathering in an open place, that something was ado in the town. Presently, marching up the Rue Aristide Briand came a body of young men in white shorts and slips, carrying the tricolour, accompanied by a band. We stood on a terrace leading to a little park, and I talked to a youngish-looking man who was watching the parade among other inhabitants of Avallon.

"Gymnasts," he said in answer to my question. "They like to show themselves off now and then and exhibit their bodily beauty."

He smiled with a look of irony.

"What happens in Avallon?" I asked presently. "How do people earn their livings here?"

The good-looking Frenchman—he had a handsome face and was of good class, as we used to say—asserted that nothing ever happened in Avallon. A good many people earned wages in the tanneries and factories. But mainly it was an agricultural district and was sorry for itself, as the vineyards were not making money.

"We are all hoping for better times," said the handsome young man, and I thought, but did not say, that humanity everywhere, and in all ages, goes on hoping for better times.

We watched the boys in white for a time while we chatted about things in general. I gathered that Avallon is not exactly a city of excitement and that life goes quietly there. Our new acquaintance spoke a few words of English and talked a little to the artist who told him that he had been wounded in France. I was surprised to hear that the Frenchman had also fought in the war. He did not look nearly old enough for that, but he had been in the first gas attack at Ypres and had been wounded once at Arras and once at Verdun.

"Now," he said gravely, "there is the menace of a new war."

I tried to persuade him that this fear was exaggerated and that I could see no such menace for several years ahead.

"Several years?" he answered. "Is that good enough? How many? Four, five, six?"

"Time enough," I said, "to make sure of peace, if there is the will to peace."

He shook his head.

"The Germans are arming again. Every German is a soldier. When they are ready they will attack France again. I am sure of that. I give them four years."

"Hitler offers friendship," I told him.

"Who guarantees his sincerity?"

"Why not believe it and put it to the test?"

"France cannot take the risk. Our life is at stake. Look what happened last time. We weren't prepared. Our generals made a mess of it. We are never prepared. Next time we shall not have the same allies, perhaps. What does England think? From the newspapers it seems that England hesitates between opposing policies—friendship with France—friendship with Germany."

"We try to build a bridge," I said.

He seemed to think there was no bridge between France and Germany, nor ever would be.

"They go on talking at Geneva! The Society of Nations is a

delusion. The English use it to postpone vital decisions. It throws dust in the eyes of the world. They could do nothing when Japan attacked China. It's a ridiculous institution, don't you think?"

It was luncheon time and Gaston was waiting for his meal, and needed it. We shook hands with a man who had gloomy thoughts on his mind. He smiled as we parted and touched his hat to three Englishmen, very politely, although he didn't get much comfort out of English diplomacy.

We had a look at the Hôtel de la Poste. It looked very good, but we shirked its price for lunch, and decided to feed more cheaply in a small restaurant near by where we could get a meal for half the price, with wine included. It was a good meal with good wine. And the company was amusing. The *patron*, in his shirt-sleeves—a burly man of Falstaffian build— was ripely humorous. He talked incessantly and boisterously to a group of young men who had lunched early and were now glad to be entertained by his badinage while they took their coffee. They seemed to be discussing politics, and I heard the name of Doumergue mentioned several times, with those of Herriot and Tardieu.

"Youth is the time of dreams," said our French Falstaff. "It is the privilege of youth to be excessively foolish."

Those scathing words seemed vastly amusing to the group of younger men, who perhaps—I was only guessing—belonged to the Jeunesse Patriote, or even to the Action Française.

"This old man is *gaga!*" answered one of them. "He is too fat. He talks the language of imbeciles."

I was tempted to join in that discussion. I was eager to hear more of this dialogue between old age and youth. But I had to content myself with overhearing chance remarks.

Down the narrow streets of Avallon were groups of those young Gymnasts who had paraded in the Grand' Place. They had broken up and were marching in small bodies in different directions, whistling, singing, as they swung their bare arms and legs. It was the only time in France that I saw anything of the kind. In Germany one saw this marching youth every- where.

8

After leaving Avallon with pleasant memories, we made a détour to see a town called Vezelay. "Don't fail to see Vezelay," a friend had said. "It's simply marvellous." Very well, I was ready to see Vezelay or any other good spot in this fair land of France. We drove through country which might have been Surrey—I mean the Surrey beyond the by-passes with their ribbon development of bricks and mortar. Here were Surrey lanes deep cut, with wild grown hedges and overhanging trees. Here were fields like those near a village I know, all strewn with silver daisies and the gold buttercups. Here even birds were singing—and, alas! birds do not sing in all parts of France, because sporting gentlemen shoot them for their pleasure. Here were little old villages with half-timbered houses and pleasant woods on which the sunlight lay, until clouds, growing larger in the sky—English-looking clouds—cast shadows across them for a few fleeting seconds.

Gaston, our Russian friend, talked to me about life.

"Humanity," he said, looking at some peasants—pleasant-looking types, I thought—working in the fields, "humanity, monsieur, is made up of sheep, wolves, and bulls. It is so in France as in other countries. There is perhaps a preponderance of sheep in the countryside. The French peasant does not think very, very much. Peasants do not think. They only know what they read in *L'Humanité* or *L'Action Française*, and that, of course, is untrue. It is impossible—or at least very difficult—to believe that these people know how to govern themselves. What do they know of government? What, for instance, is the value of their views on the Japanese occupation of Manchukuo, or even on the moral and intellectual qualities of M. Doumergue compared with those of M. Herriot? Nothing! In Russia—I am a Russian, as you know—there are one hundred and fifty million peasants. They are all ignorant. They never think for themselves. They never think. It is, then, necessary that they should be ruled by some form of dictatorship—either a Czar or a Stalin. Stalin is now the Czar, though he is called by another name. It is necessary to be very civilised before self-government is possible. And then it is not advisable! It has never yet been successful. But what nation in Europe is civilised? Minorities, yes. There are many intellectual people. Here in France there is great intelligence among certain classes. The chauffeurs with whom I talk in my garage are very intelligent fellows. We have remarkable conversations. They know life. They have travelled. They keep their eyes open. But the majority of people in the world—I am not talking only of France—are unintelligent. They must have discipline. They must be told what to do. That is my belief. But then I was once an officer in the Russian Imperial navy. And that reminds me——"

He was reminded of some anecdote which made me laugh very much along a road in France, though I have forgotten the gist of it.

We came within sight of Vezelay. It lay before us at the end of a long winding road. It stood on a hill and its houses climbed up the height like a hill town in Provence—St. Paul or Vence—and all its huddled houses were crowned by a tall straight tower, and two other towers not so high. The road twisted like a ribbon round the hill.

"If I don't make a drawing here," said the artist, "may I never draw again. But first we must go up and explore that enchanted town."

We drove up and left the car against a wall while we went to explore a noble abbey, founded eight hundred years ago by that Order of Benedictines who chose the loveliest spots for their houses and churches, and built splendidly and nobly for all time.

Nature had prepared drama for us. A thunderstorm burst over the hill. Forked lightning stabbed the dark rainclouds. There were dull peals of thunder, reminding me of the reverberations of that great *bourdon* at Sens when its rope was pulled by a little man with the soul of a poet and the passion of a bell ringer. I stood watching the storm, awed by its splendour, before going inside the Abbey of the Madeleine, with its great basilica, vast and white except for a strange pattern of black stones, and lonely and sublime. The Benedictines had gone—

old Clemenceau was one of those who forbade the last religious orders—there was not a single soul except ourselves in that great shrine. Through the windows came the flash of lightning and between the flashes it was illuminated by a cold white light, flooding its tall white columns, its rounded arches, its immensity.

It was worth a détour to see this abbey hidden among the hills of Burgundy. I shall never forget it.

9

We went on our way, or rather out of our way, en route for Semur, where our artist had spent three of the best months of his life, making many friends whom he wished to see again. This journey took us through a lovely corner of France, past an old château with massive bastions, and, later, through an old gate in which a portcullis still hung outside the village of Epoitte, and then along the walls of a noble park.

Gaston looked across the wall from his steering wheel.

"Most of the old families have departed," he said. "These places belong now to gentlemen who make chocolate or ladies' underclothes."

We came again to that fair river called the Yonne.

It led us to the city of Semur, wonderfully placed on rising ground and almost unreal in its dramatic view. Across the Yonne a bridge had been flung centuries ago, with a noble span. High above it, wall above wall, rose a mediæval city, flanked by four great towers and crowded with churches, châteaux and mansions of the French renaissance, and ancient houses with red roofs.

"It's like a fairy tale," said the novelist. "I believe the Sleeping Beauty lived here. I believe we shall see her still sleeping in one of these châteaux."

The artist must have felt like Rip Van Winkle. He inquired for old friends, but they were dead or gone away. He rang at bells which hung from old walls at old doorways, but no answer came; until a lady coming down the street stared at

VEZELAY

him a moment and then spoke his name. She lived in one of
the mansions of Semur. She opened one of the doors. We
followed into a house which seemed deserted, and she took us
out onto a terrace, where we gave a cry because it looked out
to a wide and lovely view, surprisingly. The river lay below
us, and the lower town of Semur with its bridges and deep-
toned roofs. The artist inquired after many people whom he
had known years before. Some of them had married—young
girls who had sketched with him, young men who had laughed
with him. Madame So-and-So was gone. Monsieur So-and-So
was too old to receive visitors. Semur had grown older since
his visit. We also had grown older, as we remembered with a
sense of shock.

On a wall close to one of the tall gate towers—it was cracked
from top to bottom—there was a tablet with an inscription
in old French, and very pleasant for us to read:

> *Les Semurois*
> *Se Plaisent*
> *En l' Acointance*
> *Des Estrangiers.*

Gargoyles grinned down upon us from the eaves of houses.
Little figures of the Madonna were carved in niches above
ancient doorways with renaissance mouldings. There were
wonderful wellheads here and there, like those of Italy brought
to Surrey gardens. We walked along the ramparts where once
men in morions and armed with pikes paced the walls, looking
for the approach of Frenchmen who hated these Burgundians.
The narrow streets leading to the cathedral were all hung with
flags in honour of the feast day of Jeanne d'Arc, as I heard.

We put up at the Hôtel de la Côte d'Or, and I had a spacious
bedroom with an alcove for the wash place, all for twenty
francs. Downstairs in the dining room there were modern
paintings on the wall, rather frightful, some of them, unless
one likes modern paintings with violent dabs of colour laid
on with a trowel. They were the heritage from one of the many

artists who have come to Semur with high hopes and clean canvases. The waitress who attended to our needs had been there many years but failed to remember our own artist, who had stayed there with a sketching class of young women—the first of such parties, as he believed. She had seen so many since, until something had happened to art and artists, and they came no more.

Before dinner and dusk I went up to the cathedral and fell into talk with a priest who was outside, above the steps, with an assistant. They had carried out a small harmonium, and the priest was running his fingers over the notes and playing cheerful little tunes which sounded like marching songs. It seemed to me strange. No one was in the square. Why should he play this instrument outside the cathedral in the dusk? I ventured to inquire, and he looked up at me with merry eyes in a thin, ascetic but humorous face.

"I am preparing for the procession in honour of Jeanne d'Arc," he told me. "It begins at nine o'clock this evening. We are going to have fireworks and all kinds of surprises!"

He was very amiable, and interested to meet an Englishman in Semur.

I ventured to regret that the English had not been kind to Jeanne d'Arc.

He laughed good-naturedly.

"The French, my dear sir, are not guiltless of the fire that burnt her!"

He closed down the lid of the harmonium and seemed inclined for conversation.

"What do people do in Semur?" I asked.

He answered instantly, and explosively.

"The people of Semur do absolutely nothing! That is their special character. Look at that square in front of us. It is representative of life in Semur, my dear sir."

I looked across the square. There was not a living soul in sight. It appeared that life in Semur was empty like the square.

"This is a city of *rentiers*," said the priest. "And they are sorry for themselves because the *rentier* class is not prosperous just now owing to taxation and other evils. Nevertheless, we try

to keep alive. Tonight there will be illuminations. There will be
—*mirabile dictu!*—a little excitement."

He was amused by the thought of a little excitement in
Semur. I believe he was the live wire who was arranging all
this.

Presently, after amiable conversation, he excused himself. It
was his dinner time. He hoped I would honour him by watching the procession and illuminations. He had a sister in England. He had once paid a visit there with very happy recollections, but a long, long time ago—before the war, in fact. He
had forgotten every word of English.

He held out his hand very cordially and pressed mine with
a good grip. I raised my hat to him and liked his type, so quick
and alert, and humorous, and courteous.

After dinner we went to see the procession in honour of
Jeanne d'Arc. It was dark when it began. The square in front
of the cathedral filled with inhabitants—those *rentiers* who were
so hard pressed by taxation and other worries, and the shopkeepers and their children. It was a well-dressed crowd, I
noticed. The children were charming. There was one little
boy in a sailor suit, with golden hair like an English boy. He
was restless while waiting for the procession and kept leaving
his parents, to climb up high steps, and balance himself along
old gutters, and put his head through a stone balustrade.

"Certainly that boy will break his neck," I said.

"I hope he will," said the artist, who has a pose of brutality
at times.

We stood wedged in the crowd. I was next to a tall priest
of great gravity and distinction. He was not talkative, though
I tried to chat with him, but answered direct questions civilly
enough. Perhaps—unlike the other priest—he had a grudge
against the English for burning Jeanne d'Arc. The people
were very quiet, as though in church, and spoke in low voices.
Presently came the tap of drums and the sound of brass instruments. Through an old archway came the flare of lighted
lanterns like torches flaming. Scores of young boys marched
under them, followed by a battalion of girls. They massed on
the portico outside the cathedral, and my friendly priest was

up there at the harmonium, which he began to play. A choir was singing under the red lanterns. The sound flooded the square, and many citizens of Semur joined in. It was a song with a solemn melody sung slowly.

The tall priest by my side answered a question.

"*C'est le Chanson de l'Etendard.*"

It was the Song of the Flag, written, perhaps, in honour of Jeanne d'Arc, who carried the lilies of France to victory before she was burnt as a witch.

Strange things happened after that on the great cathedral of Semur. A little figure ran along the parapet of one of the high towers. The crowd looked up and watched. A bugle sounded a long quavering note. Suddenly the black mass of the cathedral was lit up by a flame of red fire which rushed up its walls as though it had burst into flame. The whole of that great building with its tall towers and massive buttresses was red with this leaping fire. It lasted only for a few moments and then went out. The choir sang again. The square was in blackness again. That enormous mass of masonry was dark again. But the crowd waited expectantly. A rocket shot up from the tower high into the sky. The bugle called to the stars. Suddenly the cathedral was illuminated again; this time by light which turned it to a white enchantment, as though it had sprung like a dream of beauty out of the night. A third time, after a pause of darkness, was the cathedral lit up; and the last time was the most sensational. Golden rain poured in torrents down towers and pinnacles, and leaded windows, and buttresses. It was as though a cascade of golden water were pouring down it from the dark sky.

"Good heavens!" I thought. "What would people say if such things were done to Westminster Abbey?"

It seemed to me dangerous to play with fire like that on one of the glories of French architecture. Suppose that artificial fire were to set the cathedral alight with real flames! Nobody else worried. They enjoyed the scene quietly but without any demonstration of enthusiasm. A hymn was sung. The boys with the red torches marched away. The crowd went home- wards with sleepy children. Joan of Arc would be remembered

SEMUR

in their prayers. Perhaps all this illumination was symbolical of that bonfire at Rouen which had burnt her body before her soul escaped.

10

It was ten o'clock. We sat outside the Hôtel de la Côte d'Or and drank coffee and talked about these things. The people of Semur had all gone home, except a small group of boys at the corner of a street opposite. They seemed to be listening to a man who was talking to them. Presently I began to listen also. The man was speaking in a loud voice which carried across the square. It was a loud voice which went on, and on, in some queer monologue.

"Drunk!" said one of my friends.

I strolled across. The man who was drunk seemed to be talking queer stuff.

He was a peasant-looking fellow in a white shirt—not too clean—tucked into his trousers. His arms were bare and brown. He had a peasant's face, unshaven for three days or so, but good-looking and strong. He was certainly the worse for drink. He swayed slightly as he stood talking. Queer stuff! Amazing stuff.

"There is nothing I don't know," he said. "I am a peasant, but I am also a scholar. I know more than any professor of France. I know everything in history, and everything in poetry, and everything in art. I understand the meaning of life and have gone very deep, my old ones, into the secrets of nature. It is true that I am a little drunk on the feast of Jeanne d'Arc. But that does not interfere with my intelligence or spoil my memory. I do not make a boast of all this. I was born with a remarkable brain. I am a thinker. I am a philosopher. You laugh at me because you are foolish boys, and because I am a little drunk on the feast of Jeanne d'Arc. You think I am telling you lies. But that is not so. I am telling you the truth, because I am devoted to truth. I can tell you stories of heroic things which happened here in France before you were born. I can answer any questions about the mysteries which bewilder you, my poor children. Or if you will have your ears filled with music, I will recite to you things of beauty. I am not so drunk that I have forgotten, *par exemple*, the poems of Victor Hugo, the greatest poet of France. Which will you hear?"

A boy of about seventeen who was listening to all this called out the name of one of Victor Hugo's poems. The drunken man smiled.

"I remember it! I have often said it to myself behind the plough."

He was silent for a second. Then his voice rang out across the square in a noble rhythm. He recited the poem of Victor Hugo, magnificently. I stood astonished.

Another boy gave the name of another poem, and the drunken man recited it. Then another.

"You see," he said, "I have a head for poetry! But I have a head also for history. I know all the battles of Napoleon. Austerlitz—Wagram—Jena——" he recited the litany of Napoleon's victories.

"I know all about art," he said after that. "I know the master-pieces of the French painters. I could give you the names of their pictures. And I can tell you about Michael Angelo, and Rembrandt, and Rubens, and Titian. I have the soul of an artist, though I am a peasant, drunk on the feast of Jeanne d'Arc."

I spoke to one of the boys.

"Who is this man?" I asked. "He seems extraordinary."

The boy answered with a laugh.

"Certainly he is extraordinary. He does not belong to Semur. He seems to know a lot."

"Tell us about the universe," asked one of the boys, putting everything into one question.

The peasant laughed.

"That is easy! The universe? Look above your heads. Do you see those stars? They are all worlds. There are more worlds, infinitely greater than this little earth ball, than your puny minds can count or imagine. The universe is made up of whirling worlds and whirling atoms which go on to infinite distance —worlds without end."

"Tell us about God!" cried a boy.

The man laughed as if God were his friend.

"God is the Universal Spirit. And Jesus Christ was sent into the world by God to teach us the spirit of eternal goodness. I know and believe, though I am drunk on the feast of Jeanne d'Arc. Jesus Christ was a good fellow. The words he spoke might have changed humanity and brought peace among men. But men did not listen. Men prefer to be beasts. That is sad. I am among those who remain beastlike at times, and yet I have a touch of the divine fire in my soul. Drunk as I am, my old ones, I have a reverence for truth and beauty. I am a peasant—that is true—but I have great knowledge of many mysteries. I can tell you about the tides, about the life of worms——"

A burst of laughter from the boys greeted these last words.

"Tell us about the life of worms!" they shouted. But then they became silent suddenly, as an elderly man in a felt hat and overcoat above a dark suit came up and approached the drunken peasant and spoke to him sternly.

"Who is that?" I asked one of the boys in a low voice.

"The Commissaire of Police. That queer type will get into trouble."

The Commissaire of Police talked to the man in an angry voice.

"Clear out! Why do you stand shouting here? Go away before you get into trouble."

The peasant spoke to him politely, swaying as he spoke.

"Monsieur, I have not the honour of knowing you. I am doing no kind of harm. Kindly do not interrupt my entertainment of these boys, who are much amused by me. It is I who ask you to go away."

The Commissaire held a stick in his right hand and raised it slightly.

"I am not arguing," he said, "I am telling you. Go away before I send an *agent* to remove you. You are making too much noise at this time of night."

"Sir," said the peasant, "I have recited the poems of Victor Hugo. That is not a crime."

The Commissaire smiled once or twice at the man's strange

eloquence. He was very patient with him, although stern. It was six minutes or so before he moved the man on. He went away quietly with a shambling gait because of the fumes of cheap wine in his head.

I spoke to the Commissaire and walked a few paces with him.

"That is a strange fellow! Do you know anything about him?"

The Commissaire glanced at me, and then answered politely.

"He does not belong to Semur. He is a farm servant in the country outside. He is, I think, a little mad, but, as I must admit, with a touch of genius."

It was a queer experience in the quiet town of Semur. I have often thought since of that drunken fellow. "A little mad but with a touch of genius." There was something fine in his recital of Victor Hugo's poems. He had the soul of a poet. He loved the music of great verse. Perhaps there was a noble strain of blood in him, coming down to that body and brain of his, as he followed the plough, or sweated in a turnip field under the hot sun. He was not like other peasants. Perhaps his genius made him drunk.

The novelist went out for another stroll, as generally he did when the artist and I went up to bed. He met a young man who was doing his naval service. He was the son of a man with vineyards, and spoke of the depression in Burgundy. There was too much wine for the world's markets—or the world's purse and taste for wine. It would be necessary, he said, to destroy three quarters of last year's vintage. His father was feeling sad about it.

Early next morning I was awakened by noises in my room. There was a bellowing of cows so close that I thought they had walked up to my bed. Bells jangled. Pigs grunted. The wheels of farm carts creaked. It was market day in Semur.

Later, we went for a walk on the ramparts looking down to the lower town, from which rose a strong rich scent of lilac, surely the sweetest scent in all the world, with all springtime in it, and the beauty of young girls, and the lyrics of poets who loved life. On a seat under an avenue of chestnuts which

CHÂTEAU DE MONTAIGU, NEAR AUTUN

follows the line of the ramparts, I saw that one lover of pretty
girls had carved the symbol of his heart and the arrow which
had pierced it. Then he had carved some words which were
not French:

Yo te quiero.

In Spanish it means, "I love thee."

Near by was a tall full-grown poplar which had been planted
in a time of revolution. It was the Tree of Liberty, according
to an inscription, and the maidens of Semur had paraded
round it when the owners of the châteaux had fled disguised
as peasants in hay carts, or were waiting in dirty gaols for the
sharp knife of the guillotine. I thought of Madame Roland's
words which she cried out that day when she too went on her
way to the guillotine, though she had been the friend of the
men who had made the revolution:

"O Liberté, comme on t'a joué en ton nom!"

Now liberty was out of favour. "A stinking corpse," says
Mussolini. Fascists and Brown Shirts proclaim discipline instead of liberty; state worship instead of free speech; the order
of the ant heap instead of individualism; intolerance instead of
tolerance. So the pendulum swings.

II

Our next time on the road led us through Saulieu. After
the war the German Emperor's chef came to the Hôtel de la
Poste. He was received in a friendly way by the inhabitants of
Saulieu and his cuisine was famous in France. He never disguised his sympathies for the Hohenzollern, I was told, but
was a frank, good-natured fellow. He made a little fortune
at the Hôtel de la Poste and has now retired from that place
and bought a hotel in Mâcon, where he tells stories of the
Kaiser to those who like to listen.

So, through old villages again, past several châteaux with
high walls, through a countryside where there are many vineyards growing the grapes of Burgundy which make too much

wine for the world's market, we came to Autun. You remember
something about Autun? Talleyrand, that strange renegade,
that cynic of life, that betrayer of many women and many men,
that lover of France, as he always claimed—was he not made
Bishop of Autun as a young man, before he renounced his
priesthood and swore allegiance to the Revolution? In the
cathedral where he had served at the altar I spoke to one of
the cleaners and asked if there were any memorial to Talleyrand. He looked puzzled and shook his head.

"I have never heard of it," he said. "Talleyrand?"

I questioned other people in Autun, but Talleyrand did not
mean anything to them.

"I have never heard of the man," said a friendly waiter,
who had an idea that I was asking about one of his fellow
citizens.

It was this waiter in the café at the Hôtel de Commerce
who gave me some information about life in Autun as it goes
on now when Talleyrand is forgotten. Twice a month there is
a great cattle fair in the market place, farmers coming with
their beasts from all the country round. In the town itself
furniture is made from the woods in the neighbourhood. The
craftsmen of Autun fabricate "antiques," not to be told from
the originals except by the eyes of experts and the knowing
touch of their fingers.

Inside the café were groups of middle-aged men taking
their apéritifs and talking loudly. The waiter, a young man
with a laugh in his eyes, jerked his thumb towards them.

"We are great politicians in Autun," he told me. "It is good
for business in the Café de Commerce—and perhaps for little
else. Mostly they are Radical-Socialists here—followers of
Herriot, you know—but the Municipality is on the Right.
They read Léon Daudet in *L'Action Française*, and curse the
government. Then we have other specimens. There are some
mines close to Autun, and the miners—or some of them—are
Communists. At least, they think they are Communists, and
pretend to believe that Russia is paradise under Monsieur
Stalin. The Dictatorship of the Proletariat is their watchword.
They think they could rule France rather well themselves—

when they have washed their faces. First they would shoot all our politicians—and perhaps they would be right. We have another industry in Autun, monsieur. It takes place after dark inside the Café de Commerce. Many citizens are devoted to card playing. They make a lot of noise over that business. It is perhaps less dangerous than politics."

His right eye half shut for a moment. As a waiter he was an onlooker of life as it passes in Autun and was amused by it.

At the entrance to the city on one side there is a very noble gateway with double arches and an open balustrade of tall pillars above the arches. It was built quite a number of years ago—by the Romans in the year A.D. 69. And round about in the fields there are other relics of Roman civilisation. We went to see the Stadium, which is now a football ground, but could not find the Temple of Janus, which still stands by the ramparts like a Norman fort. In another field is a queer mound of stones with a top like a chimney pot. It is surrounded by bushes and railed off with hurdles. It is the tomb, they say, of the Gaulish chief Ecuen, who was a friend of Julius Cæsar when he had his headquarters at Autun or thereabouts. Beneath the soil of France, in many fields, Roman relics still lie buried, and above the soil here and in Provence, there are arches, temples, amphitheatres, standing almost as strong as when the Roman legions were quartered in Gaul and the Gauls were Romanised. France has her feet deep in history. Her civilisation is unbroken since Roman times. Her people are conscious of their heritage.

12

Beyond Autun, when we were on the road once more, we motored slowly through high woods and open country, where vineyards climbed the hills.

"Stop!" shouted the artist.

We stopped outside the château of Marguérite de Bourgogne, in the Valley of Gold—the Val d'Or.

It now belongs, we learnt, to the Comtesse de Montaigu, and is a fairy-tale castle like a drawing by Rackham, with tall towers and battlements, and high walls dropping to a deep moat in which trees are growing. The sun was at an angle which cast black shadows gloriously from tower to tower, lighting one side of them. It called out for an artist, and he was there. In fact, three artists were there, though two were amateurs with hopes higher than their skill. How good it was to sit there in the sun on a bank of flowers with that picture before us! Gaston, our Russian driver, waited patiently, thinking perhaps what queer men he was driving, or remembering his days in St. Petersburg before a revolution.

A peasant came down the road. He was a middle-aged man with Roman blood in his veins, if one might judge by his face. He had a straight back and broad shoulders and walked with dignity.

I saluted him, and we fell into conversation about life around. He spoke well, in good French, without a patois, and seemed a man of intelligence, like so many of these peasants. But he was a little sad and did not hide his melancholy.

"The earth is worth nothing now," he said. "What we grow we cannot sell. I have vineyards, but the wine is wasted. There is too much wine, they say. In any case, labour costs much money and is hard to get. Where are the labourers? The young people leave the fields. They do not like the life of the land. They go to Paris. It is always Paris which calls them—that infernal city! They are impatient with the way of peasants. We're too dull—their fathers and their mothers. They want to dance and live in lighted cities. Men come from Paris to sell us things—smart young men with quick eyes. Our boys and girls question them. They ask whether there is any chance of a place in Paris. Our girls, whom we have tried to keep good, whisper questions. Could they not go to Paris and have a fine time? Some of these men are *souteneurs*. They come especially to tempt our girls with fine stories. They tempt them away. They put them onto the streets. It is so a hundred times. Their mothers warn them. Do they listen? No. They laugh and will take the risk. So the old folk are left. And what can they do alone? The earth needs labour. I am an old *vigneron*. I love my vineyards. But I have been deserted by my sons. They are in Paris. And last year the harvest was spoilt by the lack of rain.

What does it matter? Spoilt or not spoilt! There is too much wine, they say. England does not buy. The Americans do not buy. France cannot drink all her own wine. No, sir, there is not much to be made out of the land nowadays. It was better in the old days when life was more simple and young people followed the way of their fathers. The young people now will not suffer that simplicity. They want more money, which they can earn in factories and in cities. Money! Money! That is what they say. It is the curse of the world. It is not a good life in the fields, they say—our sons and daughters. We want the cabarets, and the cinemas, and the lighted streets, and the crowded cafés. They're not content with a good quiet life in this good countryside. As a *vigneron* and an old-fashioned man I deplore this modern age. I belong to the soil. I love my vine-yards. But they do not pay. That, monsieur, is how it is!"

That is how it is, alas, in many fields of France, as I heard from other people.

Gaston had something to say about it, though he had not heard my talk with the *vigneron*.

"France is becoming depopulated in many districts. *Madame ne veut pas d'enfants!* I daresay you saw the name of that film show in Sens. That is true. Children are getting scarce in France, and in any case, when they grow up they don't like the life on the land. It is the disease of civilisation. It is of course a sign of decadence. Labour is badly wanted on the land. There are fifteen thousand Cossacks round Toulouse, all agriculturists and doing well because they love the earth."

We went through the Val d'Or, truly named in Maytime, when every petal of a buttercup is gleaming like gold dust in the grass. From these vineyards come all the famous wines of Burgundy, the noblest wines in the world, having in them this sunlight of France, and this richness of earth, and some-thing of the soul of France.

"They work hard, these French peasants," said Gaston, "and they think only of one thing—how to make a few more *sous*. When their children are old enough to understand words, their parents say, '*Il faut gagner les sous . . . Il faut gagner les sous.*' "

How lovely was France in this month of May! Every mile was like a sonnet by Ronsard, that poet who loved the living flowers of France, and the eyes of its women, and their white necks and red lips. Every yard was a line by Du Bellay and the poets of the renaissance. The air was scented with may blossom which grew in all the hedges—there are hedges in this countryside—and the earth smelt sweet, and across the fields one day, as I stood listening, a cuckoo shouted to tell us that he was here and summer was "i cumen in!" Chaucer heard him in the springtime of England. Alfred heard him at Glastonbury. And here, in France, the Roman legions, marching down their long straight roads, listened to the shout of "Cuckoo—cuckoo!" Marguérite de Valois, leaning from her casement window, heard the song of "Cuckoo! Cuckoo!" and all the children of France, making daisy chains for their hair, have laughed through the ages at this bird with its human cry of jollity. I thought of a little old farmstead in England which I had left to write this book. The cuckoo would be there.

"I have amusing conversations with garage men," said Gaston, not bothering about the cuckoo. "Some of them are Communists. And yet very decent fellows, with a lot of good sense and kindliness. They are up against capitalism, which they identify with the Comité des Forges, whom they accuse of stirring up the war fever for their interest in steel, and with the Creusot works making guns for those who may be the enemies of France—we pass very near to them—and with the newspapers which, they say, are corrupt and bought. There is truth in some of that, no doubt. It is, I think, true! But I say to them, 'That's all very well, *mes vieux*, but what about your little houses for which you have stinted and scraped until you own them? What about your personal liberty? You don't like being ordered about too much. How would you like to be under the heel of a Commissar saying, 'Do this or do that, unless you want to be shot in the back of the head?' That makes them think a bit! '*Ah ça!*' they say, 'we, of course, we shan't go too far. But Communism is the only way of getting some reality into politics. These sacred Socialists don't do a thing. They are just old-fashioned Liberals, hand in glove with

the Conservatives and ready to vote for the directors of the
Comité des Forges every time they want the government to
build new battleships or new and bigger guns. We shall draw
back when things go to extremes. Certainly we own our little
houses. We intend to go on owning them.' All that is very illogical. But man, monsieur, is an illogical animal, even in France,
where they boast of their logic."

13

We passed through Mercurey—I used to drink it, a most
excellent wine, in French inns during war time. It is a small
town with a long street, surrounded by hills and vineyards, with
tall cypress trees round an old château.

"French wine is good for the health," said Gaston. "When
one feels a chill or a stomach-ache, it is wise to drink more
wine. It's a tonic."

We had left the Yonne, that fair river, behind us, and came
to Châlons-sur-Saône, a broad stream with little islands and
many barges and tugs lying up. Women were washing their
linen in this river, and cows were feeding in rich pasture on
its bank. All along the roads ox wagons moved slowly, and here,
as on other roads of our journey in France, we were astonished
by the absence of motor traffic. Our car seemed to be the only
one in France. Nothing passed us as we drove on our leisurely
way. The sun sank a little, lengthening the shadows across
the fields, deepening the golden light which bathed all this
countryside. We were in the Mâconnais. On our left was the
Dijonnais. The Saône flowed through a plain with flat fields
and tall poplars. Every village had its avenue of trees with
spreading branches for the sake of shade in hot weather. Under
these trees old men drowsed. There were gipsy caravans on the
roads, and we met them in other countries of Europe, and
always I stared at them with interest, because these strange
people refuse to change their way of life whatever changes
come. Always they are wanderers and wild birds, never resting
long in one place, scorning the so-called comforts of civilisation,
hating its cities, loving the heath and the open fields, and the

wind, and the rain. On one of these caravans the proprietor had painted his name and legend.

MR. AZZODARDI.
100,000 Douceurs.

I was puzzled for a moment by that word *douceurs*. It seemed too good to think that any man with the name of Azzodardi, from which anything might come, should travel about the world with a hundred thousand sweetnesses.

"Bonbons," said Gaston.

We came to Mâcon, the name of another good wine, and the city was worthy of its vintage. Across the river it has a noble bridge with twelve arches; and along the river is a broad embankment, with a wide open space before the houses are reached. In the centre of this open space was a statue to Lamartine. Below its pedestal, stretching away on either side, was a line of gipsy caravans. Lean dogs prowled about, and sniffed my calves as I went up to talk to these Romany folk. Girls with gold earrings leaned out, with their bare arms on the doorways of their travelling houses. One of them was cooking soup in a cauldron below her caravan. Another was combing her hair. Groups of gipsy fellows were setting up booths for the usual kind of fair. One man sat on a wooden chair in the sunlight of this golden evening. He was smoking a cigarette and watching life on the river. He was a youngish man with a thin dark face and lean brown hands on one of which was a heavy ring. He looked up and smiled amiably when I accosted him.

"Good business?" I asked.

"Not too good! People haven't much money to spend in this place. They have to sell their wine cheap—if they sell it. There is a lot of unemployment, they tell me. I feel the pinch myself because of this poverty. I run a lottery, and that does not run as it should, unless people have a little margin for a merry game of gambling. A strange time in which we live, monsieur! One finds that out on the roads. I travel all the time. Austria, Italy, Germany, Czecho-Slovakia, anywhere and everywhere with my old caravan and this lottery. No money

Lyon
15th May 54

E. Sander

LYON

anywhere, I assure you! You may ask where has the money gone? I do not answer that. It is one of life's mysteries. What, after all, is money? Ah! Another mystery. Sometimes I try to think it out. Then I get a headache. It is better not to think too much. It is pleasant to sit in the sun without thinking. But sometimes thought comes to one. Strange ideas get into one's head. One wonders what is the meaning of life, if it has any meaning. What is it all for—this struggle to live, to amass a little money, which alters its values or disappears? People get excited about politics. In France now they are excited that way. Strange things are happening below the peace of French life. There is turbulence. There is discontent. It is better to be a gipsy. They are not political. They wander on, taking things as they come. . . . It is a fine evening, monsieur."

He raised his hand—the one with the heavy ring on his little finger—with a friendly salute. There was a smile in his dark eyes. I should have liked to talk with him more and get the tale of his strange wandering life. But he dismissed me with that salute.

On the quayside, below which a barge was lying, there was a citizen of Mâcon who looked like one of its most respectable inhabitants, though a little shabby. He was a white-collar man, as the Americans say. He was middle-aged, a trifle portly below the belt, and with a grave dignity.

"A charming evening, monsieur!" I ventured to say as our eyes met.

"It's a fine evening," he agreed.

"All goes well in Mâcon?" I asked.

He looked at me with moody eyes.

"All does *not* go well, monsieur," he answered. "On the contrary. All goes badly."

"That is deplorable," I said.

"It is deplorable," he agreed.

"Business is bad?" I suggested. "You are no doubt a business man?"

He hesitated for a moment, and then sighed.

"I am not a business man, monsieur. I am what they call a *rentier*. That is to say, I am trying to live on the interest of savings put by after a life of hard work. That is to say, I am not succeeding to live, because it is impossible, you understand."

I did not understand. At least, I desired more detailed information. He gave it with great candour.

"It is simple. It's a matter of simple arithmetic. Since the war the cost of living has increased six times. Salaries have only increased three times. Make your own reckoning. It is impossible, as I say, to live.

"Take my own case," said this new acquaintance, with a frankness which was surprising. "I have six thousand francs a year."

I made a sum in mental arithmetic. Six thousand francs translated into English money would be seventy-five pounds a year.

"You may see for yourself that such an income is ridiculous," said this gentleman of France. "Everything is taxed. Prices increase. Rents are abominable. Clothes are expensive. One does not amuse oneself on an income of six thousand francs. Yet I do not pretend that I am worse off than others. Certainly not. In France there are hundreds of thousands like myself, or with less than myself, after serving the State faithfully for forty years. I am not complaining even of the government. I am a reasonable man. It is necessary to balance the budget. The government would much like to decrease taxation but is unable to do so. It is no use urging it to lower taxation. Then the budget would not be balanced. Then the financial state of the country would be worse than now, which is, of course, deplorable. I do not see any solution. The *rentier* class is of course the most unfortunate. We have no political influence. Our deputies ignore us altogether in order to seek favour from more important classes; the labouring classes, for instance, and those who go rioting in the Place de la Concorde. We are too old to go rioting. We are too reasonable. We are loyal to France and the Republic, whatever our own poverty. Therefore we are ignored. I tell you these things frankly. There is no secret in them. But what is disheartening is the impossibility of finding a solution, in view of what is happening in the world today, when every country is on the edge of bankruptcy and trade is languishing. As a *rentier* on six thousand francs a year I deplore the state of the world!"

We deplored it together. I had no solution to offer. We decided that it was a very fine afternoon. We took off our hats to each other, and my *rentier* friend walked slowly away—homeward, perhaps, for a meal with strict economy. I doubt whether he could afford to drink the wine of Mâcon.

I leaned over the quayside, watching the river flow by. Two young men came up from a barge and sat on the parapet of the embankment. They were both very sunburnt.

"A good life!" I said. "I should like to live on a barge."

They grinned at me and found this remark amusing.

"You wouldn't like it! It's a hard life with long hours; and nothing in it nowadays."

"What's your cargo?" I asked.

"Cement from Lyons."

"Well, there's nothing wrong with that."

One of the sunburnt young men spat into the river.

"No money in it. Traffic goes by road now. Barges are being pushed off the river. Jobs are scarce. There's very little doing in Lyons. Business is dead."

I couldn't believe that. Lyons was one of the busiest cities in France when I was last there. They must be making a fortune out of silk stockings, I thought, remembering the millions of shops with ladies' legs in the windows.

Those two young bargees said, "Good-evening" politely, and edged off to have a look at the circus which was getting ready for them.

At a café I had a talk with another citizen of Mâcon, highly intelligent. He complained of bad business and rising prices in France. But he had a solution. He was the only man I met who had a solution. It was drastic.

"All this," he said, "is the fault of the middlemen"—*les intermédiaires*, he called them. "Everything, monsieur, which is sold in France passes through six or seven hands before it reaches the market or the shop. See how it works. A little man buys the produce from the peasant or the *vigneron* or the craftsman. A bigger man buys from the little man who gets his profit, which is too much. A still bigger man buys from the bigger man who puts on his profit—which is too much. So it goes from hand to hand, each one grabbing his profit—which is too much!—until at last it reaches the shop—and the shop-man puts on his profit—when the unfortunate citizen pays through the nose out of his small salary."

That was his explanation. Now came his solution.

"Monsieur, we want a Mussolini to hang five out of those seven *intermédiaires.*"

14

We came into Lyons. It was a great contrast to our journey from Paris. We have been in many little towns which had held their mediæval character hardly changed by the modern touch. We had sat by the wayside in many places of quiet beauty. We had gone into many villages with old timbered houses, where the fastest pace was the tread of the ox drawing a load of timber or dragging the plough in fields outside. Our eyes had been soaked in loveliness, and our spirits refreshed by tranquillity. Now we came to a big industrial city with trams in the streets, and shops with plate-glass windows, and picture palaces, and big restaurants, and brasseries, and cabarets. At night the streets were blazing with lighted signs, mostly flame red, advertising the cinemas and the side shows.

We stayed at a hotel called the Hôtel des Beaux Arts. It appealed to us not only because of its name—and had we not three sketchbooks in our baggage?—but because the Michelin guide had assured us of its reasonable prices. We were not deceived. For a reasonable price I had a bedroom with a painted ceiling, looking out to a square in which, far below my window, there was a handsome fountain surrounded by taxicabs. The artist had a balcony where, in his pajamas, he could draw the fountain if he so desired, as he did. After dinner we decided to see the life of Lyons. It was my job to see it.

I approached the young lady at the desk. She looked in-telligent and kind.

"Mademoiselle," I said, "be so good as to direct us to a

café where they have good music and gay company. We wish to see the brighter side of Lyons."

She looked thoughtful and doubtful, and then had an inspiration.

"Undoubtedly," she said, "it is the Café Thomassin that you want."

The hall porter, I noticed, made a grimace which was not reassuring. We left the artist drawing that fountain and the taxicabs. The novelist and I set out in search of gaiety. We found the Café Thomassin. We looked through its windows. There was no one inside. It was utterly deserted.

The novelist and I looked at each other and laughed.

"If this is the gayest place in Lyons——!"

We went up and down the streets which seemed most brilliantly lighted. We looked into several other cafés. They had few customers. At the corner of a side street were two cabarets —Les Ambassadeurs and Le Grillon. Two gentlemen in dinner jackets and black ties—rivals in business—invited us to enter. But a peep behind the blinds revealed emptiness.

There was more life outside the terrasse of the Café Riche, where an orchestra was playing. The waiters were fairly busy with customers. It was not a bad observation post for life in Lyons. There were some pretty women here taking their coffee and listening to the music. Young men—among them a group of Italians—sipped various liquids and smoked cigarettes. It was all very respectable but not exactly gay. The most exciting episode was the arrival of a very large, new, and costly motorcar which drew up alongside the pavement. Out of it, with some difficulty, emerged a large man whose stomach was obtrusive. There followed a middle-sized woman, well nourished, and two younger women who, I noticed, had dirty fingernails. The large man ordered drinks loudly. He made great trouble with the chairs. He bullied the waiter. He laughed heartily when the middle-sized lady nearly sat on the ground instead of on the chair. He laughed heartily again at some remark of one of the young women with dirty fingernails. He was a breezy, noisy, good-humoured man.

"Undoubtedly," said the novelist, "we are in the presence

of a prosperous profiteer doing good business in a time of depression."

A queer little old lady appeared. She looked like a witch. I am inclined to believe she was a witch. She had a girl's hat on her head, and on her back was pinned a newspaper with some heading about a speech by Herriot. Her hands were grimy, and she carried an umbrella in one hand and a posy of faded flowers in the other. She went about among the clients of the café, whispering secrets to them which made them laugh. To each one she had something long and intimate to say. Now and again she addressed the company in general, and I heard such words as *la vie*, *l'amour*, and *la folie*.

She came nearer to me and I heard her speech.

"*Oh, là, là!* I know what love is, my dears! A thousand years ago I was a pretty young woman. Now I am mad, of course. But I remember my lovers. Some of them were very nice. There was a young man with a red beard. He was a poet. He made verses to my beauty. Now you think I am ugly, of course. This pretty lady thinks I am an ugly old creature! Let her wait! One day old Time will claw at those pretty cheeks. She will have bags under her eyes like mine. She will fade and wither like me. And perhaps she won't remember so many lovers, because I was much loved. That is strange, is it not? My beauty made them mad! They would walk a league to kiss my little white hand. They would fight each other for my favours. I knew a young gentleman with a red beard——"

Everyone laughed heartily. She was a rare joke, they thought. Presently she climbed onto the bonnet of a motorcar and beat time to the music with her umbrella.

I spoke to a young man by my side.

"Do you belong to Lyons?"

He shook his head and smiled.

"No, I belong to Geneva. I am only working in Lyons."

"How are things at Geneva? The League of Nations, for instance?"

He was amused by this reference to the League of Nations.

"In Geneva we don't think much of that! It has failed. That Disarmament Conference is a farce."

"But what will happen if there is no disarmament?"

The young man shrugged his shoulders.

"What can one do when so many nations have gone mad —like that old woman? It ought not to be impossible to get some kind of agreement. But they refuse to agree about anything while everything goes wrong. Soon I suppose there will be another crash and perhaps another war. I am glad that I live in Switzerland! Otherwise I should have to fight in a quarrel that I have done nothing to make."

He smoked one of my Virginian cigarettes, and we chatted.

After that the novelist and I went in search of other aspects of life, but the streets were becoming deserted.

I spoke to the young woman behind the desk of the hotel.

"There doesn't seem to be much doing in the Brasserie Thomassin, or anywhere else in Lyons. It is not gay, your city!"

"No?"

She thought the matter out.

"It is of course *la Crise*. The big industrialists are suffering, and there is not much money about. Many people here in Lyons are unemployed or have to economise very sharply because of bad business. That is why they do not go much to the cafés and amusement places. In any case Lyons is not *bruyant* and animated like, for instance, Marseilles. I am sorry that you have not amused yourself."

I reassured her.

"I have been very much interested. I am, for instance, interested and sorry to know that Lyons is not very prosperous just now. That seems to me astonishing as well as sad."

"It is because of Japanese competition and English tariffs," said the young woman behind the desk.

"Excuse me," she added after the reference to English tariffs. "I speak frankly."

15

I found Lyons a fine city, very spacious and attractive, between the Rhône and the Saône, and with many fine buildings and streets. Charles Dickens on his way to Italy recorded a bad impression of it, and it is hard to believe that the city of silk should have been so dilapidated as he describes it.

What a city Lyons is [he wrote]! Talk about people feeling at certain unlucky times as though they had tumbled from the clouds. Here is a whole town that is tumbled anyhow out of the sky; having been first caught up, like other stones that tumble down from that region, out of fens and barren places, dismal to behold. The two great streets through which the two great rivers dash, and all the little streets whose name is legion, were scorching, blistering and sweltering. The houses, high and vast, dirty to excess, rotten as old cheeses, and as thickly peopled. All up the hills that hem the city in, these houses swarm; and the mites inside were lolling out of the windows, and drying their ragged clothes on poles, and crawling in and out of the doors, and coming out to pant and gasp upon the pavement, and creeping in and out among huge piles and bales of fusty, musty, stifling goods; and living, or rather not dying, till their time should come, in an exhausted receiver. Every manufac- turing town, melted into one, would hardly convey an impression of Lyons as it presented itself to me; for all the undrained, unscaven- gered qualities of a foreign town seemed grafted there, upon the native miseries of a manufacturing one, and it bears such fruit, as I would go some miles out of my way to avoid encountering again.

Lyons has changed mightily since then, as London has changed from the London of Fagin and Bill Sykes, which Dickens knew. It is well built, well drained, and has an air of great prosperity in spite of a world "crisis" which seems to be "critical" a long time.

I wandered along the Quai des Célestins early one morning before my two companions had left their beds, or at least their bedrooms. Here was a flower and vegetable market, very picturesque and amusing along its line of booths, with the scent of flowers mingling not unpleasantly with the scent of onions. There was no dirt, as Dickens described. On the con- trary, everything was spotlessly clean and fragrant, and the market folk were decently dressed and self-respecting. An old woman was knitting as she waited for customers for her straw- berries and cherries. She caught my eyes on her and smiled in a friendly way and said, "*Bon jour, monsieur! Fraises des bois?*

Cerises?" A little nun was doing her morning shopping for her convent, carrying a great bag of knitted string in which she had put a load of carrots and cauliflowers. All the stall holders were crying their wares. "*Trois têtes, vingt sous! Un kilo, trente sous!*"

I stood on the bank of the Saône, looking over at its bridges spanning the broad, fast-rushing river. A man who looked like a mechanic was leaning with his elbows on the parapet, and I had a talk with him. He told me that Lyons was depressed as far as the factory workers went. There was a good deal of unemployment, not so much in the electricity works where he worked, but in the workshops and yards. Some of the factories had shut down for a time. Others were on half time. Men were not earning their full pay. That made money scarce for everyone—the shops and the markets. But, he said, it was the same everywhere in France. Perhaps also in other countries. Something had gone wrong with the world. He was inclined to believe there was wickedness at the back of it.

"It seems strange," he said, "that men should be poor when they have all the opportunities of being prosperous. The machine working for mass production gives every man a chance of getting cheap goods. So it should be. But what do we find? No distribution of these good things. Men are cursing the machine because it throws them out of work. Should we not rather curse the statesmen and politicians, or perhaps the bankers and manufacturers, because they grasp all the money and restrict the output of good things? It is a question, I think, of control, distribution and justice. We are at the mercy of corruption and greed and bad organisation. That is how it seems to me. But I am a mechanic. I don't understand these things. I only suffer from them."

He looked across the river.

"It's a fair world," he said, "but men have made a mess of it somehow. We don't seem to have gone right since the war."

"It was the war which put things wrong," I said.

"You are right," he answered. "That is the truth. And now we talk as though another were coming. It makes one despair. You are English?"

He was just as friendly when he heard I was English.

I had another conversation that morning in a tobacconist's shop. The shopkeeper was a wizened little man with eyebrows like spiders. His wife was a buxom soul with plump hands which she folded on her stomach.

"The greatest danger to world trade," said the tobacconist, "are these little Japanese, who undercut all prices to a degree which is ridiculous. They have ruined the silk trade of Lyons. What can we do about it? I ask myself. It is sad when honest workingmen have no wages to keep their wives and children. I find it sad that they have to economise in tobacco. That is not only bad for my business, but it is a hardship upon men to whom tobacco is a comfort."

The buxom lady had something to say.

"Those politicians in Paris are the cause of it all! They talk a lot and do nothing. They are dishonest and take thieves' money. You have doubtless heard of the Stavisky case, monsieur? A real scandal! It makes one sick. Abominable!"

I had heard of the Stavisky case. I kept on hearing of it. It was an obsession in French minds.

I crossed the city and stood on a bridge called Pont Wilson, at a time when President Wilson was hailed as a great peacemaker in France, until he was denounced as an imbecile and impostor. On the bridge there was a sturdy man who looked like a farmer. Perhaps he had sold his beasts in Lyons and was resting for a while by the river before going back to his fields.

"It is of course absurd," he said, turning to me.

I asked him to tell me the latest absurdity, and he was startled when he found I was an Englishman, or, at least, as he could see, not French.

"One does not get the cost of all one's labour," he said. "I sell my beef at two francs a kilo. That is little. It is not enough to pay back. When I go home to my wife she will say, 'They have robbed you, *mon vieux!* They are always robbing you!' And that is true. They are always robbing me. It is a bad animal who robs me."

He spoke the name of the bad animal. I had heard it before.

L'Intermédiaire. The Middleman.

"In Lyons," said the man on the bridge, "beef is retailed at fourteen francs a kilo. Is not there robbery somewhere? Should not we destroy these *intermédiaires* like vermin?"

I put in a plea for them, or, at least, a recommendation to mercy.

"One must have retailers, I suppose. And they have their rents and taxes and transport charges, and all manner of costs."

"That is true," said my friend. "I am not unreasonable. I admit that in the present system there must be a retail man. But why should there be a swarm of them between me and the market—between the market and the shop? They are like lice, monsieur. They feed on the life of farming folk and those who produce the gifts of God out of the good earth. It is not just. It is, as I remarked, an absurdity."

16

I went to see an English business man in Lyons. He knew the city and all its conditions.

"People seem sorry for themselves here," I said. "Surely there is a lot of wealth in this city? What about the silk trade? What about ladies' stockings, which are the very symbols of modern civilisation? It seems to me in London, Paris, and other cities, the women's stockings are the most important things in life, judging from the shop windows. Surely Lyons takes the lion's share of that?"

My business friend passed me a cigarette and smiled.

"My dear sir, the silk industry in Lyons is desperate! Things are so bad that many of the country folk don't raise the silk-worm any more. It doesn't pay them. Many of the silk factories are not functioning. The world demand for silk has withered as far as Lyons is concerned. Artificial silk is taking its place. And worse than that, the Japanese have captured the world markets by cutthroat prices beyond competition; and not only in silk. Far from it! Why they are selling cycles—push bikes—at twenty-five francs apiece! In English money that is six-and-sixpence or thereabouts. I heard the other day that when they first arrived in Algiers the natives bought them and 'popped' them for forty-five francs at the pawnbroking establishments—until the money-lenders got wise. Very amusing, eh? Also very alarming. But there are lots of other reasons why Lyons and France are in a bad way."

"Tell me," I said.

"Prices are too high," said my friend. "People haven't any money to spend on little luxuries which keep trade going. It's partly due to——"

"*L'Intermédiaire?*" I asked. "The Middleman. Don't tell me that!"

He told me that.

"You see, it's like this. A business man—a shopkeeper—wants to make a fortune in five or six years. That's the way nowadays. He buys a shop on lease for, let us say, two hundred thousand francs. Very well. Owing to depreciation in values the shop is now worth one hundred thousand francs. The shop-keeper says, 'That will never do. I shall have to put that depreciation onto the retail price.'—Let me tell you some of these prices. They are the reason why there is rioting in Toulouse and other towns because these things cause political passion and make people discontented with their government and the whole system. Bacon, for example, is five shillings a pound in English money."

He told me other prices, but I forget them. They were all very high.

"Figure things out and you will get below the surface of discontent in France. . . . The average worker—a mechanic, let us say, gets a thousand francs a month. That in English money now is a bit over twelve pounds a month. The white-collar man gets twelve hundred a month, that is fifteen pounds. You may say that isn't too bad. But you have to bear in mind the purchasing value of money in France. It doesn't go nearly as far as in England because of indirect taxation on many articles and the rise in prices. I have worked it out that five pounds a week in England would need seven pounds ten shillings in France to equalise. So you see, a labourer on a thousand francs a month or a white-collar man on twelve hundred has a very thin time if he is a married man with a child or two."

"France is hoarding gold," said my friend after a discussion about these things.

He turned to his morning paper and looked down the financial page.

"The Bank of France," he said, "has a thousand million pounds in gold. That is half the world's supply."

"And what's the good of it?" I asked. "Isn't that poisoning the whole system? Isn't it the cause of this new unemployment and dwindling of trade? Isn't it this gold and its effect on exchanges which has killed her tourist trade and ruined her hotels and restaurants? Why doesn't France come off the gold standard——?"

My English friend smiled and lit another cigarette.

"My dear sir, so far from going off gold, the French government and people cling to gold as their last chance of safety. Any government which went off the gold standard would cause a revolution, unless I'm gravely mistaken. The French people shudder at the idea. Why, commercial firms—the very farmers even—are hoarding gold. They buy it in bars and hide it away. The government grabs gold whenever it comes on the market. The Bank of France—" he glanced at his paper again—"has a gold cover of seventy-eight per cent instead of thirty-five per cent, as required by law."

"And so France," I said, "is the richest country in Europe —and is losing her trade, while unemployment rises and there is discontent—something like despair—throughout France!"

"That is how it is," said my friend.

He spoke about the political situation in the city.

"Opinion is moderately Republican in Lyons. Of course, there are groups of hotheads. You may have seen that there was a clash last Sunday in the Park between the Jeunesses Patriotes and the Communists. Some heads were broken on a fine afternoon. How's Paris?"

I gave him my impression of Paris—restless, anxious, strained.

He was interested in my journey and worked out the cost of the car and petrol. "*Bon voyage!*" he said, after this talk of ours.

I went into a café in Lyons early one morning to reinforce
a scanty breakfast. It was ready for customers, but two or three
young men came in. They seemed to have no urgent business
for the day, but read the morning papers diligently, and then
turned to the illustrated papers. One of these young men looked
bored and restless. He walked about the café studying time-
tables on the walls, and advertisements for Amer Picon and
Dubonnet. He yawned, looked at his fingernails, and then in a
kind of desperation ordered a vermouth, though it was breakfast time. Perhaps he was waiting for a train or a business appointment. He was very smartly dressed and was a handsome
fellow of about twenty-four. Once or twice he glanced at me,
as though he would like to talk, and I was glad to give him the
opportunity.

"English, aren't you?" he asked.

He had a wish to visit England. He was seriously inclined to
learn English at the Berlitz school. He knew a bit of German,
having lately been in that country.

That was a good opening for conversation. I asked for his
impressions of Germany under the Nazi régime.

"Alarming!" he said with a laugh. "As a Frenchman I came
away with unpleasant apprehensions. Certainly they are preparing for a new war."

"What makes you think that?" I asked.

He laughed again.

"It's visible! All the young men marching about like soldiers.
All talking of the need for discipline and sacrifice. All fanatical
about the glory of the Fatherland. All very earnest in their
belief that the German people—*Deutsches Volk*—are chosen by
God to lead the world and trample their enemies underfoot.
France must not disarm. On the contrary, we must strengthen
our defences. All that talk at the Disarmament Conference is
just *blague*. How can we disarm with a nation getting ready to
lay us low? It's idiotic. What would happen to private individuals, say in a café like this, if a bandit came in brandishing a
revolver and uttering murderous menaces? They would be very

foolish if they had no means of defending themselves. Germany is a bandit nation. They are essentially militaristic. It is in their blood and spirit. They believe in war as healthy discipline and a spiritual ordeal. We can't understand that sort of thing in France. The French people loathe the idea of war. One never sees military shows in France except on the Fourteenth of July, or some special ceremony. French people want to live in peace and get on with their business. Perhaps we are too obsessed with the idea of peace! We are weakening ourselves. Our youth—my contemporaries—are too careless of the dangers ahead."

"And yet," I said, "they seem to be arming for a little private war between themselves. Isn't that so?"

My young friend was startled for a moment by that remark.

"It's not serious, all that," he said after a slight pause for inward cogitation. "The newspapers exaggerate the importance of the Jeunesses Patriotes and the Communists and all those other groups who advertise themselves by street conflicts. They are negligible in numbers and importance."

"It was a sad affair in the Place de la Concorde," I reminded him, "and since then there have been some rather serious riots in provincial towns."

He shrugged his shoulders.

"A few heads broken! A few police injured! Schoolboy stuff, monsieur, I assure you!"

He tapped a cigarette on his fingernail before lighting it.

"Perhaps there is some trouble coming in Paris. Paris is filled with idiotic people. The Parisians are neurasthenic. It is caused by their traffic, which would unsettle the nerves of a robot. They have a tradition of revolution. And they have no loyalty. Now, here in Lyons, we don't get excited. We remain calm. We have a certain contempt for Parisian hysteria. The Lyonnais are still true to the Republican tradition. We believe it is best for France. May I ask what you are doing in Lyons?"

I told him that I was only on a passing visit and that I was making a motor journey through several countries in Europe for the purpose of writing a book.

He was interested.

"That is an enchanting mission!" he exclaimed. "You will

see many amusing things. You will meet many interesting people. I should like to come with you. It would be an education. I should come back with more knowledge of human nature. It must be a fine career to be a writer of books. I am only a writer of figures in an office ledger. That is not amusing. But I have a passion for reading."

He told me about some of the books he liked. I found him a highly intelligent young man with very charming manners. We parted good friends. He took off his hat to a man who wrote books as though he had a real respect for me, though heaven knows why, now that almost everybody writes books. He wished me a good journey, without accident.

18

We took to the roads again that morning, and to the open countryside, and old villages, and the enchantment of woods, and hills under the blue sky of France—on our way to Switzerland.

We halted first for a morning apéritif in a village called Mexonieux, and sat outside the Hôtel du Lion d'Or. Next door was an old yard with a Roman pillar, richly carved round its Corinthian capital, reminding us that on this road had passed the army of Cæsar on their long marches from the Eternal City to the barbarian world, which they tamed and civilised. We were in the valley of the Rhône, bordered by pollarded willows. Beyond us there were wooded hills. On each side of us the fields were spread with flowers from which came incessantly a symphony of silver trumpets played by tiny elves. So it sounded in my ears. It was the song of the *cigales*, millions and millions of them, so that this instrumental music was shrill and loud. As we travelled, taking it leisurely, as usual, stopping frequently, the hills became higher. They were the spurs of the Jura and presently our car was climbing them until we were on a road with a sheer drop below us. We passed through a gap with a high bluff cut straight down through an immense rock, beyond a village called Poncin, where the tower of the church rose above brown roofs.

Our car followed the mountain road with innumerable wind-ings and hairpin bends. On each side of us were jagged rocks of limestone, flinging black shadows against the mountain side. Old fortresses were perched on high crags. In the old days they had guarded this valley of the Rhône from many enemies. On the very summit of the hills was the village of La Balme, isolated from all the world below, and very lonely on the height, in a clearing of woods. Dun cows browsed on the mountain slopes, with a tinkle of bells. A light railway followed the highroad, going through beech woods with their first foliage as vivid as green flames.

Round St. Germain de Joux, another mountain village, there were orchards covered with white blossom, and here, at the Hôtel Reygrobellet—strange name!—we rested awhile. A small boy came to stare at us. I asked his name, and though he was only about four years old, he spoke it gravely. Reygrobellet! I wondered at the destiny of a child born with such a name.

Across the road some woodcutters were busy with a heap of small logs. They gathered them into baskets shaped like the flower of the petunia, or trumpet-shaped. These lads were half naked. Their bodies, stripped to the waist, gleamed like copper. We talked to them, and they were very civil, and in-terested in the arrival on their hilltop of three strange-looking Englishmen, one of whom was an artist busy on his sketchbook.

"It's a quiet life up here," said one of them. "Nothing to do but work a little, and eat a little, and sleep a little!"

"A good life!" said I. "What more does a man want?"

They laughed, showing their white teeth.

The novelist took a photograph of them carrying their logs. It amused them a good deal, and they became self-conscious.

"One becomes strong at this kind of job!" said one of them. He bent his arm to show the splendour of his strength.

We continued our journey through the deep gorges above the Rhône cutting. There were snow peaks in the distance, gleam-ing white in the sun. We went down along a straight road, high above the river. A falcon poised above our heads in the blue. The road led through a French fort with a double drawbridge. At St. Cenis-Pouilly some customs officers held us up at a barrier across the road. They looked into our car. They held a conversation with Gaston, our driver, who assured them we were harmless Englishmen travelling for pleasure, with no merchandise or contraband. They accepted our word for it and saluted. There was another barrier farther on. There were more customs officers in a different uniform. They let us pass.

"We are now," said Gaston, "in the country of the picture postcard."

We were in Switzerland.

V

A Swiss Sojourn

IN GENEVA WE STAYED at the Hôtel d'Angleterre, facing Lake Leman, and not far from the Beau Rivage, which is reserved during the League assemblies for foreign ministers and their secretaries. At the time of our arrival these Great Brains, busy with the destiny of nations (according to the newspapers), and ardent in their endeavours to secure disarmament and peace (while voting for increased armaments and preparing for another war), had not yet arrived but were expected shortly. Some of their juniors had been sent in advance and were occupying the second-best bedrooms.

They were preparing the ground for what might be the last session of the Disarmament Conference, which, after many years, many plans, and many hopes—the hopes of all peace-loving people in the world—had reached an *impasse* no longer to be concealed or circumvented by any face-saving formula, unless one of those Great Brains, shortly expected, might, at the fifty-ninth second of the eleventh hour, invent one. Germany claimed equality of rights—*Gleichberechtigung*—in the matter of disarmament. It had, as a matter of fact, been acknowledged as a theoretical justice by France, Great Britain, and Italy, with other powers. But the advent of Mr. Hitler and his Nazis had, said the French, created a new situation. They declined to admit the right of Germany to re-arm until France was assured of security against German aggression—"and," said every Frenchman in his heart, "not even then!"

A nice young man named Mr. Anthony Eden—too young and too good-looking to bear the portentous title of Lord Privy Seal of England, except for his ability—had been travelling round the capitals of Europe (I had followed in his footsteps), trying to persuade Mr. Hitler, and Mr. Mussolini, and Mr. Barthou of France, to accept an English plan, very ingenious, which might give a little more security to France, at least on paper, and a certain measure of armament, strictly defensive, at least on paper, to Germany. The government of France and the newspapers of France were entirely dissatisfied with the proposition, however nicely put to them by that nice young man. Adolf Hitler, in consultation with Genral Goering and other friends, maintained his claim to equality at any level France might choose but—equality. A very awkward situation for statesmen who are elected by peoples impatient of these delays with a strong pacifist vote, as in England, likely to turn the scale of an election when convinced that disarmament was a lost cause, and that a new war might be looming close to their hearths and homes.

That was the situation when we came to Geneva, and the Disarmament Conference had failed to arrive at any agreement or even to adopt any face-saving formula even likely to deceive a schoolgirl, before we left Switzerland.

My two friends, the artist and the novelist, were scornful of me because I still had—still tried to have—some lingering faith in the League of Nations.

"It has always been a farce," said the artist, who belongs to the Big Stick school and has never recovered from his early enthusiasm for Rudyard Kipling in his jingo moods and his song of the White Man's Burden. "How could you expect any good to come out of an assembly just making eyewash for long-haired pacifists, and old women who subscribe to the League of Nations Union? It was all the fault of that schoolmaster idealist, President Wilson, who thought that nations could be made good and happy by copybook precepts of love and brotherhood. We know, my dear ass, that self-interest, patriotism, self-preservation, and the vital instincts of virile races are not to be satisfied by the smug platitudes of a sentimentalist!

And how preposterous to think that England should have her policy dictated by the votes of Nicaragua and Uruguay and Venezuela, who don't pay their subscriptions to the League!"

The novelist agreed with the artist. They did not often agree, I found, having different philosophies of life and different temperaments.

"The failure to deal with Japan when it attacked China," he said, "was the League's confession to the world that it was impotent to enforce decisions. It died then. It's no use pretending that it has any power or any life. Definitely the international idea has failed. Every nation has been forced back to self-defence. England must realise this before it's too late. We're utterly defenceless in the air. We have weakened our navy. All our pacifists are undermining the spirit of the nation. I've come to the conviction that we must abandon internationalism and rely on our own strength again. A touch of Fascism wouldn't do us any harm."

I was challenged in everything I have believed and hoped as we walked along the lake side of Geneva, green in the hot sunlight under a blue sky, with white steamers and small yachts on its shining water. We passed the Beau Rivage and I saw living ghosts there. It was on the terrace there that I had had a long talk with Austen Chamberlain before he signed the Treaty of Locarno. He was in high spirits. He believed that he had done something very big for the peace of Europe. He believed that he had given France, at last, a sense of security and a firm guarantee. There were loopholes, of course. England was not bound as much as France would have liked. There would have to be a unanimous decision regarding the aggressor. . . .

Over the loudspeaker for some weeks afterwards many voices had proclaimed the Treaty of Locar-r-r-no as the promise of a new heaven and a new earth. The temper of nations, their jealousies, and suspicions, and fears, and hatreds, had all been tamed by the spirit of Locar-r-r-no. Germany and France would love one another. We could all sleep quiet in our beds. The babies in the cradles would not be wakened up by the noise of bombardment. They would not be called upon, later on, to advance through the slash of flying steel—or, if they were, they would be glad to face that ordeal, knowing that Sir Austen Chamberlain had pledged them to uphold the sanctity of pacts signed by such gentlemen as himself with the very best intentions. It made us all feel happy, until, strangely, the French people and the French newspapers began to cast doubts upon this treaty of Locarno, and demanded more security, and started digging new defences all along the frontier.

Here, in Geneva, I had worked on hot days and nights, sending long telegrams to English and American newspapers after conversations with statesmen, and diplomats, and idealists, and enthusiasts. There had been many ups and downs of hope, many disappointments and disillusions. Over and over again the pessimists had wailed, "The League is dying!" or "The League is dead!" Some of them, hating the international ideal, had had a savage and secret satisfaction in announcing the end of all that. But the League had gone on living. It had stopped several little wars. It had stamped out many little fires which might have led to a spreading conflagration. The spirit of the League was altering men's minds, we believed. We were advancing towards a reasonable system of give and take among the nations. There was, surely, more adherence to the idea of arbitration, international law and justice. It was an educative assembly. Some of those who came to scoff remained to pray, or, at least, confessed that patriotism was not enough in a world so mutually dependent, so desperate on the edge of ruin after a world war, so sure to go down in anarchy if such a thing happened again.

There were great days in Geneva, great moments when it seemed as though the destiny of mankind had been changed to a new direction by words spoken, and things written, here in the Assembly of the League. Those words and agreements would end the long martyrdom of man, taken from the plough to be used as gun fodder, led like sheep to the slaughter because of some quarrel not of their making, or duped into popular enthusiasm for war by orators and writers, who did not share their death nor their agony. Such a day seemed to have come when Stresemann brought Germany into the League and was welcomed by Briand.

It was Briand—that shabby old man sitting hunched up, with a cigarette between his lips, and dandruff on his shoulders—who went onto the platform, threw his shoulders back, thrust the hair from his forehead, and spoke words which seemed to be touched by divine fire. He was an orator of the old school. He was an old play-actor. But on that day his own friends, cynical of his sincerity, said, "Briand was inspired!" "Briand spoke for once with utter honesty." "Briand rose to a sublime height! Perhaps, after all, there is something in this League of Nations!"

Briand welcomed Germany to the League. He pledged the soul of France to peace and good will with the soul of Germany. He turned his back, as the French people would turn their backs, upon the Way of Blood—*le Chemin de Sang*—that long road of flaming war and monstrous death, which both nations had traversed; and he faced a future when Germany and France would work together for the peace of humanity, for the safety of women, and the rescue of the world's young manhood.

Stresemann answered Briand. Standing before the delegates of all nations, he was pale, and strained with emotion. He read his speech, and it had less fire than the French statesman's, but there were noble phrases in it which moved a great audience.

"It cannot be the meaning of a divinely ordered world that men should turn their highest national achievements against each other. The man who serves humanity best is he who, rooted in his own nation, develops his spiritual and moral endowments to their highest capacity, so that, growing beyond the limits of his own nation, he is able to give something to the whole of humanity."

On that day, after those speeches and that scene in the Assembly Hall, there were many of us who believed that really and truly we had reached a time of conciliation when the countries of Europe could advance upon the same road to repair the ruins of the war and build up a common prosperity in a settled peace. It is ironical now to remember what has happened, afterwards and lately.

I remember all that on an afternoon in Geneva when I was chaffed by two friends for my faith in the League of Nations. Briand was dead. Stresemann was dead. France clamoured for new security and refused to disarm by even one gun. Germany, they said, was re-arming. There was no sense of peace in Europe.

2

We gave Gaston a rest and took a taxicab to the new Palace of Nations now being built to house the League. It lies outside the city of Geneva and when finished will cover an area larger than Versailles.

Its shell is built, and we stood looking at an enormous frontage of concrete, undecorated and unbeautiful. The hot sun beat down on workmen naked to the waist, pushing wheelbarrows along unfinished tracks, or stirring up cement, or heaving blocks of stone. A light railway for carrying heavy loads led to the area of work. We wandered about in the white dust and picked our way amidst the blocks of stone.

"I'd like to do a drawing of this House of Dreams," said the artist, grimly and with sinister intent.

"All this is a tragic farce," said the novelist.

I spoke to a group of workmen handling the stones. One of them looked up and grinned when I said something about the new palace of the League.

"We're not building a palace for the League," he answered.

"What then?" I asked.

"A new hospital for the wounded of the next war."

He spat on the ground and looked at me with blue laughing eyes, but his words had raised the hair on my scalp. I suppose I laughed, but it was a bitter and frightful phrase.

A younger man joined in the conversation.

"I know what I'm helping to build."

He gave me another version of the use to which the palace of the League would be put.

"This, monsieur, is a barracks we are building. It will be

The Palace of
the League
May 1934

E. Landon
Gordon

THE PALACE OF THE LEAGUE

ready for occupation by the Germans when they march this way."

He gave a loud guffaw which was echoed by his comrades. They all seemed very much amused.

"That's right!" said another man—middle-aged and more serious. "They will march next time through Switzerland. It's all arranged. They won't attack through northern France again. They will come this way through the plain, down from Basle. Who can stop them? Three hundred years ago we threw stones at our invaders. Now it's a different thing. Science has invented high explosives. The air will be crowded with machines dropping bombs on our pates and making a mess of our bodies. Herr Hitler will follow in his motorcar. The bands will play *Deutschland über Alles.* Those who don't say *Heil Hitler!* will be shot at dawn. Little Switzerland will become part of the German Reich. We shall have to learn the goose step. I assure you, monsieur, it is all arranged."

They became hilarious. Perhaps they took us for three Englishmen, or delegates to the Disarmament Conference. They were delighted to pull our legs. They had been saving up these speeches for any such visit. They were very bitter and jocular and voluble. In a hot sun it was pleasing to them to drop work awhile and stand over their shovels and their wheelbarrows and describe the horrors of the next war. I listened for a time, keeping a smile on my face. But that phrase I had heard haunted me:

"A new hospital for the wounded of the next war."

I repeated it to the novelist, who was startled.

"Good heavens! . . . What an epigram! . . . And to think that it comes from a horny-handed son of toil! It was worth all our journey to hear those words."

A manifesto had been pasted on the hoardings outside the palace of the League. We walked over to read it. It was addressed to the F.O.B.B., which being interpreted meant "Fédération des Ouvriers du Bois et du Bâtiment."

Workers of the Building Trade [said the manifesto]! *the Swiss Federation of Contractors has decided upon a decrease of wages. There is to be a 15 cents decrease by the hour on the wages of masons. The F.O.B.B. does not accept this. Do not allow yourselves to be starved! Be ready to defend your wages!*

Another printed placard was pasted next to this. It was longer and was, it announced, an affirmation of workmen's rights.

By the fault of Capitalism
The World dies of Misery
and Servitude.
The Bourgeoisie maintains its Privileges
By the most bloody Reaction.
Think of the Martyrs of Vienna and Elsewhere.

The incessant progress of machinery, technique, science, and human intelligence accumulate products sufficient to assure the well-being of all. Nevertheless, misery and uncertainty disintegrate the world of labour.

Capitalism is Senseless.
It is to drag down the peoples to a degrading Misery
that the Bourgeoisie wallows in Blood.
By War it destroys Social Wealth.
By Fascism it destroys Free Thought.

We Have Had Enough Of That!

Dangerous words to be posted up on the hoardings of the new palace of the League of Nations! They explained the origin of the epigrams fired at me by the workmen. They revealed the bitterness of men building, stone by stone, a new meeting place for the statesmen and ministers of nations who had failed to bring peace to the world and who were assembling again in Geneva to evade the realities of Disarmament, while every nation increased its own, ignorant of what thoughts were passing in the minds of labouring men, stripped to the waist, in a hot sun, and murmuring among themselves. I doubt whether any delegate had read those words on the walls. It is highly doubtful whether Sir John Simon or Dr. Beneš, or M. Barthou was aware of such thoughts moving in the minds of labouring men within a stone's throw of their assembly room, where they sought for a face-saving formula to cover up the failure of the Conference and a wreckage of hope among the idealists, the pacifists, the odd, annoying people who believe that war may be abolished forever by a little intelligence and a little virtue. I wondered for a moment if I might warn them. I wondered what would happen if I appeared among them and said:

"Gentlemen, unless you agree upon a measure of disarmament and create the foundations of a settled peace, there will be new revolutions in Europe, and the old order will perish in anarchy, because labouring men are impatient of a system which gives them no present comfort or future hope. If you cannot prevent new wars, you will have revolution first in all your countries, and it will not spare those who only dealt in eyewash. No dictatorship will last if it drags men to the shambles again. No prosperity is possible if nations are to be more heavily taxed for arms and armaments. Beneath this unsettled and uncertain peace in Europe there are seething discontents which one day will explode, and that day is not far distant. Is there no hope for intelligence? Have you surrendered? Is your answer '*Après nous le Déluge*?'"

I decided that there was nothing I could do about it. I was one of the common folk. There is nothing they can do about it. That is the tragedy of these times. Perhaps there is a greater tragedy. When Youth decides to do something about it, it seems quite likely that they will do the wrong things, in different coloured shirts, with different war cries, with new hatreds, with new intolerance towards their fellow men.

3

I had a conversation with an elderly woman who sold me *Le Journal de Genève*. She was in her kiosk, almost concealed by her newspapers and magazines, but she leaned forward to talk to me earnestly, after some preliminary remarks about the weather, and the coming Conference, and affairs in France, and the state of Switzerland.

"We Swiss folk are in much distress," she informed me. "How could it be otherwise? Were we not the home of the tourist in prosperous days? They were so happy to come here to our lakes and mountains—winter and summer! We were a happy country, giving happiness and beauty to all the world. Now they do not come. It is impossible for them to come because of their money troubles and the weakness of their exchange. We are still on the gold standard, whatever that may mean! That does not help us. Perhaps it kills us. Our hotels are empty. Many of them are greatly in debt. The pensions in the mountain villages receive no guests. The shops sell nothing. I sit here all day in this kiosk, waiting for English and Americans and Germans and all the people who used to buy my papers in every language. They do not pass, monsieur. Why? I ask myself why, and I answer that question."

She answered the question for my benefit.

"Because the world has gone mad, monsieur!"

"That is true!" I agreed, with deep conviction. "And yet there are many intelligent people in the world. I meet them everywhere. I am amazed by their wisdom. They are so wise— the ordinary folk I meet on the wayside. . . . What is going to happen next week when the Disarmament Conference meets again in the League of Nations?"

In times gone by I might have asked that question of one of the Great Brains, who would have answered at length, knowing that his words would go to the world's press; but I had a feeling that this elderly woman in her little box might give me more illumination and greater truth.

She repeated my last words with a kind of mockery.

"The League of Nations! . . . Ah, monsieur, what a downfall of hopes! What a tragic affair! What dreadful failure to confess to all those millions of people who have been hoping against hope that they would give peace to Europe!"

"They will arrange nothing?"

"They will arrange nothing except to increase their military strength. Year after year I have hoped that we had finished with bloodshed and the sacrifice of young manhood. Now I do not hope so much. The world is too wicked."

"It's wickedness, you think?"

"Greed and egotism, monsieur. That is what prevents peace between the nations. Everybody drags the eiderdown over his own head. If you are a married man you will understand that that is selfishness. The rich want to be more rich. That is why there are all these tariffs and trade conflicts. Capitalism has many evils, as one must admit without being an anarchist. It is Capital which makes the machine the enemy of mankind, using it for selfishness and not for the happiness of the masses. The Machine! It is a devil! It has the power of ten million devils. It turns men out of their places, making much unemployment and much misery. Undoubtedly it is the cause of great distress and discontent, which one day may lead to revolution —and then worse misery and deeper ruin, monsieur. The Machine! Yes. That is the enemy. It is the devil. It is the power of evil in the world today. But I ask again, Why? Surely God did not allow us to invent machinery to undermine our own state and to take wages from our working men? No, that is unbelievable. It is untrue. That is not the answer. I know the answer."

"Tell me," I said.

She told me, clasping her hands—thin, nervous hands—on the little counter of the kiosk.

"Monsieur, it is because the Machine is manipulated by greedy men for their own profit. That I believe is the answer."

She spoke again about the danger to world peace.

"If war comes, it will be from Germany. But how extraordinary are those people! What gain will they get from war? What will they obtain from war except corpses? They are, of course, mad. That is self-evident. Hitler is a madman. General Goering is also a madman. It is a country inhabited by madmen. They put the poison of their madness into young brains. I read the Swiss papers. I say Germany is one big madhouse, and even a little madder than other nations who are not normal. And those gentlemen in the League of Nations. What are they doing? How can they face their peoples? How can they go on talking insincerities with disaster creeping nearer? Is it impossible for them to get above all this insanity and lead the peoples back to peace and happiness? If that is impossible, then war will come again and plunge us into the blackest ruin. Because, monsieur, we cannot stand the strain of another war. It will let loose the beast in mankind. It will take us all back to the beginning of things before civilisation. I am very much afraid when I think of these things."

I put my hand into her little house, and she clasped it tightly. We were two souls on the roadside, very much afraid when we thought of these things, not because of any fear for ourselves—we were both elderly—but because we hated the thought of another massacre of youth and the letting loose of the beast.

"*Bon soir, madame. Il faut éspérer!*"

"*Bon soir, monsieur. Il faut éspérer!*"

4

We sat outside a café after dinner. An orchestra was playing merry music. Lights were twinkling along the lakeside. A bright light burned at the top of a mountain on the other side of the lake. It was warm, and with only a faint breath of air stirring. I thought of an August when the heat in Geneva had nearly killed me. It is very hot in summer and very cold in winter, but always beautiful.

The Genevese at this café were well dressed. The young girls passing were charming and elegant. There was no sign of poverty anywhere, although I had heard already, from others besides the woman in the kiosk, that Switzerland was in distress.

The novelist and I discussed these things. It was hard to believe that Switzerland—the model of nations, with several races living together in amity, with industrious people who had always been so comfortable, so solid, so "smug in their prosperity," as their critics used to say—should be stricken by this unkind wind of fate.

"I want to meet one man in one country," said the novelist, "who will say he is doing well. . . . Somehow I don't believe all this tale of adversity. Everywhere I have been in Europe before this journey, I have looked for poverty and failed to find it. The people in all nations seem to me definitely better off than their fathers, apart from the unemployed, who don't seem to starve."

I spoke to a young man sitting next to me at one of the tables. He looked intelligent and attractive for conversational purposes.

"What do you think of the economic situation in Switzerland?" I asked, as he dropped an illustrated paper and looked round. It was an abrupt question, as I was aware. It was very likely that he was thinking of his girl, or of a new suit he proposed to have made for himself, or of a climb into the mountains which he might make next Sunday—anything rather than the economic situation in Switzerland!

He looked a little startled, edged round in his chair, smiled, and answered me politely.

"Extremely unpleasant! . . . There is no business, no tourist traffic, no relief from taxation. If things don't get better there will be serious trouble. Switzerland, of course, is very much dependent on general conditions in Europe, and they don't seem to improve. In fact, they grow steadily worse. Germany, for instance, is marching towards disaster."

I questioned him about that, and he had his answers ready and gave them with a smile as though amused by this prospect of disaster.

"Germany is losing her trade. Can you wonder at it? The Jews are seeing to that. Their boycott is world-wide. They are the manipulators of money and control much business. They are seeing to it that Germany is deprived of her old markets and credits. Hitler has asked for it. That idiotic campaign against the Jews was just the most absurd thing he could have done. But then he is, of course, a lunatic in matters of finance, and perhaps otherwise."

He gave me an instance of what he considered to be Hitler's lunacy.

"The piano trade has been in a bad way in Germany. Hitler came to hear of it. He ordered twenty-five thousand pianos for schools and institutions. Not a very sound way of stimulating trade! They have to be paid for somehow. He forgets that. He doesn't seem to realise that when he builds great roads and public works to keep the unemployed busy, somebody has got to pay for it—the German people themselves! For a time it may be justified, but a nation can't live forever on public works. Anyhow, it's uneconomic, according to ancient laws."

"Do they still prevail?" I asked, doubtfully.

He thought they did.

"This Nazi business in Germany," he said, "is nothing but flag flying and shouting of *Heil Hitler*. Very amusing for the lads while it lasts, but not productive of prosperity. It won't last."

He was very definitely of opinion that Hitler would be pushed on one side by the old crowd and that the Nazi system would disintegrate and disappear.

"They may make a war first," he suggested.

"What about the Disarmament Conference?" I asked, to draw him out.

He laughed and shrugged his shoulders.

"Hopeless! . . . Don't let us talk about it. . . . In Geneva we never mention the League of Nations. It's taboo. At first we hoped. Then we laughed. Now we want to weep when we think of it."

He spoke of Germany again, having lately returned from that country.

"No German is happy unless he's in uniform. It's necessary to his soul. He has the battalion mind. He likes being drilled. He must salute some kind of a flag and wear some kind of badges. Of course they're making guns as hard as they can. France is right not to disarm. We used to be annoyed with France for putting up every obstacle against disarmament. Now, as far as my opinion goes, she is perfectly right. The Germans are just waiting until they are ready to smash her."

I disagreed with him. I too had recently visited Germany. I told him some of the impressions I had brought back. Hitler and his friends were too uncertain of internal conditions to want war with anyone. The younger crowd had their eyes on the far horizon of a new world. The older men hated war and the idea of war, having been in Flanders and at Verdun. Hitler wanted to make peace with France.

I spoke with sincerity, a little weakened by lurking doubts.

"No!" said the young man by my side. "I know the Germans. I know lots of their young men. I like them. But they are the greatest danger in the world today."

He ventured to ask what I was doing in Geneva. Was I a delegate to the League of Nations?

There was a kind of suspicion in his voice. I knew that if I had been a delegate to the League of Nations, and had told him so, he would have lost all respect for my intelligence. I told him something of my journey and the idea of this book. It was only fair, I thought, after his candid conversation. He was interested. When we parted he made a little speech, in curious but courteous terms.

"I hope your journey will begin with pessimism and end with optimism—but I don't think so!"

He lifted his hat and went away.

5

We explored the old part of Geneva—the booths and stalls in the Place de Lille, and the market along the quays under the bridges. My novelist friend was much impressed by the Monument of the Reformation in the public gardens, with a row of life-sized figures, simply and finely done, of great Protestants. Among them were Calvin, John Knox, Oliver Cromwell, and William the Silent, and I thought of all the cruelty and intolerance and frightful horrors brought into the conception of Christ's message to the world by such a man as Calvin. He lived and preached here in Geneva. Some of its citizens have not even yet escaped from the blight he put upon their souls.

Others have liberated themselves from his austere code and have gone, perhaps, a little too far in the opposite direction under the influence of American cinemas and the spirit of jazz. It was the spirit and the noise of jazz which kept me awake, in Geneva. In the Kursaal, across the way from the Hôtel d'Angleterre, there was the thump, thump, of this dance music—it is called music—and from my bedroom window I could see a few couples going round, hour after hour.

There was a friend of mine staying at the Hôtel Beau Rivage —one of those young men who were preparing for the next meeting of the Disarmament Conference before the arrival of the Great Brains. It occurred to me that he might tell me something of what had happened inside the League, and I sent my card up to his room. While waiting for him I had a conversation with one of the clerks in the hotel, busy, or looking busy, behind his desk.

"Many visitors?" I asked.

He looked up and laughed.

"Swiss hotels are empty!"

"Swiss prices are too high," I suggested. "Poor people like the English can't afford the loss in the exchange."

He laughed again and shook his head.

"All hotel prices are down by thirty per cent. Prices are cheap compared with English hotels. But still people don't come. The Germans, for instance, remain at home now. They're not allowed to bring out much money. People aren't travelling. Tourism is dead. It will stay dead until there is a stabilisation of money in Europe and a lowering of tariffs. So far that doesn't look as though it would happen. Economic nationalism is the present fashion, and it's strangling world trade. We're all in a nice mess! It's blue ruin."

He laughed for the third time. I notice that people always laugh when they prophesy blue ruin. Perhaps there is something amusing in the downfall of human intelligence after so much self-conceit in the progress of humanity. Or perhaps it is best to laugh at a world lurching towards ruin. It's much better to laugh than to weep.

My friend upstairs, in one of the second-best bedrooms, sent down word that he would be glad to see me, and I answered the message. He is a very knowledgeable fellow. He knew at this time the secrets of the Foreign Offices. He had talked with many of the leaders in Europe. He had a very close idea of what was going to happen in the next meeting of the Disarmament Conference. I gathered from him that nothing was going to happen. He confirmed the views of the woman in the newspaper kiosk, who had not his special sources of information.

"France is very stiff," he told me. "They won't compromise on their claim to security."

"And Germany?"

He didn't think Germany would yield her claim to equality in armaments.

"I'm inclined to believe in Hitler's sincerity when he talks of peace," said my friend, "but his position is not assured. Anything may happen in Germany. The danger is that militarism will prevail. There are some unpleasant minds working behind the scenes."

"So there is not much hope of disarmament?"

"I'm afraid not. . . . There's just a chance that Russia will join the League. If Russia comes in, Japan will follow. That will give it more reality. . . . There's still the one chance of getting some agreement for combined action against an aggressor. That would go part of the way to meeting the French need for security. But I must confess it doesn't look hopeful. France is moving to the Right. They insist on retaining their superiority and refusing to legalise any measure of German re-armament. The prospects are not too good."

I understood from him that the prospects were "pretty damn bad."

We had a general conversation, but he was fussed by the necessity of meeting a Great Brain due to arrive that morning.

Downstairs one of the waiters talked to me in the lounge. He was a merry little man, and one of those who laugh at the prospect of blue ruin.

"The League does nothing!" he said. "It has never done anything. It is a make-believe. Meanwhile we drift very rapidly towards disaster. What a mad world, monsieur!"

He laughed in a high shrill voice at the madness of the world.

"Switzerland is a nation of hotel keepers and waiters," he said. "I am one of the waiters. I wait for customers and tips. They do not come. There is one thing which would help to restore the tourist traffic. That would be to stabilise the world's money and unlock the gold supplies which are at present lying in the banks. That seems to me a reasonable solution of some of our difficulties. But it is not done by the gentlemen who control these things. They do not seem to have the slightest intention of doing so. It is all very remarkable. As a waiter, I find it all very absurd! In my leisure hours I play the concertina. I find that consoling for the folly of the world. It is best to play the concertina."

He was a waiter in the lounge of the Hôtel Beau Rivage. In his time he had waited on all the Great Brains of the League, and members of their deputations with their little ladies— Japanese, Chinese, Czechs, Poles, Nicaraguans, Uruguayans, and other representatives of civilisation. He preferred his concertina.

6

When we left Geneva we travelled along the south side of the lake, which belongs to France, after the Swiss frontier at Anières. Here we had to pay sixty francs for a petrol tax, which is returned when one enters Switzerland again at St. Guingolphe.

There is a territory here called *la zone franche*—a kind of No Man's Land in the way of duties and customs, so that it leads to a lot of smuggling on both sides, though I am vague as to the methods adopted. It was good country, exquisite on a May morning, along roads bordered by cherry trees, white with blossom. In the villages the lilac was out, and in the cottage gardens wallflowers exhaled their deep perfume.

Lake Leman was two miles away on our left, and the Alps rose on either side of us with distant views of snow peaks, dazzling in the sunlight. We passed through the villages of Jussy and Thonon, and saw to our right the jagged outline of the Dent du Midi with its tooth biting the sky. On the road was a travelling shop in which was a group of wax figures in the latest style of fashion. Across the car, surrounded by peasant girls and boys, was the legend *Foire et Exposition*. Beyond we passed under a bridge which crosses the road from a great château belonging to the Duc de Vendôme. A *douanier* was marching up and down, on the lookout for those smugglers who invade the *zone franche*.

At Meillerie there is a little port crowded with boats rigged with lagoon sails. Some of them were transporting stone from a quarry blasted from the face of the rocks above. We were on the lakeside again. Long fingers of light stretched across it and in its mirror were reflected the snow-capped mountains, and fleecy clouds crossing the sky. A storm gathered and broke with a loud roll of thunder following a flash of forked lightning. Across the lake we could see the Castle of Chillon black under the rain-clouds. Farther on the storm increased in violence. Wild clouds raced across the mountain tops, stabbed by the lightning. Then suddenly, with spectacular effect, the sky cleared, the sun shone down out of the cloudless blue, and the mountains gleamed as though made of metal. They were rising high now on each side of us as we drove through the broad valley. The outline of their peaks was fantastic, and they looked like an end-less line of fortresses, and towers, and battlements. Down the face of the rocks, in deep crevices, cascades fell with a rush of water, and there were raging torrents below, crossed by wooden bridges. Pasture fields for Swiss cows made green oases on the mountain sides to their barren line of rocks, which flung their shadows down on the opposite mountains. Here and there, on a high peak, was a little old castle. In the valley were Swiss farmsteads, very neat and clean, and the children who belonged to them were walking or cycling on their way from school. Along the road came ox wagons carrying loads of timber, the trunks of mighty trees. At Boveret the girls were at their wash-tubs and looked up to laugh at us and wave wet hands. So, after a long journey with many halts, we came to Sion.

7

The artist called to me as I sat in the front seat next to Gaston. "Don't you think that's good?"

I thought it very good, this first view of Sion. It was almost too good to be true, I thought, as I looked ahead at the entrance to the town. On each side was a hill, and on each hill was a castle; one of them called Le Tourbillon and the other La Valère—as afterwards I knew, too well. We entered the town and went down a street with tall seventeenth-century houses and balconies of gilded iron-work, rather Spanish looking, until we came to a fine open square.

"Which hotel?" asked the novelist.

There was a handsome-looking hotel called La Planta, but opposite to where our car stopped was another called L'Hôtel de la Poste et de la Paix.

"What about La Planta?" asked the artist.

There was no question about La Planta. The proprietress of the Hôtel de la Poste et de la Paix was advancing upon us. She took for granted, in a most charming and smiling way, that we intended to stay at her hotel. She made no question about it after we had got out of the car, doffing hats. She was a middle-aged woman who must have been beautiful as a girl and was beautiful now, in a matronly way.

"It is very nice weather," she said.

"Delightful," I answered. "We passed a storm on the way, but it was quickly over."

"It is your first visit to Sion?"

"Yes, my first. It looks very interesting."

"It is amusing sometimes. We have a great market here. There are many nice walks in the neighbourhood. You must visit the castles of Le Tourbillon and La Valère."

We intended to stay in Sion only one night. I regretted that we could only stay so short a time. Later I regretted that I had to stay so long a time.

The lady of the hotel showed us her bedrooms. They were very large and very cheap. I had a spacious apartment, with an admirable bathroom which I shared with the artist, who had an equally good room with a wonderful view of Le Tourbillon from his balcony. He came to know that view remarkably well. I believe he could draw it now in his sleep. The novelist had a room on the opposite side of the corridor, with a different view, looking over the market place. There is nothing he doesn't know of that view over the market place. He knows the shape of each tree. He knows every kind of noise which comes up from that market place. He could write a long narrative poem about it. Very likely he has written it. For many nights and days he heard those noises.

We unpacked a little—we intended to leave next morning—and went out to explore Sion. It was worth exploring. We saw the near side of the two castles on the two hills, making a wonderful picture which our artist friend intended to draw. He drew them from every angle before he had done with them. He knows how their shadows fall. He knows the contours of the rocks below them, and the old brown roofs which frame them in.

In the centre of the main street was a very fine old fountain —a lion rampant above the water basin, carved by a master craftsman. Two small boys were floating a boat in the fountain, and I spoke to one of them, for the sake of talking to him.

"That's a good lion!"

He looked puzzled.

"It's a lion."

"How long has it been here?"

"It's a very old lion. It's older than me, and I am seven."

He stared at me curiously.

"Are you French or English?"

"I'm an Englishman."

He was impressed.

"It's the first time I've seen an Englishman, and I don't know any English. I speak German."

"How's that?"

"Because I'm German. I come from Zurich. I'm Swiss too, of course."

The novelist and I found our way into an old courtyard with tall fat pillars below a balcony which had a carved balustrade. Underneath the balcony was a vast stone table with stone benches suitable for Gargantua and his fat friends.

"This is an interesting place," said the novelist. "It looks incredibly old. I wonder what is the history of that big table."

Here was someone who could tell us. It was a pretty girl who came out of a small door and walked along the balcony. It was, of course, necessary to ask her about this courtyard. She was very pretty.

"Excuse me," I said politely. "What is this building? An old cloister?"

She answered briefly.

"It's a private house."

"It's very old. Sixteenth century, perhaps?"

The girl smiled. She had a charming smile.

"Not so old as that! Seventeenth century."

"And that vast table?"

She laughed, and had a most pleasant way of laughter.

"It's for the men from the mountains. The *vignerons*. In the hot days it was very pleasant for them, no doubt, to sit here in the shade and drink wine out of the heat of the sun. I have no doubt they drank a lot of wine!"

I was sorry when she disappeared through another little door. She was charming.

Beyond the market place was a queer tower with a tiled roof covering it like an old hat. It was called La Tour des Sorcières, and was used, no doubt, as a prison for witches, when there were witch hunts in Switzerland in the time of Calvin, as there were in England in the time of John Knox—those men of God!

"There's something strange about the people of Sion," I said to the novelist. "They are very handsome, and they look oddly un-Swiss."

The novelist agreed.

"There must be Spanish influence. Look at these balconies. They might be in old Madrid."

But it was Roman influence which gave its type to Sion. The Roman legionaries had passed this way. Roman soldiers had been quartered there for centuries. The people of Sion have Roman blood.

We looked into the window of a picture shop. There were photographs of cows fighting each other, head to head, surrounded by a crowd of peasants. I questioned two young men who, I guessed, were *vignerons* down from the hills. The town was crowded with such men, broad-shouldered, bronzed, simple-looking fellows.

"What are those cows doing?"

"Fighting," said one of the young men. "They are trained to do that. The strongest cow pushes back the others until she becomes Queen of the Cows. Then she is decorated with a collar and bell. That's a good beast in that picture. She's a beauty."

"What about a vermouth before dinner?" asked the novelist.

SION

It seemed to me an excellent idea. I felt a little cold in Sion. Perhaps it was the mountain air.

We sat outside a café, watching the people pass, those good-looking girls with dark hair, carrying themselves straight as though they had pitchers on their heads. There was a young man sitting next to me. He seemed to know all the people of Sion. Other young men came across now and then to shake hands. He raised his own hand in greeting to some of the passers-by. He was interested in a Cadillac car which pulled up by the curbstone. Presently I was able to speak to him.

"This town has rather a special character," I said. "The people look to me a little different from those around."

He agreed. He told me about that old strain in them.

"They are relics of the Romans and Gauls. They live up in the mountains, and their blood is not too much mixed."

"They're very good-looking."

"Yes. Sion is famed for its good looks!"

He laughed and raised his hat to a nice-looking girl who passed.

"What do they do here?" I asked. "Any industries?"

He shook his head and greeted a young man who put a hand across his shoulder.

"Purely agricultural and wine-growing. That's unlucky! The peasants can't get prices for their produce. It's not enough to pay for all their hard work. Some of them are really impoverished. It's the same everywhere in Switzerland. We import almost everything in the way of manufactured articles, and we export nothing. Hence our troubles. We're on the Gold Standard, you know. Prices are very high. There are no tourists. They can't afford to come to Switzerland. It's very annoying."

He laughed and accepted one of my cigarettes. I ordered another vermouth. I had a bit of a chill, perhaps. I felt cold one moment and hot the next. We drifted to the subject of Swiss politics.

"There's a certain amount—quite a lot—of Fascism in Sion," said my informant. "I approve! The young men must take charge of the situation. We need new ideas and new methods.

The old men can't adapt themselves to altered conditions, and the old system won't work. It has broken down utterly. Republics are no good—not even in Switzerland. Government by Parliament is idiotic nowadays. It's too slow, and too clumsy, and too much influenced by vote-catching tricks. The mass of the people are all dumb dogs—quite senseless. What does a peasant know about economics or international affairs? They have to be led and disciplined, instead of cajoled by political humbug, or until they get angry and start a revolution, burning and killing like wild beasts, which they are then. Youth also needs discipline and a new order."

"What about Germany?" I asked. "Is youth doing any good there?"

My friendly young man was somewhat illogical, I thought, in his answer to that.

"A Republic is no good in Germany. Hitler will fail. Those people would do better under their Monarchy. They are like that. They must be drilled by sergeant majors."

He spoke about German mentality, which he didn't seem to like, and then referred to the failure of the League to bring about Disarmament.

"Germany is certainly preparing for war, and I don't blame France, although she has been asking for trouble. Now she would be silly to disarm."

We were interrupted in our conversation by another man who came to shake hands and have a few words.

"Switzerland," said the young man after this interlude, "is being undercut by Japanese competition. What can we do about it, when the Japs bring watches to Geneva—the headquarters of the watch trade—and sell them for thirty francs the kilo?"

"Good heavens!" I exclaimed.

The young man laughed.

"Fantastic, isn't it? The other day, here in Sion, a Japanese salesman was showing off his cheap watches in a wine shop where one of our watchmakers was having a drink. Something happened very quickly. The little Jap was chucked out and chased down the street!"

8

I missed dinner in the Hôtel de la Poste et de la Paix that evening. That sense of chill had left me. I felt burning. That night, much to the alarm of the artist, who was trying to sleep in the next room, I became delirious and talked incessantly in a loud voice. I was curiously aware of being delirious. I knew perfectly well that I was talking great nonsense in French and bad German. But I kept on doing it. Several times during the night the artist stole into my room, and I was conscious of him. The next day I was still in high fever. The next night I had acute pains in the left shoulder and ribs. The novelist tried his hand at massage. It is curious that once before—during the Armistice —he spent the night massaging me when I had been hurt in a motor accident. It hurt abominably. I yelled when he worked round my left ribs.

"Better see the doctor, old man," said the artist, looking very worried.

"Good heavens, no!" I said. "I shall be all right in the morning. Just a chill."

There was a tap on my door later on.

It was Madame, the proprietress of the Hôtel de la Poste et de la Paix.

She was very kind and sympathetic. She advised me to see a doctor. It was necessary, she said, and there was a very good doctor in Sion. She recommended him.

He came—a grave young man who had been the house surgeon of a hospital in Geneva. He listened to my lungs.

"*Respirez!*" he said.

I respired.

"*Toussez!*" he said, and I coughed.

"It is *la grippe*," said the doctor. "It is also a touch of pleurisy. You will have to be careful. I will order you hot compresses and send some medicine which may help a little."

It was Madame and the *femme de chambre* who busied themselves with the hot compresses. They pressed to my left side a bottle of boiling water wrapped in a napkin. It burned me like a red-hot iron. Madame laughed at my howl.

"It isn't at all too hot, monsieur, I assure you."

"It's as hot as hell!" I assured her, though it didn't sound so bad in French.

The *femme de chambre* said, "All men are babies. I know, because I once had a husband. He was a German. But he was also a baby when he was ill."

Gaston appeared in my room that evening. He expressed his regret and sympathy. He also strongly advised me to have some diabolical remedy, of which I forget the name. It was, he explained, a number of little glass cups heated in hot water and applied to the chest. They drew out the evil humours. Each little glass cup raised a large blister instantly. It was a marvellous remedy which he often used when he had a chill.

The novelist challenged the doctor's verdict. He was convinced that I had a slight touch of *angina pectoris*.

"*Penses pas!*" said the doctor when he suggested this diagnosis.

"For heaven's sake, don't frighten the fellow with talk like that!" said the artist, who was considerably alarmed by my condition. I knew by his face that he expected me to leave Sion in a wooden box. The idea had occurred to myself in the small hours of the night. I thought:

"We intended to stay only one night in this place. It will be queer if I end the adventure in Sion. Not a bad place in which to end the adventure!"

9

It was a very unfortunate episode. It became more unfortunate after ten days had passed. It was a waste of time and money. The car was standing in the garage. Gaston, its driver, was becoming weary of Sion. My two friends stuck to me close with extraordinary devotion, and they too were weary. The artist had drawn Tourbillon and La Valère from many aspects. The novelist, in sheer desperation, was writing a description in thousands of words of the scene in the market place below his window. I also knew that market place. After the fever had burnt itself out it was my farthest walk from the bedroom, and I looked down for a moment at the scene when the country folk had assembled with cows, sheep, pigs, goats, poultry, and farm produce, arranged in wooden booths.

Nuns crossed the square with small children. Barefooted monks paced by. Across the open space called the Place de la Planta—in the old days it was the Place d'Armes—was a white statue of Helvetia, who was very plump.

One day the place was astir with bugles and the tap of drums. Young recruits for the Swiss term of military service had arrived. They went by at quick march to draw their military boots. They marched back at quick pace with the boots slung over their shoulders. There was a lot of life below the novelist's windows.

And in the early morning, after troubled nights, the noises entered my brain; in my half-waking condition they seemed to invade my room. There were cows, surely, round my bed. Pigs were grunting under the bed. Goats bleated in the bathroom. Poultry clucked on the chest of drawers. A bull advanced upon me with lowered horns.

Kind folk invaded my bedroom. Madame paid frequent visits, always smiling, always motherly. The *femme de chambre* sat by my bedside, telling me of her life with a German husband. She had been with him in Strasbourg during the war. They had been bombed night after night. It was not amusing, she said. The artist was a wonderful nurse, and patient with my tossings and turnings and the general foolishness of a sick man.

A little maid with dark hair and brown eyes carried up liquid foods and held the cup while I drank and was the little mother. It was quite nice being ill in Sion.

Then one day I staggered down, and Madame clapped her hands and said, "Bravo! bravo!" and the little maid smiled, and other waiting maids, who now served on the terrasse under the big trees with overhanging branches to give shade on hot days—they were all very lovely, I thought—greeted me as though I were a long-lost uncle returned from war.

That evening there was a show for my benefit in Sion, though not arranged specially in my honour. The children of Sion had gone to Zermatt for a musical festival in which they were taking part. They had left at five-thirty in the morning. They were due back at nine-thirty, and the whole population of Sion was

awaiting them. In the hotel there had been a choir practice. I
had heard its melody rising to my room. Now when I was down
there was a rush of young women—the elder sisters of the children who had gone to Zermatt. They were making a great re-
ception of it. The castles on the two hills were illuminated. As
the children approached from the railway station escorted by
the town band, wreathed in brass and playing a marching tune,
rockets were fired from the town hall and burst in golden rain
in the dark, velvety sky. There were six hundred children of all
ages, from four to twelve or so. They had had a long day. They
were very tired, as one could see by their limping gait. But they
marched gallantly through the crowd in which were their
mothers and fathers and brothers and sisters. They tried to sing
to the music of the band. Many of the smallest ones were carrying little Japanese parasols which they twirled as they marched.
Others held long alpenstocks. They all looked very fairylike as
they marched through flood-lit streets of ancient houses. It was
the picture of the Pied Piper of Hamelin.

As soon as I was strong enough to crawl—there was still pain
about my ribs—we took to the car again and explored the
neighbourhood for fifty kilometres around. The hotel manager
—the lucky husband of Madame—suggested a trip to Sierre.
"There is the electrical factory there," he said. "Very nice."
We were not thrilled by the electrical factory, but had thrills
enough along the roads, because of the indescribable beauty of
high mountains, rising snowcapped to the blue sky, and the
loveliness of dark quiet woods through which we drove.

We halted and had a picnic in one of these woods after driving
to the lake of Chippis, where sunbaked boys and girls were
bathing in the crystal water.

Another journey we made through an old village high above
Sion. It was a village of very ancient houses made of wood, with
wooden shingles for the roofs held down by enormous stones.
We heard the clink of an anvil and stood looking onto a black-
smith's shop where a giant was beating his red-hot iron with a
jolly rhythm. We had a talk with him, and in the course of it
my artist friend showed his sketchbook to another man who had
the soul of an artist.

"You work in softer material than I do," said the black-smith. "Iron does not go so quickly as chalk and pencil! Nevertheless, one can do something good in it if one has the skill. In my way I am also an artist, perhaps!" He beat the red-hot iron and raised a shower of sparks and laughed.

We were climbing high. Far down below we could see Sion —our home town, as it seemed after so many days. There, very small, were the two castles on the two hills. We climbed higher. The road twisted and turned like a ribbon winding up the mountain slopes. We passed peasant girls with goats who bucked as our car went by, and peasant boys holding their mules on the edge of precipices to give us room. We were close to the snow peaks. In deep clefts gashed out of the rocks, cascades fell with myriads of water drops catching the sunlight. Mountain torrents raged over sharp boulders. Once across the road there was a stream of water through which we had to drive. Along the wayside the figure of Christ hung in many fields, with a riot of wild flowers at the foot of the Cross. The road was a loop twisted to a half circle, and narrow, so that nothing could pass us. Our engine was getting hot. Then we had the surprise of our lives because we left the world of reality and came into a wild dream, a waking nightmare, most fantastic and unnatural.

"It can't be true!" said the novelist. "I don't believe it."

"Do I see something?" asked the artist. "Am I unwell?"

We left the car and walked up to a witch's castle. Or perhaps it was a fortress built by ogres. Or it might have been a joke of demons and hobgoblins. They were the Pyramids of Euseignes, not built by human hands but by nature in a freakish mood. A great number of limestone rocks, dead white, immensely tall, with points as sharp as needles rose before us. On many of these needle points were immense boulders, finely balanced. They were not in line or on the level, but staggered down to a great depth in wild disorder. Immediately in front of us, across the road, there were great blocks of limestone, like the towers of a castle, and they were pierced by an archway through which we walked.

"It is not possible that such things should be," said Gaston.

"I don't understand how it could have happened. How did those great stones get balanced on the pointed rocks? Why don't they fall off? Who placed them there, and why?"

Nature had placed them there, wearing away the soft lime-stone and leaving the boulders on the needle points, carving these rocks into fantastic shapes, creating this witch world which was almost frightening when one met it unexpectedly high up in the mountains.

"There is of course only one thing to do," said the artist. "We must draw these rocks, and take home our drawings, and be told that we are liars."

He sat himself down to draw that scene, which made him feel sick after an hour or two, because the sun was hot on his neck.

"No," he said, thrusting his pencils into his pocket. "This beats everything. One can't convey it in black and white. And the damn place looks incredible. It's the delirium tremens of a drunken orgy among the gods of the underworld. How are you feeling, old man?"

I felt strangely weak in the legs. That fever had burned me up a bit. Some invisible enemy was stabbing me in several places. I envied the novelist, who jumped out of the car at Vex and announced his intention of walking back to Sion down the mountain road.

"I'll come with you," I said, with false bravado.

"Be your age, kid!" said the artist.

There was a telegram waiting at the Hôtel de la Poste et de la Paix. It announced the impending arrival of a lady who had received news of my breakdown and was worried. She had no confidence in my good sense during temporary indisposition. She was coming out to take charge. She was arriving soon after dawn the next day. She arrived and took charge. We three men had no further authority. Gaston no longer took my orders.

"I'm going to take you home," said the lady. "The whole thing is ridiculous. You can't go trapesing about Europe with pleurisy."

We had a consultation with the doctor.

"*Vous n'êtes pas guéri*," he said several times, to my dismay.

Haut de Cry

E. Lander
8th May
SION

HAUT DE CRY, SION

This book had to be written. But he decided that with care, with great care, I might continue the journey.

We had a lady in our company when we set forth again through Europe. She was a laughing lady. It was very nice to have her.

10

The Simplon Pass had just been opened for traffic after the clearance of snow when we left Sion to cross the Alps into Italy.

Our road went by way of Sierre again, and thence to Brigue, through the valley of the Rhône. On our left rose the Bernese Oberland—an immense range of giant, misty mountains with jagged outlines and masses of barren rock. The Rhône is a silver river flowing through flower-strewn fields, bordered here and there by great dark forests. In one of them a battle had been fought between the Savoyards and the Valaisiens. Along every mile of the way armies have passed since the human tribes came westward and fought each other for land and women. Dead straight runs the Roman road to Brigue, with tall poplars on either side. Cæsar, that great traveller, came this way, and his searching eyes stared at the mountains which rose before us in the mists. The valley is still guarded by old forts. At Leuk-Susten there is a noble château. At Visp there is the junction for Zermatt. At Glis the roofs reach far beyond the walls of the houses, as protection when the snow falls. It still lay white in summer sunshine on the high peaks above the town.

We halted at Brigue and put the car in a fine old square with an ancient hostelry next door to a good-looking church. At the Hôtel Couronné et Poste we called for liquid refreshment and asked to see the proprietor. I had messages for him from his mother-in-law, who had mothered me at the Hôtel de la Poste et de la Paix in Sion. He came out and greeted us with great courtesy and spoke excellent English. The hotel of which he is owner had been in the hands of his family for over a hundred years, and he is proud of it, as well he may be. But he was not pleased with present conditions and uttered a lament for the ghosts of departed English and Americans.

"Nobody comes!" he said. "And yet Switzerland is cheaper than England. People seem to be afraid of travelling nowadays. There must be many who can afford to do so in spite of bad times. I cannot understand it."

Even local business, he said, was not good. The farmers were in a bad state, getting low prices for wine and cattle and having no money to spend.

"We must hope for better times, but sometimes hope dies down. That is when one feels depressed. This so-called 'crisis' lasts too long. It is becoming a habit in the world."

His words were melancholy, but he laughed all the same.

"It doesn't do to give way to depression," he remarked. "I try to keep cheerful."

He kept cheerful then, and was pleased to receive my messages from his mother-in-law, with whom he was on very good terms. He wished us a good and pleasant crossing of the Simplon. It was not too difficult in a good car, he said.

It was not too easy. Gaston, our driver, started out in high spirits. He was glad to get away from Sion, where he had been very, very bored. He was confident that the car would cross the Simplon like a bird. For some time it went well, its engine purring beautifully in the ears of its driver. We climbed a long but easy gradient, higher and higher, leaving the town of Brigue far below and behind us, until we were among the mountains with deep precipices dropping sheer beneath us. The sky was intensely blue. The tall trunks of fir trees, climbing up the mountain sides, were splashed with golden sunlight. The road, built by orders of Napoleon after he had made his famous crossing by way of the St. Bernard, was white and dusty, with long black shadows cast across it by its wall of rock and trees above it. We came to a signpost announcing the way to Schalberg. Near by was a wooden figure of the Madonna, lovingly carved.

Gaston was looking worried. He looked more worried a little distance farther on. He got down to look at his radiator. The air quivered above our bonnet. We were on the boil.

"It will be well to cool down a little," said Gaston, taking off his peaked cap and passing a nervous hand across his forehead.

We decided to walk on and wait for him to follow. We walked quite a way and waited quite a time. There was no sign of Gaston.

"I'll go back," said the artist. "He may be unwell."

He went back and did not return.

"Curious!" said the novelist. "I'd better go back and see what's happened."

He went back and did not return.

The lady was picking flowers on the mountain road. She was quite happy to wait awhile. She found some orchids, which filled her with delight. Presently, however, she became a little anxious.

"It's time that car came!" she remarked.

It was very pleasant up there on the mountains. The air was wonderfully clean and exhilarating. I lay down on the wayside on a patch of grass. Brown butterflies flitted by. There was the smell of pines. A cuckoo was calling from the woods below. His voice of mockery was the only sound which broke the great silence. The world seemed far away. This was a high paradise. The white dust of the road was warm, as I let it fall through my fingers. There were white wisps of snow, I noticed, in the clefts of the rocks above us. How intensely blue the sky was up there! How good to lie on a patch of grass, feeling a trickle of warm white dust through one's fingers! It was nice to be alive.

"Here they are!" cried the lady with the mountain orchids.

Yes, here they were at last. But Gaston was still looking worried. He desired more water. He thought that he might crawl very slowly to some place where he might find it. The engine was still hot.

We crawled very slowly. It would be awkward, we thought, to come to a dead halt on the Simplon Pass.

"Water!" shouted the artist, who has a quick eye.

Water as pure as crystal, but not much of it. It was a thin trickle down a white rock. In the car were five cups made of celluloid, from the establishment of Messrs. Woolworth. They had been very useful for wayside picnics. They were very useful now. We formed a chain gang, each with a cup into which we let the water trickle. It was astonishing how many cupfuls were needed to have any effect upon a thirsty radiator. But it was good fun.

We went on our way refreshed, higher and always higher, along a road like a spiral climbing to the clouds. We came to a small village called Berisal at the head of a gorge. Here there were some wood cutters, who seemed astonished to see our car. Great logs were being dragged by teams of horses which wore long nose-bags like pillow cases. Later we reached the snowline and its whiteness gleamed by the roadside. There were many waterfalls coming down from great heights with foaming spray. We had reached the heights of grandeur, awe-inspiring and tremendous. Their snow peaks were lost in the clouds which now massed above them and rolled across their slopes.

Somewhere over there, among the gigantic billows of rock, was the St. Bernard Pass, across which Napoleon had led his army, those ragged legionaries, half starved, with bandaged feet, with long hair and unshaven faces, and fever-stricken eyes. Most of them were young conscripts, but among them were men who had flocked to the armies of the Republic from French farmsteads, when the cry of *Liberté, Egalité, Fraternité*, was shaking the thrones of Europe. Paris was not sending supplies. They had been long away from their homes. But they still had faith in a little man with a long grey overcoat above his top boots, who carried a stick in his hand. He had promised them the sack of cities and great wealth. Had he not promised, and did he not always keep his promise to his men? What were those words read out along the ranks?

"Soldiers, you are half starved and half naked. The government owes you much but can do nothing for you. Your patience, your courage, do you honour but give you no glory. I will lead you into the most fertile plains of the world. There you will find flourishing cities, rich provinces. There you will reap honour, glory and wealth. Soldiers of the Army of Italy, will you be wanting in courage and firmness?"

They had courage enough. It was only that their bodies were famished. How was it possible to cross these vast grim mountains? How could they drag their guns up these narrow tracks between the gorge? How could they go on with bleeding, bandaged feet?

"*En avant, mes enfants!*"

The little grey man spoke those words. He was standing by the side of Berthier, his chief of staff. He had his right hand thrust through his buttoned overcoat.

They went on. Cavalry, baggage wagons, guns, went up the narrow mule paths above the precipices. The guns were dismounted, and tied onto hollow trunks of trees, and dragged up the heights by hundreds of men tugging at the ropes. On their left hand masses of snow on the mountain sides threatened to slip down and sweep these ants over their narrow track, over the edge of it; and on their right hand, over the edge, were deep gorges, dropping thousands of feet sheer down. A false step was death for man or mule. The wheels of the baggage wagons creaked. The drivers lashed at their poor exhausted beasts. Men cursed, and boys sobbed, through sheer fatigue. . . .

The plains of Italy lay before them, and Napoleon broke his promise about the wealth they would get. Some of his men were shot for looting. "I will not be in command of a robber band!" he said. But he praised them too. "This is your title to immortal fame!" he told them. "When you return to your homes your neighbours will point you out to one another and say, 'He was with the army in Italy. He crossed the Alps.'"

Many of them never returned to their homes. Their bones were picked clean by Russian wolves in the snow. Nobody remembers their "glory" now. The word they cried on their lips —*Liberté*—is ridiculed. Liberty? Signor Mussolini has declared that to be a stinking corpse.

I thought of these things—in my mind's eye I saw a vision of Napoleon's army—as we crossed the Simplon.

We passed close to the snow. Only a few days before the road had been cleared of it. It was banked high up and was melting a little. We hoped it would not begin to slip. There was ice in some tunnels through which we drove, great blocks of ice, iridescent as it caught the faint gleams of light from the tunnel's mouth. It was very cold in there. We were six thousand feet high. The air was like wine. Every little diamond of snow was glittering. On our right was the Hospice for travellers, but we did not stop. Presently we drew our breath with astonishment. Was it a ghost we saw—the ghost of an old *diligence* with four lean horses? No, it was a real *diligence* with real horses, crossing the Simplon to Brigue.

"This is more wonderful than I ever imagined!" said the artist, with his eye on the mountains.

It was stupendously wonderful up there, with that vast turmoil of peaks still heavily laden with snow, and, below us, immensely deep gorges, cut clean down by the rush of waters in the beginning of time. There were moments when our lady shuddered. There were moments when she could not bear to look, and held my hand tight and shut her eyes, and then opened them to laugh again, because she has a laughing heart.

We began to drop very gradually. There was a broad valley ahead, but not the bottom of the mountain range—only a plateau far above the plain.

We came down to the village of Simplon, with a tall bell tower above its red roofs. Down and down we went, with a strain on the brakes. We crossed a rushing river—the Iselle—in which great boulders tossed the water. Our crossing was over. We halted in a village called Gabi, and had a bread-and-cheese lunch outside the door of an old inn.

A little grey man had been there before us. He had sat at the very stone bench on which our food was spread. He had listened to the rush of the waterfall which goes under some rocks a few yards away. He was thirsty as he sat outside this house with pink colour-wash and green shutters. It was told by a tablet on the wall.

> This is the place where
> Napoleon I
> had a glass of milk
> on the 27th of May, 1807.
> He paid with a
> five-franc piece.

Some good-humoured women waited on us. They brought out an old pewter pot which they said was the very vessel from which Napoleon had quenched his thirst. We regarded it with interest but without faith. It was a nice old pewter pot.

The women stood talking to us vivaciously. They were delighted to see us. The pass had only been opened a few days before, and all the winter they had been snowbound. But, so far, the opening of the pass had brought few travellers. They did not expect many, from what they heard. People were not travelling much. Money was scarce, it seemed. Things were still bad in the world. But they still had laughter left. They laughed with our lady, who was no longer in fear of precipices. She seemed to make some good jokes which kept them laughing.

I went into the little church and looked at a Madonna and Child wearing gilt crowns. It was a quiet place, and cool out of the sunlight, but through its windows came the everlasting murmur of water, swirling past heavy boulders under a bridge close by.

We took to the car again. We motored through a long tunnel and a deep gorge. More cataracts rushed down the rocks. The road twisted like a snake. We dropped down into the village of Gondo, the last in Switzerland.

A portly man in Swiss uniform examined our passports and thought them well and truly made. Two little girls were playing at a pump, below a tall tower belonging to a château with many windows. They were having a great game on a hot day, putting their heads under the water. I had a talk with one of them, and she was able to talk in three languages, just as I pleased—French, German and Italian. The customs officer gave us a tremendous salute. Obviously he thought us great folk.

Not far up the road there was a chain stretched across. Some little men, and one big one, in the uniform of Carabinieri, examined our passports again, looked inside the car, politely but curiously, answered a Fascist salute made by our lady, smiled, and waved us on after letting down the chain.

We were in Italy.

VI

Italy under the Fasces

THE ITALIAN CUSTOMS OFFICER at Gondo had not seen many motorists lately. He was glad to have a chat with us when he found that we understood his language at least sufficiently to ask questions and laugh at his jokes. The novelist was our best linguist in this country, having stayed in Venice many times. Not to be beaten, I thought out a good sentence and asked if the new *autostrada*, entirely reserved for motorists, was very dangerous. I had heard that it was often strewn with corpses.

The Italian customs officer regarded this as a most excellent jest. He opened his big mouth, showed a set of leonine teeth, and laughed heartily.

"Pericoloso? No! No! Molto sicuro!"

He affirmed that there were no madmen in Italy—or very few. Not many cars made use of the *autostrada*, owing to the lack of tourists. He admitted, however, that when military cars were travelling they went like a streak of lightning.

I noticed a broken column lying by the wayside and went over to look at it. It had a Corinthian capital, nobly carved.

"Roman?"

The customs officer nodded. It did not seem to him of any interest. These Roman relics are as common in Italy as broken bricks in England.

"You'll never see better roads," said the novelist. "The Italians have a genius for road making."

It is an inherited genius. The men who had left the soil of Italy stuffed with the relics of their lives were the first to make good roads through Europe for the feet of their marching legions. Had we not travelled over them in France?

The surface of the road we were on was like a racing track. It was the same on every road, and for hundreds of kilometres on the way to Milan; and each road was bordered with stones, a yard or two apart, painted black and white in stripes, except in one district where suddenly they became red and white.

"I find them monotonous," said Gaston. "They are apt to make a pattern on one's eyes."

In spite of the smoothness of the road, our car was not going well. Gaston looked alarmed. He stopped, got down, and looked distressed after a brief examination. We had broken a spring, and it would be necessary to have it mended before going far. Perhaps he could fix it up temporarily in Gondo.

He had the sympathy and assistance of several young men of the mechanic type, several small boys who gave us the Fascist salute and enjoyed our breakdown, and an elderly Italian who entered into conversation with us.

Gaston did some conjuring tricks with a block of wood and a piece of wire. It took quite a time, and Gondo is not a place of enchantment, although the surrounding scenery is magnificent. The only interest I could find in a street of mean little houses was a number of stencilled portraits painted in black and white on the walls. They represented in a few strokes the face of a bull-necked man with an aggressive jaw who beyond any doubt was Signor Mussolini.

The elderly Italian, who seemed to have no work to do and was interested in our broken spring, spoke good French. In answer to my cautious questions as to the state of Italy he gave me to understand that it was not brilliant. There were many unemployed. Taxation was very heavy. Business was bad. The government was finding much difficulty in balancing the Budget, on which there was a terrible deficit.

"It is difficult to know what will happen," he said gloomily, and his remarks were not a cheerful introduction to Fascist Italy. I was surprised by the melancholy candour of a man behind whose head, on the whitewashed wall of the "osteria" in Gondo, was the portrait of a gentleman who does not encourage criticism of his régime.

Our arrival in Italy with a broken spring had cast a shadow over the cheerful soul of Gaston. He complained bitterly of fate when I sat next to him on our way to Domodossola where there was a garage to which he had been recommended by one of the young mechanics at Gondo.

"We must have strained it crossing the Simplon," I suggested.

He would not hear of that. He told me that a spring will break just as easily in the streets of Paris. It just snaps for no reason. The devil had something to do with it, he thought.

"We are in bad luck!" he said. "Without luck one can do nothing."

Very slowly we went on our way over a hump-backed bridge which crossed the torrent of the Divaria, and between those black and white stones like an endless wall. It was in the late afternoon, and Italian peasants were coming back from work, and factory workers were hurrying homeward on bicycles. We reached the town of Domodossola, well known as a railway junction to all travellers from France to Italy. We had to slow down to a crawl because of a funeral procession ahead of us. Many people were walking behind the hearse.

"It only needed this," said Gaston gloomily. "The corpse in that coffin is probably the proprietor of the garage to which I have been directed."

I don't know why that remark struck me as being very amusing, but I laughed indecorously behind the funeral cortège.

The proprietor of the garage was very much alive. He was a courteous young man who snapped his fingers at his workmen and told them to get busy. He informed us that the spring would take five hours to replace.

Five hours in Domodossola! Not a pleasant prospect. The lady with us looked at me anxiously. She was not assured that I had regained my health. The doctor in Sion had said that I was not to fatigue myself. He had laid down a ridiculous rule of twelve hours in bed.

"How long would it take to get another car to drive us to Baveno?" she inquired of the proprietor of the garage.

"Exactly two minutes," he answered as a disciple of Mussolini and efficiency.

In exactly twenty minutes we were in a new car with a new driver, leaving poor Gaston to follow on when ready.

Our new car was of the taxi type, made of tin. Our driver was of the new Italian type, made of steel and spirit. He drove to Baveno as though on a race track. Nothing slowed him down— not farm carts crawling ahead with loads of hay, not ox wagons with loads of timber, not squadrons of young men and women on bicycles—they are great cyclists, these Italians—not young girls and old women walking under heavy burdens of hay which made them look like perambulating haystacks. We shot through Villadossola with its *castello* on the hill. A rainstorm broke above us, and the long straight road was as slippery as glass, but did not raise a qualm of caution in the mind of a young man who worshipped speed. Little girls on the footpath stared, as we flashed by, and gave us the Fascist salute. We were on a long valley road between the lower spurs of the mountains. There were fields on either side of us with stone walls instead of hedges. Haymaking was in full swing, and the sweet scent of hay was strong in our nostrils. Italian peasants were pitching the hay onto their carts. Here and there a machine cut a long swathe through the standing grass. The women had gaily coloured kerchiefs round their heads. Some of them waved their pitch-forks at us.

We passed through many villages following the course of the river Toce. At Premosella there was a tall campanile. At Ornavasso there were vines soaring up pergolas. At Gravellona Toce there was a fair in the market place thronged by crowds of Italian children, all very neatly dressed.

In all these villages there were many children, we noticed. The women leaning over their ironwork balconies had babies in their arms. There were babies on the doorsteps of the houses. Evidently Mussolini's bounties for full cradles had been success-ful in Italy. Many little Fascists are coming into the world at a time when high-souled men like Signor Mussolini are of opinion that "Peace is detrimental and negative to the fundamental virtues of man." At six years of age these babies will be enrolled in the *Balilla*, for their preliminary training in this philosophy. They will be taught the use of gas masks. They will sing the Song of Youth and salute the Fascist flag as the symbol of the State, which later on they must obey with blind obedience. They were nice little babies, I thought.

2

We had reached the Lago di Maggiore and the town of Baveno on the lakeside. There was a golden sunlight on the water, and a golden haze through which gleamed the white houses on the Borromean Islands, and the distant heights of Monte del Ferra.

"This," said the artist, "is a very good spot! I can't imagine anything better on earth."

Facing the lake was the garden of the Hôtel Suisse which had pink walls and green shutters. We were glad to sit in it and drink golden liquid on which the golden sunlight gleamed. There were big sunshades with blue and white stripes over the tables. Beyond us, only a few yards away, there was a landing stage with boats freshly painted. The front of Baveno curved round the bay. Its houses were tall and every one was of a different colour: orange, pink, yellow, blue, green, and red.

"A jolly thing to do in coloured chalks!" exclaimed our artist.

Palm trees, with broad leaves sharply spiked, grew tall along the esplanade. Green lawns under green pergolas bordered the roadway.

It is a neat and pleasant little town on the edge of the Lago di Maggiore, where the beauty of Italy is like a dream of Paradise. There are other lovely places in the world—so many! —not yet spoiled by the ugly touch of modern "progress"; but around these Italian lakes beauty is almost too enchanting. One is aware of a languor overcoming one's spirit. The hustle and bustle of modern life seem so foolish and unnecessary. It is difficult to be active and aggressive. One sinks into lethargy, and the spirit of *dolce far niente* would weaken the urge of a profiteer to make more profit by calling down his telephone, when, here, beauty offers all the wealth of life to be drunk in by the eye, to enter into the pores of one's skin, to make one a sun worshipper, to put a spell upon one's senses. On the Italian lakes it is impossible, I find, to write a letter to one's best friend or worst enemy. It needs terrific will power to address a picture postcard to one's nearest and dearest. There may be revolutions in Germany, bombings in Austria, riots in Paris. How silly! How uninteresting! There is a golden haze over the Borromean Isles. There are white-winged yachts on the glinting water. The air is warm and heavy with the scent of flowers. Beauty soaks into one's soul.

We had good bedrooms in the Hôtel Suisse, overlooking the lake. The artist had a balcony on which he could draw at his ease with the picture of the town and lake below him. The novelist, who knows Italy like a book of his own, had the look of a man who has come home after many wanderings, or that elusive mystical look of Grock when he plays soul-melting music on a little concertina with the limelight on his face.

I was in bed when there was the sound of laughing voices outside the front garden of the hotel. It was midnight. Gaston had returned with the car. He was a happy man again with a new spring.

Early next morning there were cheerful noises below the open window. Young voices were singing. Bugles were blowing. There was the tramp of marching feet. Young Italy was astir in Baveno. It was one of Mussolini's miracles. The spirit of Fascism was stronger by the Lago di Maggiore than the warm indolence of nature. I stood on the balcony in my pajamas—just the right dress for morning in Baveno—and gazed down upon the scene below.

It was very animated. For some time crowds of young men shouted and laughed while they waited for some motor coaches to start with them on an expedition. Then there came the strains of military music. A band led forward by a young drum major marched into view. They were playing a tune I had heard in Italy soon after the war. They have been playing it ever since. It is *Giovanezza*, the Song of Youth. The band was followed by a battalion of young boys in the uniform of the Balilla—black caps, black shirts, grey shorts, and a light-blue scarf over the shoulders. They were followed by little girls, also in uniform— black hats, white blouses, black skirts and white gloves—all very smart and neat, all marching like young guardsmen, all singing *Giovanezza*. Two boys held up a tall flagstaff from which hung the green, red and white of Fascist Italy, with two clasped hands in the centre. The band halted. The boys and girls marched round a white column—a war memorial—and then formed up in ranks before it. A bugle sounded. Drums beat a tattoo. Hundreds of young arms were outstretched at an angle of thirty degrees, from tips of fingers to shoulder blades, like a stage scene arranged by Reinhardt, who loves the effect of outstretched arms.

All these boys and girls looked alert, keen-spirited and happy. They were not suffering, it seemed, under any kind of tyranny. They liked this ceremony and this marching about, if one might judge from their jauntiness. It seemed to me astonishing that youth should be so active by the Lago di Maggiore.

It was active in a field near the church, from which came the sounds of organ music at High Mass. Inside they were praying to the Prince of Peace. Outside many lads were being drilled by the rasping voice of an instructor, in case they might be needed for a new war against the enemies of Italy. That morning I had read a speech by Il Duce, who makes such speeches sometimes, when he feels like it, though at other times he talks in other tones, very peaceful and conciliatory. I have already quoted some of the words.

"I absolutely disbelieve in perpetual peace. It is detrimental and negative to the fundamental virtues of men which only by struggle reveal themselves to the light of the sun. Whatever happens, the Italian people will face the future with complete discipline."

The young men of Baveno were learning that discipline on a Sunday morning outside the church. They were learning very well, I thought. I was impressed by the good clothes, the healthy look, the cheerfulness, the activity of youth, in this little town. Mussolini, I thought, has great qualities of genius. However much one may criticise his conception of government, his contempt for liberty, and his denial of free speech, he has given Italy a new sense of power and a new ardour of spirit. Whatever judgment one passes on the early brutalities of Fascism, with its cudgelling of liberal-minded men, and the imprisonment on convict islands, year after year, of intellectual and high-minded citizens, one must acknowledge that Italy now has a higher standard of life than in the days of dirt and squalor before the coming of "Fascismo," and that the people have been lifted up to a sense of self-respect and national pride.

3

So I thought in Baveno. But these thoughts were challenged by an Italian with whom I talked in the garden outside the Hôtel Suisse, under one of those big umbrellas with blue and white stripes.

He was staying in the hotel. We had exchanged salutations earlier in the morning. He accepted an English cigarette from me and sat by my side and talked in admirable English. He was a typical Italian of the northern type, such as one sees in Milan, with a strong face and sturdy frame, not unlike Il Duce himself. Like that great man he was getting a little too plump for his height.

"These young Fascists look happy," I remarked as a body of them marched by with their flag.

He shrugged his shoulders and flicked the ash off his cigarette.

"It's all wrong," he answered. "It's just Bolshevism!"

I was rather startled and looked over my shoulder to see if anyone might overhear. My Italian friend was careless of being overheard.

"The whole system is wrong," he continued. "Italy is marching steadily towards disaster."

I found that hard to believe by the Lake of Maggiore, and in the garden of the Hôtel Suisse, where everything looked prosperous. The very waiters in linen suits looked like the owners of private yachts. A luxurious car arrived, depositing an elegant young man in search of a drink, and two lovely ladies in filmy garments.

"The government," said my Italian friend, careless of being overheard, "makes roads to create work. It distributes money and food to those who are unemployed. It gives the people cheap trips to Rome and back. All very nice for them, of course! But who buys Italian produce or Italian goods? Who helps the Italian manufacturers and business men, who are being ruined —who, indeed, are already ruined, like me?"

"As bad as that?" I asked.

"Worse than that!" he said, looking across to the Borromean islands, as though staring at a scene of ruin and calamity, instead of having before his eyes a vision of dreamlike beauty.

"Property in Italy," he said, "is without value. How can a nation carry on when that happens? It is ridiculous to be a man of property in Italy, because one is the victim of the tax collector who takes away everything and then asks for more. One is taxed that the people may have cheap trips to Rome and look at the new excavations of that ancient city, made as a memorial to Mussolini. One is taxed for public works which are unproductive. One is taxed to maintain an army of officials, an army of Fascists, and an army of police. One is taxed until all the savings of one's life, put by after years of toil, are exhausted, until all one's profits have disappeared, and until one declares oneself bankrupt. All that is Bolshevism under another name. The corporations of which you hear so much are Soviets under another name. Everything now being done in Italy is a step towards Communism. The men of property are dispossessed. Business profits are nonexistent. Only the working people have privileges, and those will not last much longer because the nation itself is bankrupt."

From the interior of the good-looking car, into which the elegant young man and the two lovely ladies had now returned, came the blare of a portable radio. It was shouting out the results of Saturday's sporting events in Italy.

"Who," asked my Italian friend, "will buy a business which is overwhelmed with debt?"

I could not answer that question.

BAVENO

"I have," he told me, "a business in a town not far away. It was worth millions of lira before the arrival of the Fascist régime. Now, if you would like it, I will let you have it for a thousand lira. I do not advise you to accept that offer. There are no profits. There are many debts. The government sent its officials to me last year with a demand for taxes. I said, 'Take over my business for a year. What profit it makes you shall have in payment of taxes.' They made a grimace and would not accept. They knew too much!"

Another body of young Fascists marched past the garden of the Hôtel Suisse. They were singing a song I knew. It was *Giovanezza*.

My Italian friend accepted another English cigarette. It was the least I could offer to a bankrupt business man.

"It is, of course, an advantage to be bankrupt," he said with sudden cheerfulness. "Formerly it was a great disgrace. Now it is almost a virtue. It is even the way to advancement, if one becomes a crook. The greater the crook, the greater the honour. He gets the best jobs. He must be a clever man, they think. That is so in most countries today. France makes her crooks cabinet ministers. In England—well, perhaps in England it is different—though you have your clever gentlemen."

A group of little girls in black skirts and white blouses marched along the esplanade.

The stout Italian regarded them with a benign smile.

"I have a little niece," he said. "She is six years old. When she went to school for the first time she was asked to bring fifteen lira. She brought them. She became enrolled in the Balilla, and is taught to hold up her right hand at the name of Il Duce. Every baby born in Italy—and they keep on being born, poor infants!—becomes *ipso facto* a Fascist. No question about it. No case of conscientious conviction! 'There you are, my little one—Fascismo for you, and don't squeal about it!' Wonderful, isn't it?"

He spoke with a laughing bitterness and then turned to me with a kind of apology for so much gloom.

"The truth is," he said, "I am disgusted with this life. I remember life before the war. It was a good old world, good-natured, with a sense of peace. If a man worked hard he made a little money. If he saved it, its value seemed secure. If he did not care for saving he spent it on giving happiness to other people and himself, with a generous hand. Life then was charming, gay, light-hearted. We were not all thinking of war and poison gas. In England, for instance, where I lived for several years, learning the language as a young business man, it was peaceful and free and tranquil. There was liberty for liberal opinions. One could say what one liked, even if it were nonsense! Now, in Italy and in Europe, who can say what he likes? Where is liberty of thought? Where is happiness?"

I thought of the old war-time story of the German soldier taken prisoner by a Tommy. He began to speak of his wife and children and home and mother, until the Tommy could stand it no longer and said: "Chuck it, Fritzie. You're breakin' my bloomin' 'eart. If you say another word I'll blow your brains out."

My Italian friend was breaking my heart by the shore of the Lago di Maggiore and taking all the beauty out of its blue sky. Confound the fellow! Why had I offered him my English cigarettes? Why had he taken two, which I could ill spare at this stage of the journey?

He shook hands with me politely.

"I have enjoyed this conversation," he said. "It's nice to meet an Englishman again. One can speak one's mind freely."

He departed from me, leaving me a sadder and a wiser man.

If he had told me the truth, and I believed him, Italy under Fascism was not so prosperous as it looked. Storm clouds were creeping across its blue sky.

I reported my conversation to the novelist, who laughed heartily.

"Oh, to meet even one man," he said, "who will acknowledge that he is prosperous! I know Italy pretty well. I assure you that for the majority the standard of life has gone up prodigiously."

"But will it last?" I asked. "That melancholy Jacques who has just left me is convinced that the people are being supported by the taxation of wealth which is almost exhausted. *Panem et circenses*—can a nation exist on that philosophy? Didn't his people come to grief on that way of life nearly two thousand years ago?"

"It's nothing like that," said the novelist. "The Italian peasant is a hard worker. Italian youth in the factories is working keenly. Mussolini has brought about a new renaissance. Italy is now one of the great powers, whereas she was disintegrating and getting demoralised, and lurching into anarchy after the war."

I acknowledged some truth in this, but had a doubt in my mind. It was certainly true that the Italian worker was industrious. Had we not passed them in the fields? Had I not seen them bending over a poor patch of earth on the mountain side, scores of times on other journeys through Italy? But what would happen if they could not sell their produce? What would happen if the things they made in their factories could not find markets? How could they carry on if all their business men were advancing towards bankruptcy? Perhaps it was not quite as bad as that. Things are never quite so bad or quite so good as men are inclined to say when they get talking. The searcher after truth has to strike something off each side.

4

We were sorry to leave Baveno. The novelist would have been glad to abandon the rest of the journey and stay here a long time, yielding to the spirit of *dolce far niente*. The artist groaned at having to pack up again. Our lady laughed and gave Gaston his orders. I was overcome by the languor of the Lago di Maggiore.

But there was no great misery in travelling again. Every mile of the way was rich in interest, and we came to many pleasant places. Perhaps also it was good to get away from the heavy humid atmosphere of the lakeside, weakening to one's will power.

We passed through Stresa. It was garlanded with roses luxuriant in the gardens of white villas, climbing up the walls, and blooming in carved basins. Along the lake was Locarno, where

Sir Austen Chamberlain arranged a treaty which he thought would bring peace to Europe, but may one day call upon English boys to offer their bodies as gun fodder in a new war, if such treaties are discovered in dusty pigeonholes by the next generation of youth.

There was a clashing of bells at Stresa, calling people to church on Sunday. At Meina we slowed down through the village street, and an Italian waiter, aware that English were passing, ran out and waved his napkin at us in the vain hope that we would stop and feed at his tables. We left him behind, broken-hearted, and looked at the gardens of the Villa Boulia, with their long cypress walks, and white statues of gods and goddesses, as in the Borghese Gardens in Rome.

As the kilometres passed we saw before us a high white cliff —the entrance to the town of Arona. On the opposite side of the lake was a tall castle, white under the blue sky, and reflected in the mirror below. High on the hill above Arona was an immense statue of Cardinal Borromeo, a great prince in this part of Italy—the present Prince Borromeo takes his coffee quite often at the Hôtel Suisse in Baveno—and a great saint, who went among his people during a time of plague, with spiritual comfort which helped some of them to live, and many to die, more happily. His body lies embalmed in the cathedral of Milan.

After my conversation at Baveno with the Italian who had no good thing to say about the state of Italy, I studied the life of the people in the towns and villages to which we went. There was no visible sign of poverty among them. The children —the crowds of children—who swarmed in these little towns, were clean, well-dressed, well-booted. Every Italian seemed to ride a bicycle, and squadrons of them rattled past our car. Groups of Italian families sat outside the *ristoranti* on the shady sides of the streets, drinking cheap wine, talking, laughing, gesticulating, or playing with their babies. If Fascism is a tyranny—and it is—it sits lightly on the working people, as far as one may judge by passing observation.

The *perrucchieri* were shaving their customers. In every village they seem to be the centre of social life. The young Italian is

The Temple of Steam, Milan

THE TEMPLE OF STEAM, MILAN

careful of his hair, which he has curled and perfumed once a week, if he can afford the luxury. And these people, under the dictatorship of Signor Mussolini, have sources of wealth which no tyranny can take from them. They have the rich warm sunshine and the beauty of Italy, and the gifts of their old historic earth—wine, fruit, flowers. They were working in the fields, though it was Sunday again. The women's arms were brown up to the shoulders. The men were deeply bronzed. The children —black-haired, black-eyed, brown-limbed—were like the figures of Tanagra. They stood in fields of flaming poppies waiting for the long rhythmic sweep of the scythe. They carried immense bundles of hay. They rested awhile, lying on this sweet-smelling bed, already yellowing under the hot sun. Girls' voices were singing on high-piled hay carts. They did not seem to be groaning under a merciless dictatorship, nor starving to death in a bankrupt country. They were, I think, happy in this hay harvest, though prices might be low for their produce in the markets.

Some of these villages are ugly and dusty and hot. So it was at Nerviano. Some of them are very old and stately. So it was at Rho, with a noble church and a campanile touching the blue sky.

There were gipsies in a field this side of Milan. Their caravans were in the shade of a hedge. Lean dogs guarded them. Their tethered horses had ribs upon which they might have hung their hats—if they had had hats. Strange, wild people, speaking a language older than Sanskrit, never taking part in the life around them, possessing dark secrets as old as the East, we met them in many countries and along many roads.

5

As we neared Milan beauty fled for a while, as it does on the outskirts of all great cities. Horrible metal signs advertising the products of machine-made industry appeared along the road. We passed a big cemetery where Milan buries its dead. There were straggling houses and shacks. A green tramcar hurtled along with a jangling bell. Tall tenements had been built or left unfinished. There were rubbish heaps, pits filled with broken pots and tin pans. Gone were the languor and loveliness of Italian lakes. We entered the busy, bustling, crowded city of Milan, whose citizens are filled with a restless energy which keeps them walking up and down for no apparent purpose, in endless throngs, in crowds, at least after their working hours, in their covered arcades.

It is a noble city of broad streets and great buildings, and it has two glories of architecture, one built nearly six centuries ago and the other a year or two ago—the cathedral and the railway station.

The cathedral has been described a thousand times. Every traveller to Italy has been stirred with admiration for its Gothic miracle in stone, overloaded somewhat with decoration— every pinnacle richly carved, every wall a place for sculptured stone, the whole mass chiselled by the tools of mediæval craftsmen until it looks like lacework.

The railway station is still new and white and unsoftened by the mellow touch of time. But it is magnificent. As a railway station it takes first place in the world. Its façade is simple and austere but with a real grandeur. The Greeks at their best time would have liked it, I think. It has but little decoration or statuary, but the figure of a horse led by a naked man is nobly carved. The tall columns rise to a great height. When the sun stands behind it rich black shadows are flung from its buttresses. Inside it is like a great cathedral, pure white with a lofty dome, with flights of steps finely spaced. It is more impressive than the Grand Central in New York, which takes a lot of beating. It must have cost a lot of money. Perhaps it is part of the reason why there is at the time of writing a deficit in Mussolini's budget. Il Duce likes big buildings, broad highways, vast reconstructions, sweeping clearances, and tremendous architecture. It costs something.

We had great difficulty in finding rooms in any hotel. We went from one to another. The managers were very courteous but regretted that they had no room to spare. This, in a time when tourism is dead, was mysterious. Could it be that the world crisis had at last lifted and that tourists were invading

Italy with pockets full of money? Had something of this kind happened between Saturday and Monday?

No such thing! There was a football match in Milan between Swiss and Dutch teams. Ten thousand Dutch and eight thousand Swiss had come to watch it. From all parts of Italy people had availed themselves of cheap fares—a reduction of seventy per cent—to attend this football match. Italian business men were bankrupt, I was told. There was no profit on their products. They were taxed to extinction, I was told. But the people had cheap trains to take them to a football match. *Panem et circenses*.

By the courtesy of one of the managers who telephoned round the city, we found rooms at last. They were in a big new hotel, very expensive-looking, immediately opposite the new railway station.

"A bit of luck!" said the artist. "That railway station is the only thing I want to draw in Milan."

He had another bit of luck—a room with a balcony and a view of that great building.

That evening after dinner we went to the Galleria. That was not an original idea. After dinner in Milan everyone goes to the Galleria. It is a big arcade, glass-covered. One end of it opens at the cathedral square. It is the centre of social and business life in Milan. The citizens come here at midday to discuss business affairs over their Cinzano. Later in the day young men come here to make appointments with young women. In the evening they come here to show off their best clothes, their newly coiffured hair, to exchange glances, smiles and salutations, to discuss love, life, and all things but liberty, which is not allowed. It is very amusing to sit there by one of the café tables under the glass roof. One sits surrounded by palm trees and baskets of flowers and little glowing lamps. One watches the parade of young men and women. The young men are in the majority. One sees more young men in Milan than in any other city of Europe—that is to say, young men walking about in gangs and looking pleased with themselves, as well they might, because they are good-looking, well dressed, and with a sense of their own importance.

"No sign of poverty here!" said my novelist friend.

"None whatever!" I agreed. "This crowd is better-dressed than any one could see in London."

"Of course they are not wearing their workaday clothes," said the novelist, who knows Italy. "They have what is called a *costume di piazza*. They keep it for this Galleria. I once had a servant in Venice and wanted to make him a present. He asked for one of my old suits and especially coveted a pullover which he had seen me wearing. 'I wish to make a good appearance in the Piazza San Marco,' he said. He made his appearance, but I noticed that he was wearing the pullover inside out. It showed a tab with the name of Selfridge. I pointed this out to him, but he refused to put it right side out. 'It is for that reason I admire it,' he said. 'All my friends are much impressed when they see that I am wearing a costume which is marked Selfridge, London. I am very much improved in social position.'"

"That's a good story!" said our laughing lady.

We watched the types of humanity passing slowly by us, or sitting at neighbouring tables in the arcade. Officers of the Flying Corps swaggered by. Carabinieri chatted to each other vivaciously, with one eye on the best-looking girls. One of the Bersaglieri shook his cock's feathers from his ear. Gangs of Swiss boys and girls passed through the Galleria, carrying their national flags and singing and shouting. I can't remember whether their team had won the football match. They were followed by gangs of Dutch boys and girls carrying their flags and singing their own songs. Some of the Milanese laughed and clapped. At the table next to us was a lovely lady. She had straw-coloured hair which looked untouched by chemistry, and blue eyes which were undoubtedly natural.

"German-Swiss," said the artist. "And easy on the eye."

Some of the Milanese women, I noticed, were fair-haired, and most of them, indeed, had a northern, rather than a southern, look. So had the young men. This was a different type from the crowds in Florence or Rome. They were Franks rather than Latins.

An amusing rendezvous, this Galleria in Milan, though a little noisy, a little crowded, and rather stuffy in its atmosphere.

These people were middle-class Italians. They looked cheerful, prosperous, and unperturbed. They could afford to buy themselves small drinks—most of them drank coffee, I noticed. They could afford to smoke gold-tipped cigarettes, not very expensive in Italy. They had good boots, good hats, and well-cut jackets. There was more gaiety among them than one sees in the Burlington Arcade or, shall I say, Lyons' Corner House. By no stretch of imagination could one say that these people were oppressed or poverty-stricken. "It is obvious," I thought, "that Milan is doing well on artificial silk which has ruined Lyons. It is probable that, despite my friend in Baveno who was so gloomy about the state of Italy, in Milan at least business is good."

6

Next morning, after breakfast on the balcony with a view of the railway station, which did not turn one's coffee sour, I searched the telephone directory for a friend of mine who was a business man in Milan. He would tell me, I knew, the exact state of affairs. I could rely on his facts and his judgment. I should get nothing through rose-coloured glasses or green-coloured glasses but the unspotted truth. By good luck I found his number. By better luck I found him in his office, ready to talk.

"How's Milan?" I asked. "Prosperous, I should say!"

"Do you think so?"

He laughed and was very much amused.

"You wouldn't think so if you happened to do business in this city. Why, heaven help us!—we're in a state of complete stagnation. Nothing doing. Business is at a standstill. We're in the same state as the rest of Italy—deeply anxious and wondering what on earth's going to happen unless things improve very quickly."

"But what about the silk trade?" I asked. "Milan is the headquarters of artificial silk which has ruined Lyons. Surely that is very prosperous?"

My friend, a hard-headed business man, did not accept my facts or theory.

"Milan produces, or used to produce, real as well as artificial silk. Now many of the country folk don't bother to rear the silk-worm. It doesn't pay them. There is overproduction, and the silk trade is having its throat cut by Japanese competition. They can't stand up against it. It has captured all the markets."

My friend pulled a paper out of his drawer and looked at it attentively.

"Here are the facts," he said. "Silk yarns are down to the lowest price on record. Silk cocoon prices are exactly half those of the previous six months. Ninety per cent of the mills are closed down. The artificial-silk trade is in a bad way. No dividends. No profits. Prices have dropped disastrously."

"Everybody in Milan looks very well-to-do," I said. "I can't understand it. It's all very mysterious."

My friend laughed and admitted the difficulty of understanding these things.

"One has to get at the essential facts," he said. "When one does, they're not pleasant. People are living on a very thin margin—or getting into debt. They make a brave show in their best clothes when they walk up and down the Galleria. The truth is—well, there are certain facts not to be denied. One of them is the Deficit. Italy has a deficit on this year's budget of sixty-six million pounds, and an adverse trade balance of sixty million. Not too good! Rather alarming for Signor Mussolini and Company. Meanwhile they have just made a grant of six-teen and a half million pounds for aviation, and sixteen and a half million for the navy. Where's the money coming from? Nobody in Italy can give a guess."

"It sounds bad!" I agreed. "But the people look prosperous!"

This business man in Milan began to talk rather like my Italian in Baveno.

"Mussolini is favouring the working people at the expense of the business men. He plays up to them to keep them quiet. He arranges cheap trips on the railways for them. Seventeen lira to Venice and back! It's simply ridiculous. And all the people go rushing round Italy, not doing anything for the towns they visit, because they take their own food and spend next to noth-ing. But that sort of thing can't go on. The government itself knows that the limit has been reached. Mussolini has admitted that himself in a recent speech. 'Taxation has about reached its limit,' he said, 'and the taxpayer must be given a rest.' About time too! The poor devil has been bled white."

"How is he going to raise money?" I asked.

My friend shrugged his shoulders.

"He is going in for a régime of drastic economy, and his danger lies in the necessity of cutting down workmen's wages. Up to now he has avoided doing that as much as possible. But he must get prices down in order to cheapen costs of production and find markets for Italian wares. There are going to be cuts of ten per cent on all salaries. Workmen will be paid reduced rates. As an offset, the landlords will have to pull down their rents, and retail shops will be forced to lower prices. There will be ten per cent knocked off the rents of private houses and apartments, and twelve per cent off offices. Mussolini has issued a decree to that effect. It's a process of deflation and will lead to the inevitable results: Less money all round. Unemployment. More doles for the unemployed. The vicious circle. Another economic crisis!"

I groaned slightly.

"Is the world ever going to set its house in order?"

My friend in Milan smiled and shook his head.

"It's the end of an era. We shall have to adapt ourselves to a new chapter. I don't know what it will be like. I doubt whether it's going to be very pleasant."

"Italy always has the sun!" I reminded him. "That's an asset. And the old brown earth still gives its fruits."

We shook hands after further conversation about things in general, and I reported his facts to my travelling companions, who were waiting for me outside a café near by. The novelist laughed light-heartedly.

"Look at all these people!" he said. "Do they appear miserable and worried?"

I looked at them. They put up a better show than we do on a week day. They looked more smartly turned out, neater, and with more attention to their footgear. There were no grey flannel bags looking as though they had been slept in. The young

Italian men, mostly hatless, had their hair curled. Italian girls in summer frocks were spotless. They passed by, laughing with each other.

"Perhaps they get happiness on the cheap," I suggested.

I bought a straw hat in a shop down one of tne big streets of Milan. It cost me a pound in English values. I couldn't get one for less. It wasn't a bad hat, and Gaston was pleased with it, as I could see by his look of admiration. But it was more expensive than in England.

7

We were glad to get out of a great city and to get the scent of fields again, and the vision of the Italian countryside, with distant hills, wonderfully blue on the far horizon. We were in the plain of Piedmont. In its flat fields rice was growing, heavily irrigated. Old farms with flat roofs stood away from the road-sides. The villages had pink and primrose-coloured houses, and big churches, and tall campanili. We passed a canal where women, with bare arms and bare legs, were washing clothes. Down the canal floated long narrow barges. In one of them were three horses, and a load of chickens in crates so tightly packed that they must have stifled.

We went through Villa Fornaci, a long village with an inn called Trattoria della Madonna.

"Tell me," I said to the novelist, "what is the social distinction of these Italian inns?"

He obliged with the information. It goes down the scale, starting with the *albergo*, followed by the *ristorante*, then by the *trattoria*, then by the *osteria*.

To our left, faintly visible, was the range of the Bergamese Alps. Over there was Como, and I thought of a month I spent in its neighbourhood, when it rained every day and the mountains were shrouded in wet mist, and all its beauty was veiled.

We crossed the river Adda—a full, flowing stream—and for the first time the black-and-white posts which we followed through Italy became red-and-white posts.

I remember Boltiere. We were back in the Middle Ages there. The houses were old as the Medici. Through the arched streets young men with parti-coloured tights and slashed doublets and daggers in their belts, had passed, or stopped to look up to one of these ironwork balconies, to kiss the tips of their fingers to pretty girls whom Boccaccio knew. There were many immense churches in the town, and a tall campanile high above the roofs.

But Bergamo was more spacious and on a nobler scale. Many of its streets are arcaded. Its houses are very tall and stately, their old windows shaded by orange-coloured blinds. At the end of the town, beyond the walls which look far over the Plain of Lombardy, there is a great castle with square towers and battlements dominating the whole town with its spread of red-tiled roofs. We passed through an old gateway and came into the Piazza Vecchia—the Old Square. One side was a noble old palace approached by a flight of steps worn by the footsteps of many centuries in Italian history. The palace itself was built in 1199, the year of the death of Richard Lion Heart of England. It is guarded by stone lions which stare into the sunlight from the shadows flung across the square by the fine old palace behind them. There are other palaces in this Piazza Vecchia, and near by is the Duomo and the Baptistry and the church of Santa Maria Maggiore, all as old as the beginning of the splendour of Lombardy, when its great princes vied with each other in magnificence of building and patronage of art.

We took lunch in a restaurant called *Il Ristorante del Sole*, which wasn't built yesterday. It was, in fact, an inn as far back as 1365, according to an inscription and the affirmation of its host, who is a very trustworthy man, not without fame, being the friend of a thousand artists who came to Bergamo before they starved to death or grew lean during a world crisis. In return for his admirable cooking, his excellent wines, and the atmosphere of his old house, they were pleased to paint his portrait and present the result to him. Several of these portraits hang on his walls and old beams, and they all depict him as a smiling, cheery, plump-faced man, which in truth he is, as I can tell. It was interesting to wander round the long low rooms of this ancient *albergo*, with its arched roof supported by great beams. It is hung with an immense number of pictures and caricatures. I suspect that many artists paid this way for good dinners. Beyond the rooms is a garden with a pergola, shaded by an immense wall belonging to the church of San Michele. A pleasant spot, directed by the host himself, who speaks perfect English and was delighted to welcome English guests, so long absent from his house and garden, at least in any numbers.

I thought of recommending him to the novelist as the man he had been searching for—the man who did not complain of poverty but was pleased with life and the profits of his business. But this could not be done because, alas, after chatting very cheerfully, with gusts of Italian laughter and keen delight in his pictures and treasures, he confided to me that business was bad, and that Italy was not prosperous, and that taxation was ruining the middle class.

We made friends in the Piazza Vecchia with an Italian policeman. His police duties did not prevent him from acting as a guide to English visitors. He spoke fairly good French in which he was at least talkative, and he was anxious to accompany us round the town so that he might show us the things best worth seeing. He had very bright smiling eyes under his steel helmet, and I was abashed by his good-nature and his anxiety to please us. He was, as I have said, a policeman. He was not so good-natured to an elderly gentleman who lay on the steps leading down from the Piazza Vecchia. He lay sleeping in the sun very happily and harmlessly, I thought. But our friend kicked the soles of his feet and spoke to him sternly. He awakened reluctantly and asked why he should not sleep in the sun. Had not God created the sun in order that men might sleep in it? That seemed to me a pleasant thought, but the policeman kicked the soles of his feet again and ordered him away. He apologised to me for this episode.

"Why can't he sleep off his wine elsewhere? There is plenty of room in Bergamo. The sun does not shine only in the Piazza Vecchia, and it is not pretty in the centre of the town."

That seemed to me a reasonable point of view, after all.

Our policeman led us down some ancient ways with very old houses on either side, belonging certainly to the sixteenth century.

"In a year or two," he said, "all these will be swept away. There is a plan of reconstruction which will be very fine."

I was dismayed. That plan of reconstruction would sweep away so much of the charm of Bergamo, so much of its mediæval character.

"In Italy," said the policeman, "we believe in getting rid of old rubbish. We are making our towns modern."

I was sorry about that.

But this young man had an eye for natural beauty. He led us to the ramparts below the Castello di San Vigilio.

"*Lombardia!*" he exclaimed. "*E molto bella!*"

He pointed out the two rivers which run through the plain, and the town of San Pellegrino, from which comes an excellent mineral water, and the peaks of the Bergamese Alps faintly visible.

A delicate moment arrived when we parted. The artist had been in conversation with him about the war and other subjects which might interest a policeman. It was the artist who handed him discreetly some Italian paper money. It was rejected. He gave us to understand that it had been a pleasure to him to show us round. It was in no way done for money. He had been an officer in the Italian army. He was charmed to talk a little French and a little English.

8

The posts went black and white again after Bergamo. We went through the plain of Lombardy which we had seen from the ramparts of San Vigilio, and past a hill our policeman had pointed out to us. It rose abruptly from the plain. Every village on our way had its campanile and old brown roofs, and fountains with water basins in which the children splashed their brown hands; and iron balconies over which plump women leaned with plump babies. Here and there we passed the walls of an old fortress which guarded the valley when Colleoni came riding this way on his fat horse with his freebooters. We drove through Italy of the Middle Ages, not much changed since then.

We came to Brescia, with its flour mills and factories. It dates back to Roman times but has been industrialised and American-ised. It is not, however, completely modern. There is an old duomo there, and an old part of the town. But suddenly we came into a square which gave us a mental shock. It filled me with horror, as I must confess, though the lady with us was delighted.

"I like it," she told us with enthusiasm. "I prefer it to mouldy old houses!"

We were in a modern piazza—so modern that there was even a skyscraper in the American style, though not so high as the Americans make them. The banks and the postoffice were in the pure style of Fascist art—boxlike buildings without decoration, and with straight lines this way and that, most austere. The skyscraper was of yellow brick and, in my eyes, an atrocity. The shop fronts were of black marble. The whole square was brand new and in the modern spirit, which is good for those who like it.

On one side of the square was a tall statue of a naked young man. His limbs seemed to me wobbly in their lines. The sculptor had taken liberty with nature in his idea of the beauty of young manhood. On the other side of the square was an open pulpit from which, no doubt, Fascist orators praise the nobility of Signor Mussolini and the blessings of Fascismo.

I read an inscription on one of the walls. It told that the reconstruction of Brescia had been made by the will of the Fascisti of that town, from the design of Marcello Piacentini—Fascist artist, October, 1921–1932.

On the sides of the open-air pulpit were young Fascists in *basso relievo*, and the face of Mussolini, with an unpleasant expression.

I fell into conversation in the square with a man who spoke German.

"Who paid for all this?" I asked.

He told me that the new buildings had been built by the Banks and Insurance Companies, who had lent the money to the Municipality. Then he told me other things about Brescia which I found interesting. It was an industrial city. There were great metallurgical works and textile factories.

"Unfortunately," he said, "the metal works are mostly at a

standstill; and the textile works are doing very little. There is considerable unemployment. For some reason which I do not understand, we are unable to sell our products. The world has fallen into a bad way. It is perhaps the fault of the United States. The collapse in that country shook the whole structure of civilisation. Now they have gone off the gold standard and do not buy from Italy. Nobody buys from Italy at the moment. We have, as you know, a very heavy deficit on the budget, and an adverse trade balance which is very serious. The Fascist régime has not been able to avert this economic distress. Mussolini himself cannot work miracles. That is too much to expect!"

At the mention of the great man's name he looked across his shoulder. I was aware that he thought he had been talking incautiously to a stranger. He was, I think, the only man I met in Europe who suspected me of sinister questioning. A sudden fear came into his eyes. He raised his hat and walked away. Perhaps the local Fascisti were suspicious in Brescia.

We went on our way, and it was a good road through villages with Venetian red houses, and past old barns—half farmstead and half fortress; past ox wagons crawling slowly; past two monks on bicycles with their habits tucked up and their beards wagging as they rode; past Lonato with a dome like a soap bubble as seen at the end of a long avenue of chestnut trees; and so to the Lago di Garda, of enchanting loveliness.

From Desenzano we looked across the water with its golden ripples to little islands lit by the sun, with white houses gleaming against green hills and, beyond, a background of mountains with their peaks jagging an Italian sky. Our hearts were tugged to stay there. Here was another earthly paradise. How pleasant to linger there, to bathe in those golden waters, to row out to those little islands, to lie in the flower fields, to forget a troubled world and all its hatreds and its ugliness!

We resisted the temptation, having a long journey to go, but we kept along the lakeside as long as possible. The sails of the fishing boats in small harbours were reflected in the water. The fishermen were singing. An old barrel organ, of the type which used to visit London—I haven't seen one for years—came along in a donkey cart, followed by small children. A band of gipsies had pitched camp by the water's edge. Their dark eyes stared at us as we passed them.

At Peschera di Garda there is a great fortress, formidable and grim. Italian soldiers were looking through the gates. At Castelnuovo there was a castle on the hill, and we were back in the Middle Ages again, forgetting the skyscraper at Brescia, and boxlike buildings of Fascist artists with their passion for straight lines and plain surfaces.

Then we came to Verona.

9

It is good to come to Verona for the first time. It is one of the noblest old cities in Italy. Every stone in it vibrates with history, back to the days when the Romans built the very gates through which one walks, and the great arena, still standing, almost undamaged by time, opposite the outdoor cafés where one sits in its shadow; and the old bridge across the Adige— the Ponte Pietra, with its Roman brickwork still carrying the traffic of human life. The Scaligere were the great people here in mediæval Italy—great fighters and murderers and lovers and princes. Cangrande, the Big Black Dog whom Dante knew, was one of them. His tomb stands in a narrow street over the door of a church. He rides in stone—a strange grotesque figure on a comic horse, draped from neck to heels. It was his successor who first rode across the bridge and under the iron-toothed gates of the Castel Vecchio—that great fortress on the river with fan-shaped battlements, so oddly Oriental in their aspect.

Where before had I seen red walls like that, and fan-shaped battlements like that? I stared at them with amazement. Good heavens! It was in Russia—in Moscow! The Kremlin above the Red Square was like this fortress of Verona.

"Easy to explain," said the novelist, who knew this Verona and all its history. "The Kremlin wall was built by an Italian architect named Pietro Antonio of Milan."

Great walls, massive bastions, high ramparts, tell of the

times when the citizens of Verona had to fight for their lives against many enemies who tried to storm their gates and cut their throats, and often did. But other stories are told in stone —the story of Renaissance Italy when beauty was worshipped, and the builders had a light and delicate touch and strove for grace instead of brutal strength.

In the Piazza dei Signori, and the Piazza della Erbe and the Piazza Dante, there are marble colonnades of exquisite grace, and every detail is touched with art. They wrought their iron into flowerlike shapes for their well-heads and balconies and sign-boards. Benvenuto Cellini and his master craftsmen gave stone and metal a new vitality and charm of fantasy. The princes of Verona wanted palaces instead of fortresses. They lavished their wealth on painted ceilings and gilded panellings and gorgeous tapestries and silken hangings. They had their shields carved over great mantelpieces, and paid handsomely for any craftsman, painter, carpenter, iron-worker, sculptor, moulder and mason who could produce some new miracle in wood or metal or stone or glass or gold. Their stone lions lie couchant at the top of winding flights of steps leading to their banqueting halls and council chambers. There are fountains in the squares below their windows. The Lion of St. Mark stands in the Piazza dei Signori. There are little statues in the niches of old streets. Every step in Verona stirs something in one's spirit. The men of mediæval Italy gave life to their handicraft. They worshipped art. They were passionate for beauty, though very cruel.

We sat outside a café from which Garibaldi in his red shirt— the first to wear a coloured shirt as a symbol of political force —made his famous speech before the March on Rome. "Rome —or death" was his watchword, and on his lips was another word which has gone out of fashion. It was the word "Liberty."

In front of us, across the roadway, were the immense walls of the Roman amphitheatre, in which now there are sports and games and spectacles for good Fascists. Shakespeare is played there sometimes. Did he not write *Two Gentlemen of Verona?* And the other day there was a fireworks display of which the most sensational item was the Monster of Loch Ness!

"Who is going to visit the tombs of Romeo and Juliet?"
asked one of our company.

The answer was a laugh. It's a pity to make a fake like that
in Verona, where there are so many relics of its history and so
many ghost memories.

One ghost paces the stones of the city. It is the ghost of a man
with a thin face lined with spiritual agony and inward passion.
He wears a long gown and a hood. He mutters to himself.
His eyes seem to see some strange vision. He must have been a
very melancholy man and not good company at any festive
board. There was hatred in his heart for the follies of mankind.
He had had no tolerance of men's frailties or passions. He had
no mercy for evil, and no pity for those who had done him
harm. He wished his enemies in hell. He put them there in a
book he wrote. A man of wrath, he was, with smouldering fires
in his soul as he walked through Verona in exile, past those
very walls of the Roman amphitheatre upon which we now
look with living eyes. But there was a sweetness in him somewhere. He was a great lover. There was a girl he loved. He had
met her on the Ponte Vecchio in Florence. Her name was
Beatrice.

We stayed at a good *albergo*. The young manager had learnt
English from a book, and learnt it very well. He knew enough
to tell us he was a sad man, although he laughed quite merrily
as he told us.

"I am sad," he said, "because few visitors come now to
Verona. There are not even any Germans, who used to swarm
here. They have been kept at home by Herr Hitler. They are
not allowed to take money out of Germany, and it is likely
that they have no money to take. Where are the English?
They do not come! You are the first I have seen for some
months. Where are the French? They do not come! It is not
amusing to keep a hotel in Italy just now. The taxes are too
high. Every year we pay all we earn, and more, in taxation.
The cost of living goes up. It is always going up. Hope is very
difficult to keep alive! We have been hoping for fifteen years.
That is a long time for hope to keep alive without a little food.
So you see I am sad!"

Verona
29ᵗʰ May
Saturday.

VERONA

I did not see that he was sad. He looked remarkably cheerful. He was even a little too stout for his age. But his cheerfulness was due perhaps to courtesy. He smiled because he did not want to weep, like my friend the waiter in the Hôtel Beau Rivage at Geneva.

"Things are getting better," I assured him. "Slowly but surely the economic state of the world is improving."

I spoke my hopes rather than my conviction, to cheer him up.

"Not in Verona!" he answered quickly. "Not in Italy. We are getting worse. Taxation is too, too much! Mussolini says so himself, and I see no way out."

Down in the market, which goes through the Corso and spreads into the Piazza della Erbe, where Dante walked, there was great cheerfulness. Plump Italian girls offered me their fruit and flowers and were good enough to give me their smiles free of charge. Priests and monks and nuns went about among the market folk. Italian Carabinieri shouldered their way through the crowds. Bersaglieri with long cock's feathers hanging over one eye or one ear, lurked in the shadows of the tall houses. There were many soldiers about, I noticed. Verona is strongly garrisoned.

Early next morning the novelist and I explored the Castel Vecchio. After passing the guardian at the first gate we were alone in that vast palace and fortress. There was something uncanny, but also enchanting, in being alone and untrammelled by any guide. We walked up long stone stairways leading to the battlements, and looked over the high walls to the broad river below. We crossed the bridge which leads straight through the castle, easily closed against any enemy by heavy hanging gates with iron teeth. We wandered through a hundred rooms with painted ceilings and polished floors, and enormous fire-places richly carved. We gazed at the portraits of the tiger men who once dwelt here with their passionate and lovely women. We touched the furniture on which they had sat, and the treasures of art which they had touched. We leaned out of casement windows to gaze upon the roofs of Verona which they had seen. We tried—and failed—to bring back life into these empty rooms, these little chambers, these great banqueting halls where they had walked, and loved, and hated, and plotted, and died. The passion of many centuries had vibrated in these bricks and panellings. We could not tune in to them. The tiger men, the wolf men, the lion men, the poets, the painters, the women with white necks, the lovers, the musicians, the jesters, the gentlewomen, the little pages, the scholars, who had thronged these rooms, left no sign of their presence nor spoke a whisper to us.

"It's all very marvellous," said the novelist.

"It's all very dead," I answered. "Let's get back to the sunlight outside."

It was an Italian in Verona who told me a fact which I wanted to know.

"An unemployed man," he said, "gets three lire fifty a day for a period of three months."

It is not a handsome allowance. He can't spend much of that in riotous living. I paid nearly as much as three lire fifty for a cup of coffee in the Piazza di San Marco, in Venice.

10

We did not go to Venice or Rome on this motor journey, but I had been in both those cities a short time before—Venice on the way down from Vienna, and Rome afterwards for a special inquiry into political affairs.

In Venice I went to the Hotel Danieli, for old times' sake, and for another glimpse of an old Venetian palace which still retains its atmosphere of faded splendour, although it is now— or was before the world crisis—the haunt of English and American tourists, who drink cocktails in the lounge, where formerly great nobles and merchant princes assembled for banquets, watching women in silken gowns below their white shoulders, who passed between the arches high above the floor and leaned over a painted balcony which looks into the central hall.

No such tourists were there when I sat in this room on my last visit. There were no tourists, English or American, but only a few people waiting in Venice for a boat out East. The waiter who brought my cup of coffee as I sat by the enormous fireplace with its heraldic carvings deplored the emptiness of the Danieli.

"One hears the sound of one's own footsteps," he said, as though living in a haunted house. "The Germans have stopped coming. Germany is going rotten, like most other countries. The world seems to be advancing towards a new disaster."

"How is it in Venice?" I asked.

He shrugged his shoulders.

"The Venetians walk up and down the Piazza di San Marco. When they have walked one length of the square they turn and walk the other way. They get free music in the evenings, but wear out their boots. There is nothing else doing in Venice. The new road which has opened up the city to the rest of Italy, for motor traffic, takes away as many as it brings."

But it was pleasant to sit in the Piazza di San Marco and see the people walking up and down. They are a good-looking people, although the men have long noses. The women still wear the Venetian shawl tight about their hips and flung over one shoulder. They have a peculiar and attractive way of walking with a swing of the body about the hips. When they get tired of the Piazza they walk down the Merceria, under the clock with the blue face, and into the narrow streets along the canals and across the bridges. They also keep on walking up and down the steps beyond the Danieli; and when I think of Venice I think first of those steps, and the crowd of women in black shawls, with soldiers, and monks, and white-gloved policemen, and brown-legged children, going up the steps and down the steps all day long. And then I think of the cries that come up to the open windows of the bedrooms in the Danieli from the Grand Canal—an incessant repetition of the word: "Gondola! Gondola!"

Nothing much had changed in Venice since my last visit. But something had changed since an earlier visit soon after the war, when the walls were scrawled in black paint with the name of Lenin, and sullen and hungry-looking men stared through the ironwork over the lower windows of the Danieli, and cursed the American and English tourists sitting there in evening clothes with liqueurs close at hand. Once a stone was flung at one of those windows, smashing some panes of glass and frightening the women with bare shoulders and backbones, with ropes of pearls round their necks.

Stories were told of theft and violence. An American woman had her rope of pearls snatched from her neck by a hungry-eyed man, in one of the little streets beyond the Merceria. Italy was falling into anarchy. There were strikes every day, almost, especially on the railways. They were lightning strikes without notice, and very annoying to travellers who had packed their baggage and hired gondolas only to be told that they could not get farther than Bologna. So it was once when I was there, held up for several days.

Now, on my last visit, a short time before this motor journey, there were no hungry-eyed men in Venice. At least, I did not see them. The name of Lenin had long ago been obliterated and that of Mussolini had replaced it.

I walked past the Ponte di Pieta, straight along towards the public gardens in the direction of the Lido. The way passes through the poor quarter of Venice, and I remembered it as a slum crowded with squalid, dirty children. It was still crowded with children playing on their doorsteps or the broad stretch of pavement between the shops and tenements. But they were not squalid or dirty. They were clean and well dressed and plump and healthy. It must be said for Mussolini that his spirit and energy have given a better chance to childhood and cleaned up the slums of Italy. Perhaps that has been the best result of his dictatorship—the most meritorious.

These people have the sun. Glory be to the sun! They have the warm waters of Italy and are lucky. To England, the Lido is a famous place. It is known to Hollywood. But it is only depicted as a place where ladies with lip-sticked mouths show themselves in shorts and brassières, and where film stars and other celebrities enjoy their magnificent wages of folly. That part of the Lido is outside the Hotel Excelsior which has its private plage for those who can afford it, and private *piroscafi*, or motorboats, to bring them from the hotels on the Grand

THE RIVA, VENICE

Canal. But there is another Lido. It is very democratic. It stretches in a city of wooden huts for a great distance along the sands. All Venice comes here on a Sunday—the little shop girls, the factory workers, the young men who look like haberdashers on week days and gods on Sundays. No attention is paid to the austere modesty of Mussolini, who issues edicts on the fashion of bathing costumes. No heed is given to the exhortations of the Church, old-fashioned in its fear of the human body. The Venetians wear the least possible and are not ashamed. These Venetians are finely made. They are good swimmers. The little shop girl is as beautiful as the Roman goddesses—and not so fat—when she leaps on the sands by the Lido of Venice. And though there may be a world crisis, and though the economic state of Italy may leave something to be desired, here they find happiness, and laughter, and sunshine, and warm waters, and lose no virtue thereby, as far as I am aware.

II

I was in Rome at the end of a Holy Year, when the Pope was receiving innumerable pilgrims of faith from all parts of the world. It was also when Signor Mussolini was in active communication with Herr Dollfuss of Austria who had just bombarded the dwellings of his Social Democrats.

The pilgrims were still in possession of Rome when I arrived. It was almost impossible to get rooms in the city, as it had been difficult in Milan. The Albergo Flora, which is my favourite habitation in Rome because of its closeness to the Pincio Gardens, was filled on every floor with priests and their flocks —mostly middle-aged women and young girls. I was directed to a *pensione* which was clean but uncomfortable, from which I sneaked, feeling unkind, to the greater comfort of the Hotel Bristol—still Victorian in atmosphere and furnishing—where there happened to be one vacant bedchamber of small size and moderate price.

The pilgrims came mostly from Streatham, Brixton, Clapham, Tooting, and other London suburbs where the middle class dwell with a faith unshaken by the evil example of cocktail parties in the smart set, and with a faith uncontaminated by the morals of the picture palace.

They had a hard life in Rome but seemed to enjoy it. They were up for early Mass in St. Peter's. They attended the Papal ceremonies, and were received in audience by the Pope himself. They visited innumerable churches under the guidance of their priests. They went down into the catacombs and thrilled to the memory of the early Christians, whose bones were here and whose altars remain. I doubt whether they had much time or inclination to study the relics of Pagan Rome, with its great baths, and ruined palaces and gates, and temples and amphitheatres.

I had little time myself for sightseeing, but drove one morning down the Via Imperiale in a *vettura*, which is so much better than a taxi, if one has time. The driver—a genial man—turned round on his box seat, waved his whip, and said, "Made by order of Mussolini." On the whole I regretted that order of Mussolini, which swept away many old houses and uncovered many broken columns, and made a broad dusty highway past the Forum of Trajan to the Colosseum. It is magnificent but hot and shadeless. And I liked those old Roman houses, and taverns, and arched vaults, where good wine was kept.

I combined business with pleasure that afternoon. I had an introduction to a very old gentleman who was also very wise and full of knowledge. His name is Cardinal Gasparri. He is now living in retirement—if he still lives when this book is read—in a palace presented to him for his services, near the Baths of Trajan, beyond the city gates. Outside his own gate on a Sunday afternoon was a man in black livery talking to a soldier, and a few servants who were sunning themselves. They straightened themselves up when I stepped out of the hired carriage and asked to see the Cardinal.

"His Eminence is not receiving today," said the man in livery.

I presented the letter and spoke a few words.

"*E molto importante.*"

The man in livery shrugged his shoulders slightly but condescended to take the letter. I knew my chance was slim. But a few minutes later he returned from the courtyard and was deferential.

"His Eminence will see you."

I waited in an antechamber which led into an immense drawing room with a painted ceiling and heavy candelabra, and long curtains which kept out the sunlight. There was a faint scent of polished wood and old furniture. An unseen hand touched some electric switches, and the candelabra were lighted one by one until their cascades of crystal were all glittering. There was a shuffle of feet along a corridor. The man in livery appeared, said, "His Eminence," and bowed, before retiring, with a sign that I should enter the great drawing room.

An old man in a black gown, with a red sash and a red skull-cap, stood in the centre of the room, peering at me.

"Why have you come to see me?" he asked in French. "I do not understand."

I tried to make him understand. I was travelling in Europe, I told him, trying to find out what was happening below the surface of an uneasy peace—the new groupings of powers—fears and dangers of some new catastrophe. I knew His Eminence was in retirement, but doubtless he was interested in all these things. Something of the sort I said in French.

He shook his head, and a faint smile twisted his thin old lips.

"There's nothing I can say," he answered. "I am in retirement. I have no first-hand information."

He made a sign to me to be seated and then sat down himself, wearily, on an uncomfortable couch of the Empire period, very stiff for an old man's bones. I think I must have disturbed his afternoon nap. He gaped behind a thin, transparent hand several times, and once or twice, when he talked, seemed to doze off for a moment, pulling himself back to wakefulness with an effort. But he talked, and I listened attentively.

"The situation is, no doubt, grave. There is no real peace in the minds of nations, no sense of security. Everybody speaks of the need for disarmament, but everybody increases armaments, even England now! It is all very unwise. It is all very dangerous."

He sighed deeply and pushed his red skullcap—a Cardinal's cap—on one side.

"We were very near war not long ago," he told me. "If German Nazis had invaded Austria, Italy would have taken action with her army. It was a delicate situation. Some accident may happen like that, any day, to light the fires of war again in Europe. One never knows! One reads the headlines of the morning papers with apprehension, because anything might happen to stir up the fires of war again. There is Germany, of course. Germany cannot be ignored. She has a hundred thousand officers fully trained—the *cadre* of her army staff. All her young men are drilling as soldiers. There are evil minds in Germany, though the mass of the people are good and honest. So far they are not sufficiently armed with rifles and guns. They can do nothing. Germany is not going to attack France for some time. Herr Hitler is sincere in saying he wants peace, for some time. The internal situation in Germany is not good. It is far from good. They may have another revolution. There will be a struggle for power among the leaders, and a conflict between the Left and the Right. Herr Hitler has his work cut out, without attacking France."

It was at this moment that he seemed to doze off—pulling himself back to consciousness with a start.

"Excuse me," he said, "were we talking about Signor Mussolini?"

I was very glad that he should talk about Signor Mussolini.

"He has a strong will power and a considerable genius," said His Eminence. "His word is law. The people obey him and believe in him. Fortunately he is working for conciliation in Europe. Mr. Mussolini wants to pacify Europe. He dislikes the idea of a new war. That, after all, is something! He has done great things for Italy in many ways. But what will happen when one day he dies? Ah, no one can answer *that* question!"

He had something to say about the spread of Fascism in Europe.

"It is the impatience of youth and their need of leadership. But there is, of course, a danger that there may be a revolutionary movement against dictatorship. That is always the danger of dictatorship. The only way of criticism must be revolutionary. England will never become Fascist. With France it is different. There is much corruption in high places in France. French youth is roused against the government. Their political groups are arming against each other. I foresee much trouble in that country."

He was silent for a few moments and struggled again with the desire for sleep.

"Shall I tell you what is the real danger for Europe?" he asked after this interval.

I begged him to tell me.

He shifted forward a little and peered at me.

"Japan has captured Manchuria. Next she will dominate China. There will be six hundred million Asiatics under discipline. As a Japanese gentleman said to me the other day: 'When that happens, Europe will have to be careful!' That is true! Europe will have to be careful. It is better for the European nations to stand together. It is indeed urgently necessary. Even now, Japanese competition is becoming irresistible in the world's markets. The Japanese labourer works ten hours a day for six sous a day. In Switzerland the Japanese are selling cheap watches by weight, like potatoes!—at thirty francs the kilo. What can we do against that? His cheap production has already destroyed England's cotton industry in the East. Meanwhile European nations are quarrelling and re-arming for another war. That is the way of suicide! It is very unwise, don't you think?"

I agreed. I listened to this old cardinal who had been at the Vatican for a long period, closely in touch with foreign policy. He was still very wise, with the dispassionate wisdom of old age —very old age, which looks back at life as though already from another world. He was so tired—so tired—but his mind was working with a balanced judgment, and with the simplicity of one who sees the truth of things without prejudice or passion, apart from the human struggle. I had many conversations in Rome, but none impressed me so much as that with this wise old gentleman. He knew. There was nothing he didn't know. His forecast of Germany has already come true.

12

Rome is the noisiest capital in Europe. The Italians like noise.
It seems to give them an exhilaration of spirit. It is their way of
expression, vitality, dynamic purpose, and the joy of life.
The motorcar has given them an easy means of indulging in
this form of self-expression, and they make full use of it. Their
motor horns have a strident and ear-piercing timbre not pos-
sessed by any other make of horn in any other country; and
Italian drivers let forth blasts without a pause, as they rush
through the narrow streets. A walk down the Corso is a nerve-
shattering experience, as though one walked through some
infernal highway with yelling demons on either side. The
young Italian, inspired by the spirit of Fascism, likes to tell
the world he's coming. He comes very often, at sixty miles an
hour between the blocks of traffic. He comes in a racing car
with an open exhaust. He blasts his way through the Eternal
City; and the Roman crowds, so far from resenting this assault
upon their ears and nerves, gaze at this outrageous fellow with
admiration. He is alive! He adds to the music of life. He is
cleaving his way through the world with triumphant trumpet-
ings. So they seem to say with their eyes, though the foreigner,
coming perhaps from London, which is not without traffic,
cringes at this incessant bombardment of his eardrums. Fortunately Rome goes to bed early, and the Roman nights are
quiet, with a quietude which is very deep and startling, because of this contrast between day and night.

These Roman nights are enchanting. The air is warm and
still. The darkness is very dark in the shadow places under the
old walls, beyond the starlight or the moonlight which touches
tall cypresses, or the ruins of the ancient city, with silver.
One seems to hear one's own heart beat; and I have noticed
that groups of friends, coming late from some restaurant or
villa, talk in hushed voices.

On these Roman nights one feels the past. All that is modern
and vulgar is obliterated by the spirit of antiquity in this age-
old city. One is aware of its ghosts. Time alters its beat. One
stands close to Cæsar, Nero, Constantine. One stands and

listens, conscious in this stillness of the brevity of one's own little life, one's own insignificance. A thousand years are as nothing when one hears the footsteps of the ages in the silence of a Roman night.

One hears in one's spirit the rhythm of Time's waves. One touches an old wall, a broken pillar, a stone within reach of one's hand in this darkness. There are very old vibrations in it. A Roman soldier leaned against it when Christ was talking to Peter on the lake of Galilee. A Christian girl leaned her head against it and wept, because her lover was waiting for the cages to open in the Colosseum. This bit of masonry vibrated to the shouts of Roman crowds hailing a new emperor, or a general bringing back prisoners from Gaul or Britain. Its vibrations go back to the night when Cæsar's body lay bleeding with wounds like mouths. Under these stars, above these stones, a million crimes, murders, infamies were done by men more cruel than the wild beasts they kept for their shows. Under these stars, above these stones, a million agonies, loves, dreams, martyrdoms, happened yesterday, or the day before yesterday, in this mystery called time. In this quietude, by these pillars, touched and silvered by the old moon, saints prayed for the Kingdom of Christ on earth, and scholars peered into the mysteries of life, and emperors, who ruled the known world, tossed sleeplessly as they thought of the hordes they must fight to hold their empire against the outer barbarism.

Rome! It was the headquarters of civilisation, the capital of Christendom; the city to which all roads led across the world. These pebbles, under one's feet, were trodden by men who had made and marched along the roads of Britain; who had put up altars to their gods in Gaul; who had seen the camp fires of the yellow-haired tribes in German forests. Peter and Paul may have passed here in chains.

And afterwards—a few moments, or a few centuries, afterwards (what is Time?)—Raphael watched how lovely was the Roman night from the Trinita dei Monti, and Michael Angelo saw through the darkness colossal figures writhing their way from a stupendous block of stone; and painters, poets, and craftsmen of the Renaissance went to their workshops to carry out the orders of Lorenzo the Magnificent for some new thing of beauty. The moon shone for a moment now and then on the flash of a dagger or the shiver of a sword. The stones of Rome are soaked in blood.

But in the silence of a Roman night there is a living and eternal spirit which speaks to one. . . . Or is that just make-believe, after a flask of Roman wine at the Concordia, where good company dines late?

13

I dined late at the Concordia. It is not a grand place, but one of the old Roman eating houses, not smartened for a tourist crowd. The company was good. They sat at a long table with their elbows touching—men and women mixed. There were men here who knew many secrets behind the scenes. They had been in many capitals. They sent news of high diplomacy to the world's press, leaving out the most interesting things they knew, being their own censors.

Next to me was a young man whose relatives I had met in Asia Minor where, at Burnabat, there is an English colony, long established. We discussed the affairs of Austria, then in a state of siege, and the intervention of Mussolini. He was a knowledgeable young man and had a cool judgment. In his opinion Dr. Dollfuss would be supported by England and France as well as Italy, against the rude embrace of Germany. But the danger might come from within. There were many Austrians who believed that only Germany could give them trade and some future hope. Most of the peasants in South Austria were of the Nazi frame of mind. Italy was making a pact with Hungary as well as Austria. It was a balance of power against Jugo-Slavia and Czecho-Slovakia.

"Now that Austria has turned Fascist," said a friend of mine, "there are Fascist states from the Mediterranean to the Baltic. Rather formidable! Mr. Smith"—it was the name used in public for a certain gentleman in Rome—"is the leading mind in this new system of European government. He sees every move on the chessboard. He moves his own pieces rather more rapidly than anyone else. But what staggers me

sometimes, as an old-fashioned liberal, is the decay and death
of individualism over so large a part of Europe. France and
England are the last strongholds of democratic liberty, and
France is changing, from what I've heard. There's a lot to be
said for Fascism. It has done much for Italy. But what about
the progress of the human mind under this new system of life—
in which Russia must be included? The individual has to swear
blind obedience to the State. State worship is the new religion.
No criticism is allowed except in whispers. The press, in all the
countries, is under strict censorship, and the people only get
a little news which is thought to be good for them. The theatre,
and all art and literature, must conform to the State creed
and the State philosophy of life. Children are trained from
babyhood to obey the leader with a blind devotion, even if in
manhood it leads to death. In the infant class and the school-
room the child's mind is bent and twisted to the right mould.
The loudspeaker roars out propaganda. The film screen flashes
the same kind of picture made by Fascist producers under
orders from the chief. How is art to survive? How is intelligence
to grow and advance? What is the value of man's struggle for
liberty through a thousand years of political conflict and many
martyrdoms, and executions, and imprisonings, and burnings?
We are back to intolerance and secret police, and the decree
of the tyrant who may be benevolent like Mussolini or—not.
It's a new phase in history—this sweeping victory of the Fascist
creed. Is England tainted by it? I hear strange things of a man
called Mosley."

In Rome I met an Italian friend of mine whom I was glad
to find alive and well, and still laughing at the ideals of Fascism.
There was a time in this city when he did not expect to remain alive and well. He was known to be a critic of the Fascist
system, when criticism was knocked on the head by sticks
and bludgeons. In his room he waited often for the arrival of
a group of young Fascisti armed with those weapons. A foot-
step on the stairs caused him to listen attentively. He kept
listening for four or five years, which is a long strain on the
nerves. But this Italian has a laughing temperament. He saved
his life, I think, by laughing and giving an edge of humour to

his critical remarks. He laughed delightedly when we clasped hands again, and he answered my questions about the state of Italy with ironical good-humour.

"Economically, Italy is pretty desperate. Politically, Mussolini is playing his cards well. The façade of Fascism is still a bluff which impresses the outside world and the working folk."

He told me that most of the Fascist ideals were on paper and not carried into reality. The Corporate State, for instance, was just a phrase. The Corporations didn't function. The whole administration was in the hands of Mussolini and his lieutenants. The business world had no voice in the affairs of the country. They were told what taxes they had to pay, what wages they had to pay, and that was that. It was government by decree, and the people had no share of self-government, in spite of a prodigious amount of rhetoric and eyewash.

From this Italian, and other citizens of Rome, I heard judgment passed on Mussolini's mind and diplomatic purpose. They gave him credit for throwing his weight against the chance of another European war. He was playing for the leading position in Europe as a mediator between rival groups of powers. The arrival of Hitler had worried him for a time. He had no desire to see Germany linked up with Austria and menacing the Italian frontier beyond the Trentino. That was why he had backed Dr. Dollfuss and his Austrian Fascists, with a pledge to support the independence of Austria as soon as they had routed out their Social Democrats in Vienna—his price for support. But he recognised Germany's claim to equality in arms, and many of her other claims for revision of the Treaty of Versailles. He holds that peace in Europe will be impossible in the long run, if France and others endeavour to keep Germany in a position of permanent inferiority. It was for a policy of revision that he invented the Four Power Pact—stillborn because of French dislike and the passionate suspicion of the Little Entente. But Mussolini did not change his view because of that failure, and held it impossible to prevent the re-arming of Germany, by consent or without consent. The only alternative to which he still held was a measure of general disarmament. He was eager to persuade France that her safest policy was to admit German equality under a general bond of control and defence. Meanwhile he was anxious to end the hostility between the Danubian states, paralysing trade, and keeping nerves on edge with the danger of new war. By economic concessions to Hungary and Austria and Czecho-Slovakia much might be done to make Italy the centre of a new block of powers. France, racked by internal disorder, was, it appeared, willing to give Mussolini a clear field, provided he prevented German union with Austria.

"At the moment," said one of my friends, "Mussolini is the leader of Europe in the game of diplomacy and is playing for high stakes. It's a pretty dangerous game, but he has a subtle mind and a cool head. Fortunately he believes in the tradition of Europe, menaced, as he believes, by the Yellow Peril. He is on the side of peace. He is friendly to France and fair to Germany. Perhaps he will build a bridge across that gulf. He is, in the tradition of his Romans, a builder of bridges."

14

I had a very able exposition of Mussolini's policy of peace, his belief in the heritage of European civilisation, and his hopes of creating a new structure of prosperity among the nations, from a young man in the Palazzo Chigi, which is the Foreign Office in Rome. It was, of course, propaganda, but spoken with sincerity, I think. It was interesting, anyhow, as the official view, and I was impressed, being a simple soul without undue suspicion. I felt it necessary to say so. I acknowledge my admiration for Mussolini's genius, though with mental reservations regarding his contempt for liberty and his Machiavellian mind, ruthless when he puts an idea into operation. The Foreign Office young man accompanied me to the door and laughed as we parted. He put his head outside the door and spoke with smiling eyes.

"You have not been very friendly to Fascism," he said. "I have read some of your books."

I was rather abashed. It is always dangerous to write a book.

"I will be more friendly next time," I said.

And indeed I feel more friendly to Fascist Italy and Signor Mussolini, for certain reasons which have already been given. The people have better conditions of life. The children are cleaner and better dressed. The slums have been cleared in many cities. The Italian peasant sings at his work, although he lives under a dictatorship. There is happiness in Italy, in spite of economic depression, though none among business men and industrialists. And if it is true that Mussolini is a builder of bridges for the sake of peace, we must wish him well. He has great qualities of courage and kindliness. He wants to raise the standard of life among his people. Like Robin Hood, he robs the rich to feed the poor, which shows a kind heart— towards the poor—though it may lead to the ruin of the nation. On the other hand, one remembers certain episodes in his career, certain phases of his mind, which do not put an aureole round his head.

In order to get a reduction in railway fares granted to all visitors to Rome, I had to go to the Fascist Exhibition and through all its rooms, until I reached the ticket office. It was guarded by Carabinieri in steel helmets, and by State Guards in tricorner hats and tail coats and white gloves. There were pictures of the March on Rome and other triumphs of the Fascisti. There were also relics of the war, and among them on the walls were some posters which halted my footsteps. I had seen them before on English walls. There was a portrait of Kitchener's stern face. He was pointing his finger. In big letters across the poster I read familiar words: *Your King and Country Need You.*

It was twenty years, almost, since those words first called to the spirit of England; since they were answered by millions of young men who volunteered for death. How strange to see them again in Rome! There was no settled peace in Europe twenty years after all that sacrifice of youth. Behind the scenes, in the war offices of the world, staff officers were studying their maps.

15

After our journey through Milan, Brescia and Verona we turned north out of the last city, and drove through the valley

of the Adige towards Trento, which, once, under Austrian
rule, was Trent. The Italian armies in the World War marched
this way; dragged their guns up the mountain peaks; were
blinded by flying rock splinters; and had their brown bodies
smashed by high explosives. For four years these mountain
ranges and the long fertile valley below resounded with the
roar of gunfire along the Austrian front. Now all was quiet.
There was no motor traffic on the road. Along the whole way
to Trento we passed only two cars. On our right, after leaving
Verona, there was a chain of mountains with great walls down
which deep fissures were gashed. Italian workmen were labouring in sandstone quarries under the hot sun. There was a great
heat in that valley. The villages looked sunbaked by many
centuries of such weather. The children carried their shoes and
walked in the grass by the roadside.

We went through a deep gorge, at the end of which is a fort
on the hill above the Adige which here makes a sharp bend. At
Ceraino there was another fort on the hills across the river;
and all the way along there were fortresses, old and new, guard-
ing this valley, which is the pass to Verona and the heart of
Italy. It is thickly populated. We counted thirty villages almost
linked together on the way to Rovereto, past Borghetto-sul-
Adige. The mountains above them were clad with green, and
on the lower spurs were ruined castles, white churches with tall
campanili, and hamlets and tiled roofs. The names of these
villages were like Italian songs: Dolce, Ala, Pilcanto, Santa
Margherita, Chizzola, Lizzana, Volano, Acquaviva. Some of
them were not beautiful, being modern and dusty and mean:
but others were very attractive with their pergolas, and colour-
washed houses, and green shutters, and shady little market
places with fountains and stone benches. The vines were growing high, as in old Roman days before grapes grew in stunted
bushes. Along the dusty highway marched Italian troops, as in
the days of the World War; their faces deeply tanned and wet
with sweat, their backs burdened by heavy packs, their legs
dragging a little after a long and weary march.

Through the old village of Volano with narrow streets from
which the sun was kept came a body of young conscripts with

flowers in their caps. They marched briskly and looked keen and ardent. Most of them were young peasants from the mountain villages, as wiry as the young goats up there.

These mountains were higher and wilder as we went along the road. Here and there drifts of snow still glistened in their clefts under a blue sky. Peak after peak they reached away into the blue haze, a marvellous vista from which one could hardly turn one's eyes, and unforgettable.

We had laughter with us on the way. Gaston was pleased to have the lady next to him. He was telling some very good stories. We three men smiled because of his vivacity at the wheel, against which he had been warned by the lady herself. I wondered if he were telling his story of a Russian gipsy in Moscow who had put a spell upon a lady after she had refused to cross her palm with silver. It was a very strange and humorous story. But he had many others just as good. So with laughter at the wheel and beauty on the roadside, we came to Trento.

It was Austrian in the last war, as I think I have said. Now it is Italian, and undoubtedly its inhabitants were mainly of Italian origin while they were under Austrian rule. They were all speaking Italian as we went about the streets, and took our lunch out of doors at an old inn which faced the Bishop's palace with a gigantic tower which I tried to draw. Near it was the Duomo, built in the Romanesque style with a high nave under a double range of round arches. Two staircases of stone led to the triforium and clerestory on either side.

It is a handsome old city, built mainly at the time of the Renaissance, when the middle and merchant class began to get wealthy. Many of its houses are richly decorated and painted, and nearly all the streets are arcaded as shelter against the fiercely beating sun. There was a prince bishop here in old days, and Trent was rewarded by his wealth and power with fine fountains in which old Neptune plays with his nymphs and sea horses, and stately mansions for the prince bishop's court and friends.

It was here that the Council of Trent was held in 1545, when the Catholic Church reformed herself from within to check the ravages of the Reformation, which had been followed by frightful wars, making a mockery of Christian faith and charity.

We had a pleasant time in Trent, and I had a good conversation with an Italian tobacconist, who was very friendly, in his little shop. Because I was an Englishman he was not afraid to speak frankly on political and social subjects, and only paused when one of his customers entered for a box of matches or a packet of cigarettes.

"This world crisis!" he said, speaking with his hands as well as with his lips. "It bears down on this old city of Trento. What had happened in the United States—what is happening in Germany—makes a difference to the money in my till, and to my friends who carry on business in this city. That is the tragedy of modern times. We are so much dependent upon our neighbours, and yet we go on hating them and trying to ruin them! A most foolish proceeding! Then there is this passion for dictatorship. I have no quarrel with Signor Mussolini in any personal way. He has done good things for Italy. But it must be admitted that he has not mastered arithmetic. Arithmetic is not subject to dictatorship, perhaps! We have cement works here. There are many unemployed. Twelve per cent has been taken off salaries. That is not good. Deflation, as they call it, is the very devil! It would be better if salaries were increased, so that people had more money to spend—on cigarettes and tobacco, for example!"

My tobacconist thrust his fingers through his hair, which was black and greasy. He shook his head at the interference with the laws of arithmetic.

"It is all very strange," he continued, "this human nature and the way it works! Mussolini, for instance, is a highly intelligent man. He was formerly, as you know, a Socialist. He changed when he found he had the support of the capitalists. Now he has changed again and has killed the capitalists! They are taxed to death. Business is at a standstill. Not long ago an important bank closed its doors. Thousands of small people were ruined. There are, of course, mysteries. They mock the intelligence of man. One of them is the question of the gold standard. No one understands that! Gold has always been an evil thing. It has destroyed many human souls. For gold they have sold themselves to the devil. Now gold is at the bottom of the world's troubles. The old devil is laughing again, while humanity sinks deeper into distress, and labour—the strength of man's right arm, or his skill in craftsmanship—are worthless. What is going to happen in the future? Ah, that is a riddle!"

I bought some picture postcards, and we parted, without even attempting to answer that riddle of the future.

We headed the car northwards again. The journey was through dramatic scenery, after leaving San Michele sul Adige, where the stairways of the houses are outside their walls—very high walls with shuttered windows. Small castles were perched along the way on high peaks.

"How do those eagles' nests get their food and water?" asked the artist, and no one answered him. That was another riddle.

We went through Salerno and Sallaio and Villa, old, old towns with tall bell towers. In the fields beyond Villa there was a picture to please the eyes of Augustus John. It was a gipsy camp with tents made of red and blue blankets, and horses tethered about the camp fire, and swarthy fellows lying on the grass, and brown-limbed girls sitting on the steps of their wheeled houses, combing their black hair.

Beyond Bronzolla there was a *Campo Santo*—God's Acre, as it used to be called in old England—and over its gateway was the word of promise—*Resurrectionis*.

16

We arrived at last in Bolzano, which, like Trent and all the villages we had entered that day, was Austrian until the end of the World War. Unlike Trent, which had an Italian-speaking population, Bolzano is still Austrian in blood and speech, though Italianised as far as the decrees of Mussolini can alter racial instincts. These people in Bolzano have to Italianise their names, and that is not easy if they happen to be Schmidt or Wolff! Their children are not allowed to learn German in the schools; and, until a recent revocation, to speak it in their homes. The names of their streets are altered to those in other Italian towns.

Bolzano
May 1924

BOLZANO

In the Cathedral square there stands a statue of Walther von Vögelweide—one of the old Minnesingers whose poetry in German is still remembered and learnt by heart. He was a knightly man and a minstrel with sweet songs in his heart. But the Italians wished to pull down his statue. It was too German, they thought. It was better to have a statue of Mussolini. A cry went up from the people of Bolzano, a cry of horror at such sacrilege. It reached the ears of Mussolini. The statue still stands in the Cathedral square, plastered over with the stencilled portraits of the Dictator, and with his name printed in black letters and pasted on to the base of the monument. Il Duce. Il Duce. Il Duce.

Bolzano is a fine old city on the Isarco. Like Trento its streets are arcaded. Below its bridges the river rushes turbulently over rocky boulders. Its old houses have a German character. The fifteenth-century Pfarrkirche on the south side of the Piazza di Vittorio Emanuele—until 1925 called the Waltherplatz, and still so called in the minds of the citizens—is of German-Gothic. Many of the children are fair-haired and blue-eyed. No decree from Rome can alter that. But the Italians have built a new monument to their glory. It is a memorial to the Italian soldiers who fell in the Great War. It stands at the edge of the countryside, across a bridge. It is in the form of a Greek temple, with the Fasces on each side of its columns, and in the centre a statue of Christ, finely done. This memorial, guarded day and night by two Italian policemen in cocked hats, is one of the most beautiful things I have seen, because of the background against which its columns stand. It is a background of mountains set on fire every evening when the sun sinks in splendour. Simple and white, the temple is framed by that astounding glory. But there is no memorial to the Austrian soldiers who fell in the Great War. Their courage and their sacrifice are not remembered in stone.

We spoke German in Bolzano, and the people were pleased to speak it with strangers. The lady who had joined our party asked a question of a shopkeeper who was serving us with a small souvenir.

"Are the people happy here?"

It was an innocent question, but the shopkeeper—an elderly

man—seemed startled by it. For a moment or two he did not answer. There was an Italian officer in the shop and it was not until he had gone that the answer came in a low voice, emotionally.

"How can they be happy? There is much misery here and sadness of heart. Are we not Austrians? How can we be happy when our children are not allowed to learn German in their schools?"

His hand shook as he wrapped up a parcel for us. He waited until another customer had gone.

"All the people in Bolzano, except the officials," he said, "are Austrian. We were born Austrians. We shall die Austrians. But we are cut off from our own folk. They are not allowed to cross the frontier. We are not allowed to visit them. Anyone is arrested who tries to cross without a special permit. Meanwhile the tourist traffic by which we used to live has been killed by politicians and international troubles."

We sympathised with this elderly man; and because of this sympathy his eyes were wet for a moment. Then he made an admission, which, I think, told the real truth.

"It is the old people who feel the situation bitterly. The young take all this for granted. It does not break their hearts."

He tied up our parcel, and we left his shop, afraid of getting him into trouble if we asked more questions before two customers who came to his counter.

No doubt there was much heart burning—perhaps some heartbreaking—when the Italians first took possession of Bolzano. In the early period of their new régime the Italian officials were not tender towards the feelings of the Austrian population. The process of Italianisation was rigorous and imposed by force. But it has become less insistent since the new alliance between Italy and Austria; and no one can say now, I imagine, that there is any intense passion against this Italian occupation.

At a café in the Piazza di Vittorio Emanuele, facing the statue of Walther von Vögelweide, a young citizen of Bolzano gave me his views on this subject and others, while a military band played in the square.

"Italian rule is not harsh now," he admitted, though he was of Austrian blood. "Of course, middle-aged people still resent being under Italian rule, but the boys and girls don't mind very much. They go into the Balilla when they leave the nursery, and in due course have to do their military service. Some like it. Some don't. But they accept the new conditions of life which have given them Italian nationality. There is no spirit of revolt."

He began to talk about the affairs of the world, and didn't like the look of them.

"There will be another war in eight years," he prophesied quite calmly, as though he were telling me that rain would fall tomorrow.

"God forbid!" I exclaimed in German. "What makes you think that?"

The military band was playing light music very well. The people of Bolzano were walking up and down the square and looked cheerful. They were all Austrian in appearance. The girls were smart and pleased with themselves.

"It's boiling up," said my friendly young man, who had a noble type of face, thoughtful and gentle. "Germany is going mad again—*Verrückt*. All that Nazi enthusiasm is dangerous. They go marching and parading and asking for trouble. It's in their nature. They love military discipline and military symbolism. The Austrians aren't like that. And the German government is in the hands of a bad crowd. Low-class characters! They will certainly make trouble. I don't believe Hitler will hold his power. There will be another revolution and then war. Everybody in Europe is in a nervous state. Many nations are seething with political passion which doesn't make for peace. Look at France! I was in Paris lately. There is a revolutionary spirit among the young men. There will be barricades in the streets again, from all I heard. If it happens, there will be bloody fighting."

We spoke of France, which he seemed to know well. We agreed that it was the last stronghold of liberty in Europe, apart from England, which is outside the Continental system.

"There's something happening in the minds of the younger generation everywhere," he said. "Young Frenchmen are adopt-

ing the Fascist ideal. They are disgusted with Parliamentary
government and don't think much of liberty or democracy.
It's the same everywhere. The younger men want power. They
want to get rid of the older men. They want to seize the reins of
the horses. It may be good for some nations, not yet sufficiently
civilised to share in their own government. But it's bad for others
who have known liberty. Anyhow, it's an adventure towards the
unknown!"

He asked me about the influence of an Englishman named
Oswald Mosley and the number of his English Fascists.

"It would be a blow—the last blow—to liberty and free
speech if England goes Fascist," he said, very gravely.

He impressed me as an unusual young man. I should have
liked to talk more with him. But he had some friends at the table
next to him who were getting impatient with this conversation.

There was an amusing waiter at the Grifone, where we
stayed. He spoke very good English and had excellent memories
of England. He had been a waiter at Margate and Hampstead
and the Hans Crescent Hotel in London before the war. He
had had a girl at Rottingdean and still remembered the colour
of her eyes. He had been in a Jaeger regiment during the war,
on the Italian and Russian fronts. It was on the Italian front
that he was wounded in the leg and taken prisoner. He disliked
the idea of being a prisoner, and was much attracted by the
look of a horse which happened to be grazing near the camp
where he was put behind barbed wire. One morning he sprang
on to that steed and was away like a flash of lightning, until he
took to the cover of some woods. He was not far from Verona,
and having sent the horse back, he made his way to the Austrian
front. His knowledge of Italian, which he spoke perfectly, helped
him to escape.

He told us this story with great detail and vivacity, laughing
heartily at his good luck in escaping. Then he surprised us by
telling us that although he fought on the side of Austria he received a war pension from the Italians, like all the other ex-
soldiers in Bolzano and Trento and the zone now taken over by
Italy. That seemed to me very fair and generous on the part of
Italy.

It was another ex-soldier and ex-Austrian who spoke the last words we heard in Bolzano. He too had been talking about his war adventures, mostly to our artist, because of his wounded arm. He had been laughing and joking, but suddenly his expression changed.

"There is talk of a new war! If any officer comes to me and says, 'You are wanted for a new war,' I shall shoot him dead on the spot! The last war was enough. What madmen will make another?"

17

Those words of passion rang in our ears as we left Bolzano and travelled along a road which rose high until we were twelve hundred feet above the valley, where the river ran white with snow water although it was full summer now. There was a noble view at Campodazza, and a fine old castle at Castelrotto stood on a high bluff above the Ponte all' Isarco. There was snow on the high peaks above the villages, which were like those in the Austrian Tyrol—as this once was—or in Bavaria, with church spires of red brick, and farmsteads with tiled roofs on long poles jutting out beyond the eaves.

Along the mountain paths came young men dressed in the Austrian way, with tasselled shorts above their bare knees and embroidered braces over their white shirts. We went through an enchanting village called Varna, like the coloured picture in a fairy-tale book—one of Grimm's—and then past a forest where Red Riding Hood might have met the wolf—a fir forest with tall trunks like the pillars of a Gothic church through which the sunlight slanted. It was guarded—being close to the frontier—by Alpini in their Robin Hood hats. An immense fort with battlements and bastions surrounded by a moat stretched across the valley for its defence. At Fortezza we were two thousand two hundred feet high, surrounded by forests where timber was being cut and heaved down the mountain sides.

They were haymaking in Mezzaselva, and the fields were covered with small haycocks, golden in the sun, with crinkled gold strewn about them.

At Vipitono we drove through an old arch below a tall grim

tower. We were still following the Isarco, and at the Colle Isarco a torrent was rushing through a great hole in the rocks across a water wheel, and into little canals irrigating the gardens and fields. It was all bubbling and frothing, with the noise of a strong wind rushing through a beech wood.

We reached Brenno and a post across the road. Italian officers of the Carabinieri examined our passports carefully.

It was good-bye to Italy, the loveliest country in Europe, with the oldest cities in which this civilisation of ours reached its first splendour, from which the Roman legions marched to all the known world, followed along the same roads by Christian pilgrims from the city of Peter's tomb. The Renaissance, with its faith in beauty and its revival of learning, came also from the land we were leaving. Our own Shakespeare was steeped in its spirit. We learned our manners, and fashioned our clothes, and rebuilt old mansions, in the style of Italy.

Now Italy has a new Renaissance, and there is a new Cæsar there, leader and tyrant to his people, though without foreign victories. He has revived their spirit and pride. He favours youth with its song of *Giovanezza*. He is very partial to the multiplication of babies. He has raised his country to the status of a first-class power. His active and subtle mind plays a great part in the diplomatic game behind the scenes. He has real qualities of greatness. But, as my friend in the tobacco shop observed, not even Mussolini can alter the laws of arithmetic. His budget is unbalanced. Business in Italy is strangled by taxation and suffering a loss of markets. The conversations I had had did not reveal a sense of prosperity or security. It seemed to me, looking back on all that I had seen and heard, that Italy was expecting some new crisis and was nervous of a new war. Only youth was singing.

VII

The Austrian Tragedy

I WAS IN VIENNA A few days after the fighting between the
Austrian Heimwehr—a Fascist army under the command
of Prince Starhemberg and Major Fey—and armed bodies of
Social Democrats, firing from the great blocks of workmen's
dwelling which had been built for them by a Socialist municipality. Faced by rifle and machine-gun fire, the Heimwehr
had brought up artillery and bombarded the tenement houses,
crowded with women and children, until the Social Democrats
—mostly boys and unemployed men—were forced to surrender
after heavy losses in killed and wounded and were led off to
prison camps for trial and execution.

It was a tragedy which shocked the world—or that part of
the world which is still capable of being shocked by such bloody
episodes in what we are pleased to call our civilisation. It was
difficult to believe that such civil war should have broken out
in Austria, among those easy-going, good-natured, art-loving
people, for whom all nations—even their enemies—have had a
romantic affection, though it did not prevent them from cutting
the old Empire into pieces and leaving Austria itself, a small
state with a great capital, without the means of self-support.

Even the Germany of Hitler professed to be deeply shocked
by this attack on a working community. The German Press
denounced it as "barbarous"—forgetting brutalities against
Jews and Communists and not yet stunned by the cold-blooded

murder of their own leaders in a revolution at headquarters under orders of that god-like man—did they not worship him? —Herr Adolf Hitler.

There was panic, or at least, the gravest apprehensions, in the Foreign Offices of Europe. It might mean another war. Italy was behind the action of Prince Starhemberg and behind the dictatorship of that midget man, Dr. Dollfuss. Czecho-Slovakia was deeply alarmed by this Italian influence. The German Nazis, who had sworn to bring Austria within their system, were roused to fury by Italy's guarantee of Austrian independence and by French and English support. If they crossed the frontier in armed bands to link up with Austrians in favour of union with Germany—as they threatened—Italy would send her battalions into Austria to defend this "independence"— whether the majority of the people liked it or not. All the fat would be in the fire. Europe might be in flames again.

The Chief of Nazi propaganda in Austria from the other side of the German frontier was one of Hitler's lieutenants named Habicht. By powerful broadcasting stations he had blasted his propaganda into Austrian ears month after month. With that delicacy and tact for which the Germans are so justly renowned he had called upon the Austrian people to unite with their German brothers in allegiance to Adolf Hitler or to take the consequences of being blown up in their railway trains by high explosives and routed out of their meeting places by stink bombs.

After the bombardment of the Community houses in Vienna, Herr Habicht had graciously given the Austrian people a fort-night to think things over. At the end of that time there would be the devil to pay, he threatened, if they did not rise against the Dollfuss government and proclaim their Nazi faith.

This ultimatum expired on the evening when I reached Vienna. The nerves of the people in that city were on edge. They had been shaken by the noise of gunfire during the fighting around them, and by the state of siege in which they were still living. There were thousands of prisoners in the jails and camps. Thousands of women were waiting to know the fate of their men, seven of whom had already been hanged, while the others were awaiting trial; many of their sons were still in hiding

—wounded and afraid to ask for medical help. There was the menace of starvation in many working homes who had lost their breadwinners. Even those who had not been arrested had been dismissed from their work, if they belonged to any of the Social Democratic institutions, which included almost every branch of social service in Vienna, including banks, children's clinics, and municipal baths. Their political opponents, the middle classes, who had been heavily taxed against their will to support the Socialists, were by no means free from fear. No one knew whether the provinces—hostile to the Heimwehr and anxious for union with Germany—would remain quiet. Now, if the German Nazis marched across the frontier, Austria might be the battleground of a new war. They were having sleepless nights in Vienna.

On the evening when Herr Habicht's ultimatum expired, I sat in the room of a high official who was in touch with every source of information. He was a delicate man, with thin, transparent hands and a look of nervous exhaustion, though he talked with extreme rapidity in the most perfect English.

He was talking to me about the fighting in Vienna and its consequences. He assured me that Dr. Dollfuss—who only recently had received great hero worship in England—would not be vindictive against the Social Democrats who, in his judgment, had been misled by their leaders. He would be merciful and conciliatory. He wished to establish a new form of constitution which should not be a dictatorship but a partnership between employers and labour in a corporate state, carrying out the principles of Leo XIII's vision of a Christian nation. It was, of course, official propaganda, to which I listened politely, fascinated by the charm and courtesy of this delicate man, who seemed so frail that his body could hardly support his active brain. But every minute he was rung up on the telephone, and his answers to questions which came into his earpiece were more interesting and more dramatic than anything he told me. From his answers, spoken in German, I could guess the questions.

"No. It is untrue that German Nazis have crossed the frontier. ... I say it is quite untrue. You can rely upon that."

"That is inaccurate. Austrian troops are not massed on the border of Czecho-Slovakia. We have no need to do that. Precautions have been taken, of course, on the German frontier. Naturally!"

"What is that? Grave incidents reported in many directions? Certainly not. I am in close touch. I should know immediately. No such incidents have been reported to me."

"The German bluff has been exposed. An ultimatum is ridiculous unless it is followed by action. No such action is in progress. Herr Habicht has made himself look very foolish. Not for the first time!"

Across the telephone that delicate-looking man smiled at me. Certainly, Herr Habicht, the German propagandist, had made a fool of himself. His master, Hitler, had withdrawn him. Hitler himself was not going to risk a war in which he would have no allies but all the great powers against him. His own régime was in jeopardy.

2

I was anxious to visit the workmen's dwellings which had been bombarded during the civil war, and to talk with the people who had had this frightful experience. I had seen some of these buildings before. These great community houses for the working folk were an object lesson to all countries in beauty and convenience. Built round spacious courtyards with green lawns and flower beds, they provided cheap flats for thousands of families. The men who had built them had taken a pride in them. They were nobly planned. In the opinion of many foreigners who had visited Vienna in recent years, Social Democracy in that city had made a good job of the municipal government. Now its leaders had been hanged or imprisoned, unless they had escaped. All their work was destroyed.

It was not easy to get an entrance into the *Gemeindehäusen*. They were still guarded by police and Heimwehr men, who had orders to keep out any inquisitive people. No inhabitant could enter or leave without a police pass. Some friends of mine in Vienna, closely in touch with some of these working people, arranged a little subterfuge. At the corner of a certain street I was to meet an elderly woman and a young girl carrying a washing basket. I was to make an offer to help them. I would pass in with them.

This idea seemed to me very thin. It turned out to be so. I had hardly gone ten yards with the washing basket when I was approached by an enormous policeman with a rifle slung over his shoulder.

"What do you want?" he asked sternly.

I dropped that subterfuge, and the washing basket, and answered frankly that I wanted to see the bombarded dwellings. I mentioned the name of the Save the Children Fund which had done so much for Austria in the hungry years. I was connected with it, and its name was a good password.

"I will show you round," said the policeman. "Follow me."

He led the way into the courtyard and showed me how the walls were spattered with bullet marks and pierced by shell holes. The beauty of that building was hideously scarred. Then he took me up flights of stairs, down long corridors, and into rooms utterly wrecked by shell fire. Every bit of furniture in them was smashed into small splinters. The children's cots were dust and twisted wire. The household treasures were in smithereens. There were great holes in the walls. I had seen many such rooms in war time.

Suddenly I was aware that this giant policeman, who had seemed so stern and gruff, had tears in his eyes. They were rolling down his cheeks.

"It is a tragedy!" he said, in a broken voice. "The people built these houses themselves. They were proud of them. Now look at this ruin!"

He turned away to hide his emotion, but all the time I walked with him into many rooms like that, he had moist eyes and could hardly bear to see this wreckage. It was not pleasant to see. I realised its dreadful tragedy, especially when I talked with women who had lived in these rooms and now had come to search in this ruin for any rag or remnant that might remain. They didn't weep, I noticed. They had hard, thin lips pressed tight. Their husbands were in the prison camps. They had lost everything. They had no means of livelihood, except the charity of their neighbours, who were also suffering.

As we passed through a courtyard I noticed a separate building much damaged by shell fire.

"That was their cinema," said the policeman.

The name of the last film shown before the civil war began was *Die Küss in Spiegel*—"The Kiss in the Looking-glass."

I went to the suburb of Floridsdorf, across the river. It was here that the Social Democrats had put up their strongest defence, and had caused most trouble to the Heimwehr, until the guns were brought up.

A young clerk was my guide. I met him in a street of Floridsdorf where crowds of working-class people were passing with haggard, anxious faces. He himself was nerve-racked and looked very ill. He had been in his office when the fighting began and could not get back to his young wife, who had a flat in one of the model dwellings. For thirty-six hours he lived through an experience which had shaken his nerve to pieces. He was in the line of fire. The young men of the *Schutzbund*—the defence force of Social Democracy—had taken up positions in some factory yards from which they kept back the Heimwehr troops by rifle and machine-gun fire. They had only two machine guns, I was told, but they were sufficient to sweep the line of approach. They retreated under gunfire, and those who were not wounded or killed took up a new position farther back. Other small bodies of men were on the roofs of the big block of dwellings, firing at the Heimwehr troops. The young clerk could see what was happening down below, at the risk of his life from rifle fire. He could see the wounded lying on the pavement. He could hear their screams of agony as they lay in pools of blood. They were mostly boys of eighteen or so. There was no Red Cross work on either side. No doctors came to attend the wounded. They were left there for two days.

I talked with other people who lived through the bombardment. One was a working family of father, mother, and one small son, and an old grandfather. They knew nothing of any preparations for a siege until the shooting began. They had nothing to do with politics. The first thing they knew was that bullets were coming through their walls and windows. They crouched down, expecting to be killed. The firing was so intense that they dared not stand upright or risk the chance of rushing to the cellars. The boy had been terrified. There was still the remembrance of terror in his eyes when I spoke to him. The old grandfather had cried out to God and moaned all the time.

I was taken into other apartments, those which had been most wrecked by gunfire. I was introduced to families who had fled from them when the first shells burst. They all denied that they had had any warning before the bombardment. Probably it was given, according to the official statement, but it did not reach many inhabitants in those great blocks of dwellings. They had been utterly ignorant, they told me, of any plans of a general uprising of the Social Democrats. They had had no orders for a general strike. The thing just burst upon them. Groups of the younger men belonging to the *Schutzbund*, formed to defend Social Democracy against the Fascist Heimwehr, had rushed to arms and taken up positions without informing the inhabitants who would be in the line of fire. Now thousands of young men, their sons or brothers, had been arrested, after brutal treatment, they said, by the Heimwehr men, who had beaten and kicked some of them unmercifully.

"I don't know what is going to happen to us," said a young man who had taken no part in the fighting. "I have been dismissed from my job like most others. Here is the dismissal notice."

He showed me a small piece of paper informing him that his services were terminated.

He looked round at his flat. It was well furnished and undamaged. He had a piano and some good pictures. It might have been a flat in Knightsbridge. Several well-dressed young women—one of them his wife—were listening to our conversation with anxious eyes.

"It's the end of everything," he said. "I shall never get another place. And my wife and I were rather pleased with ourselves. We liked this little home."

His wife put her hand on his shoulder with a caressing touch, and I was sorry for them.

"The workmen's dwellings were built as fortresses," said the propagandists of the Dollfuss government. If that was so, the work was badly done. The bullets of the Heimwehr had gone clean through the inner walls of lath and plaster. The outer walls had been pierced by shellfire like brown paper.

3

All one's instincts of fair play and sympathy were on the side of the Social Democrats, but it was difficult for a foreigner to pass judgment. I heard horrible stories of the brutal treatment of prisoners, including delicate women kept in overcrowded prisons without any sanitation, but I could get no first-hand information, and these things were denied by government officials. "We are a civilised people," they said. "We don't ill-treat our prisoners. We are Austrians."

Among my own friends, including English residents of Vienna, there was a difference of opinion as to the provocation which had caused the conflict. Some of them blamed the leaders of Social Democracy for political abuse of the Dollfuss régime and for inflaming the younger men with political passion, knowing that if it came to a fight they would be wiped out. They believed that the only policy for the happiness of Austria and the peace of Europe was for all moderate-minded men to support the Dollfuss government against the forces of anarchy and the Nazi element who wanted union with Germany.

Others accused Dr. Dollfuss of surrendering his conscience to Mussolini and his power to Prince Starhemberg. They thought that the Social Democrats were justified in defending their organisation against the long-drawn menace of the Heimwehr Fascists. They knew that an armed struggle would have to come one day. Were they to surrender to the forces of reaction and the spirit of the bully as tamely as German Socialists? Were they not right and justified in storing up arms—mostly old stuff kept after the Armistice by ex-soldiers who were the defenders of the Republic which Dollfuss had betrayed? Was not the *Schutzbund* the defence force of liberty against oppression? . . . So they argued.

I heard such an argument among the Austrian people. It was in a private house to which I was invited on a Sunday afternoon. The people present belonged to the professional class. They seemed to me highly intelligent and with all the charm of Austrian character as one likes to think of it, and as it still is, in spite of political passion.

"If I had been a Social Democrat," said a pretty woman with gold-spun hair, who sat next to me at the tea table, "I should have fought with a rifle in my hands. At least they weren't cowards. They had a right to defend themselves. It was better than a pitiful surrender, as German democracy surrendered."

There was a silence at these words. Everyone looked at that pretty woman, who spoke suddenly, with intense emotion.

A young lawyer on the other side of the table looked at her with a faint smile.

"One must admire courage," he said. "Those boys were heroic. One must admit that. Even Dollfuss and Starhemberg do so. Personally I am sympathetic towards the Social Democrats, but critical of their leaders. They betrayed the rank and file. They were fools and madmen."

"The whole world is mad," said an old gentleman who sat at the head of the table. "It was the war which drove us all insane."

The young lawyer turned to me and tried to explain his political view.

The leaders of Social Democracy in Vienna—men like Dr. Otto Bauer—were always mouthing red-hot stuff which was not intended to be taken very seriously. It was their métier. It was stuff in which they did not believe very seriously themselves. Platform rhetoric. Political propaganda for party purposes. The only people who believed in it were young unemployed men and theoretical Communists. The other people who belonged nominally to the ranks of Social Democracy had become moderate and bourgeois and non-political. They only asked to be left in peace with a decent chance of livelihood, and pride in their little homes—cheaper in those model dwellings than other citizens could get.

"What about the secret stores of arms?" I asked.

He shrugged his shoulders.

"Nothing much in that. They were stored up, not to over-throw the government but to resist the Heimwehr—a Fascist and illegal organisation which, until recent events, might have been against the government. I don't blame them for enrolment in the *Schutzbund*—those boys who tried to defend their party and faith. I want to be fair."

"What was the immediate challenge?" I asked.

"It was not immediate," said one of the women. "The Heimwehr had declared war on them for years. It was only a question of when it would come."

The young lawyer passed by this interruption.

"In my opinion it was brought to a head by the conversations between Dollfuss and Mussolini, and then—by the visit of Suvich of the Italian Foreign Office. The *Arbeiterzeitung*—the Social Democratic paper—insulted Suvich violently, calling him an Austrian traitor who had deserted his own country. There was some truth in that, but it was not pleasant reading for a distinguished visitor who had come to make a friendly alliance. The paper was suppressed for a time. When it reappeared it was even more provocative. Its editors guessed, and guessed rightly, that the price of Italian support for Austria, by Mussolini, was the wiping out of Social Democracy."

"Would you have had them surrender?" asked the pretty lady with the gold-spun hair. "Mustn't men fight to defend their liberty?"

The young lawyer did not seem much in favour of fighting anyhow.

"The younger men were the dupes of their leaders," he insisted. "I don't believe the leaders wanted the conflict at all. But they had talked wild words and couldn't climb down. They funked the consequences and bungled everything. The orders for the general strike only reached about ten per cent of the workers and was answered by less than that number. The majority were stunned and bewildered when they heard the shooting. Many of the leaders were arrested before they could give any order. Others fled, leaving their men in the lurch."

That seems to be near the truth, as far as I could get it from a variety of sources in Vienna. The general strike was only sectional. Most of the Social Democrats were unaware of it until they heard the noise of fighting. It did not spread at all to the heart of the city. The young men who had resolved to fight hadn't a chance from the beginning, being vastly outnumbered and unsupported. They hadn't even the key to the whereabouts of the hidden arms. They had no general plan of action.

"Many of the Social Democrats will go over to the Nazis," said the old gentleman who sat at the head of the table. "It's their only chance of opposition to a government which has destroyed their organisation."

"What about Dr. Dollfuss?" I asked. "Hasn't he lost all his influence? Isn't his government doomed, anyhow?"

There was a long silence in the room. These Austrian people of the middle class seemed to be thinking deeply. They belonged to the intelligentsia. They believed in liberty and civilised ideals. But they were afraid of revolution and the chance of war.

"Anything is better than civil war," said one of the company. "Perhaps anything is better than a Nazi régime. People of moderate views like ourselves—am I right in saying that?— ought to support the Dollfuss government as long as it can carry on. It's the only chance of peace in Austria. I'm a peace-loving man. Perhaps also I'm a coward. I dislike bloodshed. I dislike bludgeoning. I want to be left alone by all extremists. Dollfuss is the only moderating influence in Austria. He has good intentions."

"He's in the hands of the Heimwehr," said another member of the party. "If he ever had any conscience he surrendered it to Major Fey and that rattle-pated youth, Prince Starhemberg."

"Poor Austria!" cried one of the women. "When I think of all we have suffered——!"

I thought of all they had suffered. I was in Vienna soon after the war, when they had no light, no fuel, and very little food. I saw their rickety children in the hospitals and children's clinics. I knew people who had belonged to their aristocracy and now were starving. I went into the Hofburg, the palace of the Hapsburgs, when it was a soup kitchen and when foreigners were feeding the hungry children. I knew what they had suffered.

There was one episode of chivalry in this time of fighting. It was the act of an old man—Prince Schönberg-Hartenstein, Commander-in-Chief of the Austrian army. With one bugler he went into the courtyards of the workmen's dwellings while sniping was still taking place, and he summoned the people by bugle call to gather round him.

"My dear people," he said, "Dr. Dollfuss has promised an amnesty to all men who will surrender their arms by a certain time, which is now running out. I want you to know this and to take advantage of it. I want the wives and mothers to persuade their men that this is the best thing to do to avert further bloodshed."

The old man's words had a good effect. Many of the young men laid down their arms.

I read placards on the walls of Vienna calling upon the working classes to coöperate in the reconstruction of Austria. They were told that they had been duped by their leaders, who had betrayed them into fighting against their fellow citizens. They were urged to forget these tragic happenings and to join in a loyal effort to make a peaceful and a happy Austria in a system of government which would safeguard the interests of the working classes and give them a share of self-government.

Groups of people read these placards silently. No comment was made in the streets. Moody eyes stared into mine, as haggard-looking men walked away after reading those manifestos. It was too soon for any of the Social Democrats to forget or forgive. Twenty thousand people in Vienna were threatened with starvation by the loss of their breadwinners and by dismissal from their posts. Frau Dollfuss and Cardinal Innitzer established a relief fund and distributed food, but many women would not take bread from the wife of a man who had ordered, or allowed, the bombardment of their dwellings and the shooting of their men. The promises of clemency had not yet been fulfilled. The prisoners were still in camps and jails, horribly overcrowded, according to stories told of them, and with many beatings and brutalities, according to other stories. Dr. Dollfuss proclaimed his good intentions and his mercy. There would have been more hangings but for the plea for clemency urged by the French and British ambassadors. But wounded men were still being hidden by their friends, who had no faith in the merciful instincts of Dr. Dollfuss and his friend Major Fey.

Yet there were still people in Vienna who could take a joke. After all, I heard many jokes in Flanders when it was strewn with dead.

"Dr. Dollfuss is walking up and down under his bed, thinking out a new Constitution," I was told when I asked for an interview with that pocket dictator, whose tiny stature was a cause of constant jesting, until it was carried in a little coffin to the Stefankircher, after terrible events.

I was promised the interview, if I would postpone it until my return from Budapesth, to which I was going for a few days. But when I returned I found all doors closed in official quarters. As I heard afterwards, I was made responsible for an article hostile to the Dollfuss régime, which I was supposed to have written, but which, as a matter of fact, I did not write. I missed a talk with Dr. Dollfuss; and I shall never have it now.

4

Four months or so had passed when I entered Austria again from Italy, with a novelist, an artist, a lady, and a Russian driver. The frontier was guarded. No Austrian was allowed to cross without a special permit. Passport examination was rigorous—though Italy was in alliance with Austria.

The first village we entered was Steinach-im-Tyrol, and it was all that one might expect or hope for as a typical little town in a country which used to be the most charming in the world because of its sense of art, its good-natured people, its ease of life, its love of light-hearted music. The houses of seventeenth-century architecture were all painted with floral decorations, or with romantic pictures of knights and ladies, or with portraits of famous people. It is a pity that English villages are not picture galleries like that, though perhaps the results would be atrocious if such a habit spread.

Opposite the *Gasthaus zum Wilden Mann*, where we had lunch, there was a house which, according to an inscription, had been the headquarters of the organ-building art for two hundred years. On another house was the portrait of Max Emmanuel, Kurfurst von Bayern. All down the street were fine old inns and good solid houses, built at a time when Austria was a great Empire with a traffic of princes, and nobles, and rich merchants, who liked good food and good wine when their coaches stopped in villages like this. Now it seemed dead in Steinach-im-Tyrol. We were the only visitors. There was no life in the village street. There was something sinister in its quietude, I thought.

We fell into conversation with a young woman who waited on us. She was sympathetic with the artist because of his broken arm, and cut up his food for him. She laughed pleasantly at the jokes of our laughing lady, who can jest in German. But presently, after our meal, which was very simple, she became serious on the state of Austria, and seemed to know a lot about it, with a shrewd judgment.

"It seems very peaceful here," she said. "That is an illusion. Almost every day there is something unpleasant going on. The Nazis are making trouble. I can't see what good it does them. They put bombs on the railways and let them off in public buildings. Then the Heimwehr arrests a lot of people, and the innocent suffer with the guilty. It's all very silly."

She laughed at the silliness of things in Austria.

"How are the Social Democrats getting on?" I asked.

Her answer was decisive.

"Social Democracy is dead!"

She told me that the Nazis were strong in South Austria, but she thought that Dr. Dollfuss was getting more support from middle-aged people. It was the young men who made all the trouble. Meanwhile there was a lot of unemployment and very poor trade and much misery. The unemployed are paid two and a half Austrian shillings a day, she told us, or a little more, if they have a family.

"Just enough to keep them alive," she thought.

"Hasn't the treaty with Italy done something?" I asked, confident that she would know. She was one of those young women who keep their eyes and ears open, and their sanity, when men go mad with politics and passion.

"It hasn't made much difference. The Italians still tax Austrian goods. It is difficult to sell our timber across the frontier. There is a lot of talk about Mussolini's treaty with Austria. It is mostly newspaper eloquence, and the Austrian peasant is still without a market, while Austrian girls are idle."

"Idle? I can't believe that!"

"Thrown out of work. The hotels are cutting down their staffs. So are the shops, and the middle-class families who used to have maids. Women haven't much chance of earning a livelihood in an honest way."

She spoke some words which ended with a sigh and then a laugh.

"One must go on hoping—until one gets old and hope is worthless. That is life nowadays."

I thought of the interview I had missed with Dr. Dollfuss in Vienna. I have no doubt this girl had told me things which I shouldn't have heard from him. She gave me the point of view of the working woman—the hope and the hopelessness of many Austrian girls of her class.

We went into other Austrian villages on the way to Innsbruck. At the entrance to their streets a banner was strung across the way, and the words on it were a warning:

Avoid Politics
And Strife
And Be Good-Humoured.

On the walls of some of these villages—perhaps all of them —were other warnings of a sterner kind. They announced that the punishment of death would be given to any person or persons found guilty of placing bombs or other high explosives with intent to do damage, or to any persons found conspiring against the State.

We had a wonderful drive through the Austrian Tyrol, with an endless vista of high mountains barren at their peaks and clad with fir forests below. Then suddenly there was a wide gap between the mountains. On one side was a great castle, and below, outspread like a map, was a broad plain and a red-roofed city.

It was Innsbruck.

5

Innsbruck was very quiet. The last time I had been there it was crowded with visitors from Germany, England and other countries. I remembered the traffic along the main street with its gilded houses, and the densely packed restaurants where farming folk down from the mountain villages were having heavy meals and much beer, in holiday time. Now the restaurants were empty, and I saw no farming folk, nor any foreign visitors. The inhabitants of Innsbruck had their city to themselves.

They did not spoil the picture of this lovely old town, with its vista of mountains at the top of its high street, beyond the statue of the Madonna with a golden circlet. Young men with the look of mountaineers wore their short jackets—green, blue, or cherry-coloured—and tasselled shorts and Robin Hood hats. The young women, with straw-coloured hair and eyes as blue as cornflowers, wore white bodices and sprigged pinafores above their short frocks, as though they were the chorus of a musical comedy with music by Strauss or Lehar. Barefooted monks passed, swinging the ends of their rope girdles. Nuns went by with downcast eyes. Child beggars, wizened and pale, came into the restaurants and cafés. University students—boys and girls —walked hand in hand and looked into the windows of the bookshops. A company of soldiers marched along in steel helmets and war kit. Innsbruck, the city of pleasure, had a dejected look. Pleasure had gone from it. It was in the hands of armed men.

We stayed at the Grauer Bär, an old inn with a vaulted roof above its restaurant. In the courtyard I spoke to a nice-looking fellow who had given me the old Austrian welcome of *Grüss Gott!* —so much better than *Heil Hitler!* He raised his hands when I asked him about Austria, and then smiled in a melancholy way.

"The situation is strained," he said. "It does not seem to get any better. Too much political passion."

"Still?"

"More than ever. It is partly due to the economic situation. There are half a million unemployed out of six million inhabitants. That is a high percentage, and unemployed men are apt to get savage and do savage things. Austria depends so much on the tourist traffic. Now there are no tourists. Germany is cut off from us. They have to pay a thousand marks for the privilege of paying us a visit. That is a bit too stiff! In any case, the frontier is closed to them because of Nazi propaganda."

"Is the government secure?" I asked indiscreetly.

The young man, who wore a jacket of blue and white check above an embroidered waistcoat and buff-coloured shorts—I envied him that costume—looked round cautiously before he answered.

"Dollfuss can only hold on if things get better," he said. "He has many enemies. In this part of Austria we are all for union with Germany. We have no love for Mussolini and his sham friendship."

He smiled and raised his Robin Hood hat.

"This is a dangerous subject of conversation," he confessed, "I don't want to get shot or put into a prison camp. You have perhaps seen the notices outside the Austrian villages."

He repeated the words.

"*Avoid Politics: and Strife: and Be good-humoured.*"

"It is well to keep that advice," he remarked, and that was the last word he said to me before touching his hat and walking away.

That evening we strolled through Innsbruck. It was a summer night with a blue sky above, almost black, but scattered with stars. There were few people about, though it was not late. Many of the streets were deserted except for armed police. But the city was illuminated as though for victory. The house of the golden roof—*Das Goldne Dachl*—was flood-lit and looked like a picture in a fairy tale. The statue of the Madonna with the golden circlet was touched by the white finger of a searchlight.

We spoke in low voices because of this loneliness about us.

"It all seems very sad!" said the lady.

"It's all very magical!" said the artist.

"If only one could get at the drama in these people's homes?" said the novelist.

I sat alone next morning in one of the cafés of Innsbruck. It was in the middle of the morning, and only a few people—not more than two, I think—sat looking at illustrated papers over their coffee. One of the waiters seemed interested in me as an Englishman. He had been to England in the old days, like so many foreign waiters. He would like, he said, to be in England now.

"England is always a safe place," he told me with a smile. "It is the land of liberty. No revolutions! No excitement beyond cricket or a football match! The English know how to live. They are civilised. They are tolerant of other people's ideas. When I was in England . . ."

After he had enjoyed himself in English reminiscence, I asked him about Austria.

He glanced over one shoulder. There was only one person left in the café—a girl at the far end of the room, writing a letter on the marble-topped table. It was probably a love letter, judging from her smile.

"Outwardly," said the waiter, "Austria is peaceful. *Underneath it is a powder magazine!*"

He gave me some details of that powder magazine in the spirit of the Austrian people. They were very bitter, many of them. Many young men were desperate and ready to resort to any kind of violence. They were already making bombs and setting them off. That was not with murderous intent exactly, but as a demonstration against the government, which they hated. If they were Social Democrats they hated the government for the bombardment in Vienna and the suppression of their party. If they were Nazis they hated the government for playing into the hands of Italy and preventing their union with Hitler's Germany.

"I am not involved in any of that stuff," said the waiter. "But all the same, it is impossible for Austria to stand alone. The Peace Treaty made that impossible. We were cut to pieces. All our industries and natural sources of wealth were stripped from us and went to Czecho-Slovakia and other countries.

CORPUS CHRISTI NIGHT, INNSBRUCK

There are no markets for our timber or cattle—pedigree cattle, as you know. This Italian treaty is a fake. Italy only increases our debts by subsidising the Heimwehr and granting loans. Germany is Austria's market. There is no other. We must either join up with Germany in an economic union or go down in ruin. That is, in my opinion, the truth of things."

He flicked some tables with his napkin, hurried to another part of the room when two customers entered, and then returned, when they had gone, a quarter of an hour later.

"As we were saying," he remarked, "the world is mad!"

I did not remember any word he had said about that, but I agreed. Almost everybody agrees about that.

"The press is to blame," said my confidential waiter. "The journalists ought to be shot first, in every country. Then the rest of us could live in peace and prosperity. It is the press which stirs up international hatred. It is the press which prevents international agreement. When I see a journalist I wish to kill him because he is a disease spreader. He is the infecter of the human mind. He is essentially evil."

I dared not confess to him that I had done some journalism in my time.

He continued his conversation. He picked up a paper—one of those detestable papers written by journalists—and showed me a paragraph relating to the bombing of a railway line in Austria.

"The situation cannot last," he said. "A people cannot live in these conditions. So much passion must lead to an explosion. And what good will that do?"

He was a pacifist. He didn't believe in violence. He was a hater of cruelty—except against journalists.

"Perhaps the Dollfuss régime is the best for Austria," he said. "I do not know. I cannot see the alternative. I can only see that the present state of Austria is very dangerous."

He spoke of England again. Because I was an Englishman he shook hands with me heartily.

"England," he said, as a parting word, "is not mad in a mad world."

I hoped he was telling me the truth.

6

I wakened at six o'clock in the Grauer Bär, and got out of bed to look out of the window. A company of infantry was passing in steel hats and full marching order. They were preceded by a band playing a good march tune. Long banners were flying from all the houses. It was the Feast of Corpus Christi, and the people of Innsbruck were already on their way to church to pray at the altars of the Messenger of Peace and Good Will on Earth. I thought of the waiter's words: "Outwardly Austria is peaceful. Beneath, it is a powder magazine." Already they were assembling for a procession through the streets. It was a remarkable procession, and I watched it from the balcony of my bedroom. No one would have thought, looking down on those men and women and children, walking in honour of the Crucified Christ, that there was any civil conflict in their land, or anything but peace in their hearts.

It was beautiful and impressive. They came on with tall banners, with their flagstaffs garlanded—staffs so tall and heavy that the young men could hardly carry them. A group of boys in sailor dress marched first, followed by battalions of young girls in white frocks with wreaths of daisies round their fair heads. Tiny girls like fairies scattered flower petals in the roadway. Nuns with white coifs and long black robes walked at the head of the girls' detachments, reciting the Rosary. Battalion after battalion, the boys and girls marched with perfect rhythm to the music of their bands. There were girls in flower-coloured frocks, making human bouquets as I watched them from above. Others wore white veils above their muslin frocks like brides going to the altar. University students passed by with their little flat caps and short tunics. Behind them stepped the Student Corps in duelling kit—strange costume for the Feast Day of the Christ Who said, "They who take the sword shall perish by the sword." They wore blue jackets, white breeches, and Hessian boots. Behind them came their professors—old gentlemen with bald heads and whiskered faces, whose knees were stiff as they walked in the hot sun on the hard pavement for the love of God. Monks with shaven crowns and brown habits and sandalled feet stepped into the sunlight from the shadow of the *Jesuiten Kirche* opposite the Grauer Bär. There were, I counted, a hundred and eight of them, and they were followed by two hundred and fifty priests in their surplices and black gowns, chanting a hymn of praise in unison with the choristers, whose boy voices rose to my balcony yet did not overwhelm the song of birds in the trees of the hotel garden. A bishop and canons came in vestments of gold and white. The sun gleamed on the mitre of the bishop and made a mockery of the lighted candles which were carried by acolytes. The military band was playing. The men in steel helmets marched with a kind of goose step. They were the guard of the Blessed Sacrament carried under a canopy across the flower-strewn street. They marched in lines of eight with packs on their backs, as though on a field day. Behind their rifles came a company of Mary's Children, singing an old hymn which I had heard in English churches—"Star of the Sea."

It was a procession which took two and a half hours to pass my balcony.

"I must say I'm mightily impressed!" said the artist, who has no definite religion except a general benevolence to mankind, with certain private exceptions whom he has put on his black list for sudden death if he ever gets the chance. "People don't go marching about in a hot sun for the fun of the thing. Some of those old professors looked very baked. Some of those kids were tired all right. I must say I have a great respect for the Catholic faith. And they did it all damn well—with a sense of beauty and reverence. Amazingly good."

The novelist was equally impressed. The poet in him overcame a certain cynicism which now and then breaks his sympathy with human faith—so inconsistent with human action.

The lady with us watching on the balcony had once walked in such a procession.

It was unfortunate that almost at the end of the procession my glasses fell off my nose onto the pavement beneath. Without them I was lost. I gave a cry of horror which startled the people thirty feet below. A girl picked them up and laughed up to my balcony. They were unbroken. They were not even cracked. I hesitate to call it a miracle, but it defied the laws of nature.

How does it happen that in a Catholic country like Austria, among a people who are pious as well as good-natured, who are very strong in their Christian faith, there should be civil war, the bombardment of workers' dwellings, shootings, bombings, beatings, murders, in the name of political and passionate hatreds which find vent in violence? Dr. Dollfuss was a Catholic, yet he ordered, or allowed, the attack on the Social Democrats with machine guns and field guns. Prince Starhemberg is a Catholic, yet he commanded the Heimwehr. See how these Christians love one another!

I talked with another young Austrian about the situation in his country. He was perfectly frank and did not seem afraid of expressing his thoughts—which were very dangerous.

"There is no hope for Austria," he said, "except in union with Germany. It is beyond all argument. We can't stand alone. Germany is our natural ally. Italy is simply making Austria a catspaw between herself and Jugo-Slavia. One day there will be a political explosion. The Dollfuss government will disappear. We shall unite with Germany. It is inevitable, and it is our only way of escape from ruin."

He spoke those words before a day in July when the explosion happened, and when Dr. Dollfuss disappeared after bleeding to death from a mortal wound; and when there was heavy but futile fighting throughout Austria by groups of Nazis, who had no chance against the government forces, and whose hopes of union with Germany were unfulfilled.

7

We left Innsbruck and went into the villages again. They are good villages, like most in Austria, and the scenery around them is more than good; it is magnificent, as everyone knows who has ever seen pictures of the Tyrol and made a vow in his heart that one day he would go there and see those snow-capped peaks and those flower-spangled fields and those peasants who dress in old costumes.

The peasants greeted us as we passed with that best of salutations, *Grüss Gott!* Bronzed young men—they didn't look like murderers with bombs concealed about them—strode along the mountain paths with the sun shining on their knees. Old fellows, still upright, with knees more bony than those of youth, puffed at enormous pipes. Women knelt before wayside calvaries or crossed themselves as they came out of little churches with tall red steeples. The rocks of the mountain range were rose-red in the sun of summer evenings. A young fellow had his arm round the waist of a girl on the banks of the river Inn. There was tension in Austria, but they were lovers and all was well with them. In one village we passed an old veteran wearing— for God knows what reason—a row of medals and a big sword.

We came to the village of Nassereit—an old, old place with elaborately painted houses, one of them by the master painter in whose imagination these wall paintings lived, and who trained good prentices in that lovely and homely art.

We took a meal in the garden of the Gasthaus of the Green Tree—Der Grüne Baum. The host thereof was a friendly and obliging man. He was delighted to see us, having good memories of Hastings, Brighton and Kensington. He deplored his ill luck in having no visitors, whereas a year before his house had been full. He was enchanted when our artist asked for his terms, and he put them as low as six Austrian shillings a day, which would ruin nobody who earns a little more than a living wage. It was pleasant in his garden. A smiling wench waited on us. If our lady had been a princess of the Blood Royal she could not have received more courtesy and reverence. In the absence of all other tourists we were wonderful people and greatly loved.

An Austrian business man of the neighbourhood entered into conversation and put his life into our hands by the extreme indiscretion of his speech. On a wall not a stone's throw away from him was a warning to him:

Political Crime, Scandalmongerings,
Or Political Strife
Will Be
Punished by Imprisonment.

I was astonished at his open defiance of such an edict.

One of his first remarks might have been denounced as something worse than "scandalmongering."

"If Dollfuss hadn't the Heimwehr to protect him he would be shot like a mad dog."

He informed us that in southern Austria eighty per cent of the people were Nazis, and the only thing for Austria was to join up with Germany. For Prince Starhemberg he had nothing but contempt.

"He is paid by Italy," he said. "He has sold himself for Italian gold."

He uttered an aphorism which reminded me of the waiter in Innsbruck.

"In this modern world there are too many politicians and too many journalists. They both belong to corrupt and dishonourable trades, who prosper on adversity and strife."

It occurred to me that he was somewhat of a politician himself, but I did not put that point to him.

Another man was more cautious in his answers to my friendly questions. It was in another Austrian village where we stopped.

"What do they think of Dr. Dollfuss in this district?" I asked.

He stared into my eyes, and answered enigmatically.

"Do you see many portraits of Dr. Dollfuss in the shop windows?"

I cast my mind back to all the shop windows I could remember in Austria. No, I had not seen a single portrait of the little dictator. That was unlike the publicity given to Adolf Hitler, whose face with mystical eyes—are they mad, those eyes?—stares out from millions of plate-glass windows in Germany—or did until the thirtieth of June, when something he did to his friends may have made him less beloved.

We turned our car towards Bavaria. All of us were sorry to leave Austria so soon. In spite of its distresses, nature there was glorious, and the old hills were serene under the blue sky, and the villages looked like the abode of peace.

We took the hill road to Garmisch, a corkscrew road which twisted and turned along the mountain sides, looking down to deep ravines clothed with tall fir forests, and looking up to walls of rock which shone like metal in the sunlight. Far below;

at one turn of the road, was a green lake which looked immensely deep. It was of emerald green and lay there like a jewel in a black frame. Beautiful grey cattle with big ears grazed on the lower slopes. Ahead, beyond a place called Lermoos, there was a great mass of rock, stupendous against the sky.

"That looks like a hill," said the artist.

The lady behind him knew its name. So, by an odd chance, did I.

"The Zugspitz! . . . We must be close to the German frontier. Not far away is Garmisch."

Perfectly true. Griesen was the frontier village. There were Austrian customs officers. A few yards away were German customs officers. They were very friendly to English travellers, but the examination of our passports and of Gaston's papers took a considerable time. The German officer was ready to give information, but I was doubtful of its accuracy.

"Ninety per cent of the Austrian country folk are Nazis," he said. "Fifty or sixty per cent of those in Vienna have the same opinion. And yet that little man called Dollfuss ignores the wishes of his people!"

There were occasional scuffles on the frontier, he told us. Boys were thrashed for trying to get across without permits. Business was made difficult. Tourism was killed.

The German officer excused all this by a general amnesty to human folly.

"It is all very silly," he said, "but great men will do these things."

They certainly will—God help them!

A post across the road was raised. Uniformed men saluted us. The road to Germany was open.

8

"Outwardly," said my friendly waiter in Innsbruck, "Austria is peaceful. Underneath it is a powder magazine."

It was only six weeks after he spoke those words that a trail of fire spread through Austria; and in Vienna two shots which killed a little man with a big heart resounded across the world.

Dire consequences might follow that act of madness—even that new war which was a haunting fear in many minds.

The narrative of what happened still seems unreal in its melodrama. An American film producer could not have imagined anything more sensational or wildly improbable. It began at a few minutes before midday on Thursday, July 25th, when a small group of Austrian Nazis entered the wireless station in Vienna, overpowered the attendants, and sent out false news to the Austrian public.

Dr. Dollfuss has resigned. Herz Rintelen the Austrian Minister in Rome has formed a new government. Austrian Nazis your hour has come. . . .

Still more like melodrama, as one finds it in the picture palace, was that scene, at the same hour, in a room overlooking the Ballhausplatz in Vienna, near the entrance to the Hofburg, which was the palace of the Habsburgs. It was in the Chancery. Dr. Dollfuss was holding a council of ministers. A slip of paper was brought in and handed to the little Chancellor. It brought news that an attack was being prepared against the government at the Heimwehr barracks. For a moment there was silence. No one yet has told exactly what happened in that room when these rulers of Austria looked into each other's eyes and wondered whether all the forces of passion and revenge which were seething below the surface of Austrian life were now at flash point. They went to the windows and looked out. They saw a number of private motorcars filled with armed soldiers. Were they friends or enemies? They had not long to wait before they knew. The council chamber was invaded by men wearing army and police uniforms, but with drawn revolvers pointed at the heads of these ministers of state. Dr. Dollfuss and a minister named Karwinsky were forced to leave the room. Then, at the pistol point, Major Fey and his other colleagues were ordered to go to a small room adjoining the council chamber.

Major Fey himself told a story which still stands as the authentic narrative of this amazing and tragic episode.

"At two-thirty a patrol asked us to go over and meet the Chancellor. We found Dollfuss there, heavily wounded, on a sofa. He asked us to look after his family when he was dead and to inform the other members of the government that he had been killed. We were then escorted out of the room again and had to spend three and a half agonising hours, during which the Nazis, armed with rifles, threatened several times to kill us."

The alarm had been given in Vienna. Other ministers had been holding a meeting at the Ministry of War. They received news of the capture of the Chancellor and other colleagues. They were actually rung up by Major Fey himself—a prisoner with a pistol at his head, over there at the Chancery.

Amazing situation in the heart of Vienna! People were going about their business, doing their morning shopping, sitting in the cafés, ignorant of this capture of the Chancellor and of any sinister happenings, unless they had heard that message on the wireless. Police and Heimwehr troops surrounded the Chancery. Wild rumours spread through the city. Suddenly in the Ballhausplatz there was a movement among the police and troops. Someone had appeared on the balcony of the Chancery. It was Major Fey, the leader of the Heimwehr. He was shouting down —astonishing words, unbelievable words. They understood him to say that the Chancellor was seriously wounded; that he had resigned to save the country further bloodshed; that Major Fey himself was negotiating with his captors.

Inside the Chancery, as we now know, the Nazi invaders were getting anxious about their own way of escape. They were frightened by the death of Dr. Dollfuss. He had bled to death after being shot by a man named Otto Planetta, at close range. They allowed Major Fey to use the telephone, and agreed to spare his life and the lives of his colleagues if he would arrange for them to get a safe conduct across the frontier. Major Fey agreed to this condition. He came onto the balcony again and shouted down to the officer commanding the police, asking him to desist from all action.

"We shall soon be coming downstairs," he is reported to have said.

A new figure appeared on the scene. It was Herr Rieth, the German Minister in Berlin (what had Berlin to do with this

affair?). He had received one of those telephone messages from
the Chancery. He had been asked to act as intermediary for
the safe conduct. Reluctantly, he says, he undertook this commission, and had an interview with the rebels, and signed a
paper for them, agreeing to their free passage across the frontier
to his own country.

Major Fey did a lot of telephoning, it appears. He had spoken
to the Minister of Defence—Herr Neustädter-Stürmer—who
now came into the Ballhausplatz, and shouted up to the rebels:

"In the name of the government," he called out, "I promise
you a safe conduct if you evacuate the building in twenty
minutes and if nothing has happened to anyone."

He affirmed that he heard of the Chancellor's death only
when Major Fey left the building at the conclusion of the negoti-
ations for the safe conduct; but at the trial of Otto Planetta, who
shot Dr. Dollfuss, he made another statement, in answer to a
question about any reservation regarding the safe conduct.

"I gave my soldier's word of honour. A soldier's word is given
to soldiers. I leave it to the court to judge whether it was the
behaviour of soldiers to deny medical and priestly succour to a
mortally wounded man."

The rebels relied on his promise, which was not fulfilled. It
is a nice point whether a soldier's word of honour was violated;
or whether it should hold under duress of such kind; or whether
it should have been given at all.

Meanwhile, there were risings in many parts of Austria.
At Klagenfurt there was fierce fighting between the Nazis and
the Heimwehr. In Styria and Carinthia the Nazi flag was raised
over public buildings. There was fighting round Innsbruck and
Salzburg, and many of the villages through which I had passed
on the journey for this book.

After a few days it became clear that the government forces
were holding the situation and were strong enough to prevail.
What then about all those repeated statements that there was
an eighty per cent majority for the Nazis in Austria, and especially southern Austria? There had been no general rising. The
fighting had been done by bands of young men, taking a desperate and hopeless chance against the government forces.

These peasants, as most of them were, had no organisation for civil war, and, perhaps, no spirit for it after the first news of what had happened in Vienna. They were Catholics, and it is possible that something turned in their hearts when they heard of the murder of Dr. Dollfuss, who was refused the last sacraments as he lay bleeding to death. It is also likely that events in Germany—on the thirtieth of June—had weakened their faith in the blessings which might follow union with that country under the dictatorship of Adolf Hitler. In any case, it is certain now that these Austrian peasants were not prepared to risk their lives on a wild chance of civil war, without arms and organisation beyond the smuggled rifles, and explosives, sent by secret agents across the German frontier, and hidden by the younger men.

Those desperate boys, inflamed by political passion and the Nazi spirit, had one chance of destroying the Dollfuss régime and raising the Sign of the Crooked Cross. It failed them, and betrayed them, at the very outset. Had they not been urged on by Germany? Had they not listened, night after night, in beer-houses and farmsteads, to German speakers broadcasting from Munich, and inciting them to rise against a government which blasphemed against the gospel of Adolf Hitler and thwarted their desire for union with their German comrades? Was not the whole weight of Hitler's Germany behind them? Did not Herr Habicht—that man of flaming words—promise them, night after night, from that wireless station in Munich, the aid of the whole German people in their struggle for racial union? What arms they had were German-made. These boxes of tricks, which they hid in haystacks and granaries, came from Germany. Across the frontier, near Munich, were three thousand Austrian Nazis—their brothers and cousins—fully armed, and well drilled by German officers, ready to rush to their aid at the first signal of revolt. It was from Germany that they would get their most powerful and irresistible aid. So they thought.

Fortunately for the peace of Europe—unfortunately for bands of boys with the Nazi madness in their minds—Germany failed to fulfil any of these promises. At the first news of what had happened in Vienna—the assassination of Dolfuss—Herr Habicht was recalled from the microphone. The Austrian Nazis near

Munich, ready for their rush, were forced back from the frontier, surrounded, and disarmed. German statesmen denied before the world any complicity in this Austrian insurrection—and were not believed. They "deplored" the death of Dr. Dollfuss which they had incited. As a gesture of friendliness and conciliation Adolf Hitler announced his intention of sending his "dear friend," Herr von Papen, as envoy to Vienna. The Austrian Nazis had no help from Germany in the hour of their insurrection, because the rulers of Germany were afraid of the passionate anger aroused against them by all the friends of Austria—and because of another fear.

Those men in Berlin knew that war might happen—would happen within twenty-four hours if they gave armed aid to the Austrian Nazis. Italy was moving troops to the Austrian frontier. Four divisions—forty thousand men—fully equipped for war, were ready for action. There is no doubt that messages were being sent to Hitler by Mussolini, warning him to be very careful, as otherwise Italian troops would move.

Hitler acted rapidly—with lightning speed. The last thing he wanted was war. He could not risk a clash with Italy, which was supported morally, if not by force of arms, by England and France. He recalled his propaganda hounds. He repudiated their promises. He denied his own dream of racial unity with the Germanic folk—or postponed its fulfilment. Fate was against him for the time. The whole world was against him. He decided to be very careful.

Dr. Dollfuss was buried with solemn ceremony, made sinister, in St. Stephen's Cathedral, by strong bodies of troops. There were people who remembered that this very day, twenty years ago, the World War had begun in Austria after the murder of an Austrian archduke. Was history going to repeat itself with variations?

The little coffin on its way through the streets passed between lines of armed men in steel helmets. The bells of Vienna were tolling, and half a million citizens stood bareheaded. Dr. Dollfuss in his death had more power over the minds of his people than in his life. Pity and horror and fear might lead at last to a truce in Austria.

In the cathedral the body of the Chancellor—so small, but
now no cause for jesting—was received by Cardinal Innitzer,
his friend, who praised him as a faithful son of the Church and
as a good Austrian who had died for his ideal of a Christian
state.

The President—Dr. Miklas—who had no power, said that the
dead Chancellor had tried to prevent Austria from being turned
into the battlefield of a new war and from perishing in a Central
European chaos.

There were other tributes in the world's press, and they made
a martyr of him. But now that he is buried and his murderers
are hanged, it is possible to judge his character and career
with less emotion. He was, as many of his friends have told me,
a charming little man, with a merry heart, a peasant's courage,
and a Christian faith. It was against his will that he found himself in a political arena where fierce passions raged. He loved
Austria and desired its happiness and peace—so all his friends
say—but he had to act between fiercely conflicting parties, all
armed for strife. Between the Heimwehr on one side and the
Social Democrats on the other, no bridge could be built. There
was a third party, growing dangerous and hating him. The Nazis
were out for his destruction and proclaimed a creed which he
believed was anti-Christian and very brutal in its paganism.
It threatened the independence of Austria, because, if these
Nazis triumphed, Austria would become a German province
under the rule of Hitler and his lieutenants. Yet Austria could
not stand alone. That was a clear and undeniable fact; and
every day that passed made it more evident. To whom should
Austria turn? The question was answered by Mussolini. He
offered financial and military support—on one condition. The
Social Democrats could not be tolerated. They hated Italy and
the Fascist régime. There could be no Italian help if that crowd
held power in Vienna. Out with them!

Little Dollfuss agreed to that condition. Prince Starhemberg
and Major Fey would support him only if he allowed them to
fulfil it; and it was only their Heimwehr men who could keep
his government in power. His enemies say that he sold his soul
for power. At least, they said so before he bled to death. It is

kinder, and I think more true, to say that he deplored this attack on the Social Democrats, but allowed it for the sake of Austria, and for that Christian state which he desired to make and, in moments of mysticism, believed he was destined to make, as a bulwark against the paganism of Nazidom.

In any case, Prince Starhemberg and Major Fey were determined to use their Heimwehr against the Socialists. He could only retire when they did that job, and then use his influence for mercy. That is what he did. One cannot look into the soul of that little man, now dead, who tried to be merry and moderate when the wolf instinct had taken possession of so many minds among a people who had once been lighthearted and easy-going and lovers of laughter. Those who stood near to him loved him; and even his enemies gave him credit for a plea of mercy when the hangings began and when the jails were filled with boys who had fought for their belief in liberty.

All that I had heard in Austria on my journey was fulfilled in tragedy; and the story is not yet finished.

VIII

Hitler's Germany

I WAS IN BERLIN in the early part of this year. I had been in Germany several times since the war, studying the minds of a people who had suffered the defeat of all their pride, the downfall of all their gods, deep humiliation lasting for years, economic ruin, and great agonies of spirit; but this was the first time I had been in Berlin since the triumph of Adolf Hitler and the domination of his country by National Socialists under his dictatorship.

I walked down the Wilhelmstrasse and stood outside the house where Ebert the saddler had been President of the first Republic, and had done his job well, I think. It was guarded by two soldiers of the Reichswehr in steel helmets, which look grimmer than our old tin hats. A group of people—among whom were some schoolboys and university students—waited outside the railings. I spoke to one of the boys and asked what was happening.

"*Hindenburg kommt!*" he answered.

The old Imperial flag hung beside a new banner bearing the Sign of the Crooked Cross. As I waited, a heavy motorcar came slowly out of the iron gates. There was a cheer, and the schoolboys waved handkerchiefs. For a second I saw the old tired face of Field Marshal von Hindenburg, the victor of Tannenberg, the hero of the retreat when he brought a defeated army—the Germans say it was undefeated—home from the front after a World War. He raised his hand to the salute. On the first day of

August he raised his hand for the last time, and the whole world paid a tribute to this old German soldier who had stood like a rock in a sea of trouble.

"If you will come with me," said the German schoolboy to whom I had spoken, "I will show you Herr Hitler's house."

I followed him for a few yards, and he stood outside another house guarded by two more soldiers in trench helmets. The old Imperial flag and the new red Swastika flag hung above it.

"That is the Leader's house," said the boy. "He is away today in Munich. It is a pity. Otherwise we might have seen him."

"You like Herr Hitler?" I asked.

The boy was astounded by this simple question.

"He is our Leader—*der Führer!* The whole German nation obeys him. We are willing to die for him. It is our duty, if necessary."

I thought of Adolf Hitler, the builder's labourer—an Austrian who had been a corporal in the German army. He was now Chancellor of the German Reich, with greater powers than any previous ruler of the German folk. By some magic spell in his personality—a simple-looking man with a toothbrush moustache and fanatical eyes—he had stirred the whole nation by his flaming words, his harsh voice rising to a scream, his denunciation of Jews, the Peace Treaties, the Reparation Payments, the French government, the German Communists, the humiliation and weakness of the German spirit. He talked mad stuff at times. He had strange theories—borrowed from other minds—about the need of racial purity—German blood uncontaminated by alien strains—and about the God-ordained destiny of the German people to link up with other peoples beyond their frontiers of the same Nordic stock.

He had been arrested and imprisoned for an abortive attempt to overthrow the Republic, in company with Ludendorff, who had gone *gaga*. In Munich taverns he had gathered a band of comrades, a queer company of adventurers, of no great quality or character in the opinion of intellectual Germans. They had formed a body of volunteers who wore brown shirts with the Swastika on an armlet. They had fights with local Communists, brutal on both sides. Men were murdered in cold blood on both sides. As a political move it had not been taken seriously in the early days—not seriously until, year after year, their numbers increased all over Germany, and they sent many deputies to the Reichstag. Not even then seriously, until in a general election they obtained an enormous number of votes, giving them an absolute majority.

The old crowd had tried to deprive this man of the fruits of victory. Hindenburg had offered him the Vice Chancellorship in a government which would tie his hands. The man who had been a builder's labourer rejected this offer. He had the whole body of German youth behind him. Now he was Chancellor, and more than Chancellor. He was *Der Führer*—the Chief of the German Tribes—the Dictator of all Germany. Any word he spoke was law. Women worshipped him. His Brown Shirts, his old comrades, the men who had fought with him, were in command of the key positions. In every state they had taken over the entire administration. It was Germany under the Nazis.

For the first time in history there was a sense of national unity. Even Bavaria—proud of its own traditions and independence from Prussia, Catholic in religion—had sworn allegiance to the Nazi faith. This man with the eyes of a fanatic and the speech of a demagogue had put a spell on the people of all classes. He had promised them release from their humiliations, and they believed him. He had promised to build a new world for them with the spirit of his Brown Shirt troops, and they believed him. He proclaimed the end of unemployment, national despair, broken pride, and they believed him. German youth would make Germany strong and feared again. National Socialism would bind all classes together in a unity and loyalty which would stagger the world. The German race would advance to its God-ordained destiny. The Jews would be expelled from all the places they had taken from pure Germans. Germany would demand equality with its enemies. The nation would be purified, strengthened, and revitalised. . . . And for a time the Germans believed all this, and, by believing, regained their sense of pride, a new exaltation of spirit, a kind of ecstasy, a kind of madness. *Heil Hitler!*

2

On this first afternoon I spent in Berlin—it was a Saturday
—there was some excitement in the streets. Groups of Nazis
suddenly appeared and notified their presence by trumpet calls
which held up crowds of young clerks, and typist girls, and
shop assistants, who were hurrying homewards after business
hours. It was, I learnt, a special collection day of the Berlin
district on behalf of unemployed comrades. The man who told
me this laughed.

"There is nothing very special about it, really! We know
those collecting boxes. It's a daily tax on our pockets."

They were a smart-looking crowd, those Nazi officials. Most
of them were young men of about twenty onwards, in brand-
new uniforms of yellowish brown, with many badges on their
chests, and with the arm band of the Swastika. They looked
good-natured—not at all as though they would beat Jewish
intellectuals or kick them to death. They seemed to be enjoying
themselves and on good terms with the crowds as they rattled
their collecting boxes, and made speeches from the seats of
motorcars, and heralded their coming by bugle calls.

Groups of staff officers dashed along the streets in good-
looking cars, answering the salute of outstretched arms. There
was a rush from the sidewalks when one car passed. Inside
was a handsome man in what looked like a naval uniform.
He had a clean-shaven, powerful face, not unlike that of
an actor, or a film star, who might play the strong silent
hero.

"General Goering!" said a man at my side.

He was saluted with respect and enthusiasm. The young
women, I noticed, were most enthusiastic.

One man, who looked like a staff officer of Storm Troops,
jumped out of his car and dashed to the crowds on the sidewalk
with his collecting box. I saw him do that several times in
different streets, and always the crowd gathered round him
and laughed at his remarks, which I could not overhear.

"Who is that?" I asked.

It was Prince August Wilhelm, youngest son of the ex-

Kaiser, and now in the service of an ex-corporal of the German army who was the ruler of Germany.

All that afternoon and evening there was no escape from the collecting boxes. Even when I sat at lunch in a small restaurant along Unter den Linden, two of the Nazis came in, clicked heels, and collected tribute from the company. I noticed that everybody dropped some kind of coin into the slit. There was no compulsion. There was no sign of bullying. But perhaps it was best to pay up in the smallest coin and keep things pleasant.

3

I was awakened very early next morning in my bedroom at the Fürstenhof by the shrill calls of bugles, the beatings of drums, and the marching of feet. It was six o'clock when I sprang out of bed and looked out of the window into the great square of the Potsdamerplatz and saw battalions of young Nazis marching to the beat of those drums. They marched in perfect step, with a splendid rhythm. Scores of banners with the sign of the Swastika were carried high above their heads. All day long banners were flying, drums beating, and bugles calling.

It was the fourteenth anniversary of Hitler's campaign, started in a Munich beerhouse, where that night he was to make a speech to his comrades—Roehm, Heines, Ernst, Hess, and others who had been with him during the early struggles. All over Germany, and here in Berlin, hundreds of thousands of young men were assembling at fixed points to swear an oath of allegiance to Hitler, as section leaders of the Nazi organisation, or as guards of honour to those who were taking this oath.

That morning I watched the march of the Storm Troopers and the battalions of the Hitler Jugend—young boys of the Youth movement who would one day, they hoped, be Storm Troopers sworn to service of *Der Führer*. It was impossible not to be impressed by the splendour of that German youth, as it is impossible not to be impressed by the vitality and the freshness of youth wherever one meets it in the world. Those boys marched solemnly. Their faces were grave. They were handsome, in the mass. They were trained to a perfect discipline of march step. They seemed to carry their banners—hundreds of banners—as a sacred charge. There was something stirring in the sight of this army of young men.

There was also, at the back of my mind, a sense of apprehension. This pride and discipline of youth could be so easily used by evil minds for sinister purpose, later on. This devotion to duty, this readiness for sacrifice—I remembered what that boy had said outside Hitler's house—might lead a nation to the shambles again. I remembered something told me of one of these German boys. He was of the Catholic faith and made his first Communion—the most sacred day in Catholic life. He was very friendly to an English governess. He confided to her, and to her alone, the prayer he had made when kneeling at the altar. It was a prayer that he might die with a French bullet in his heart. . . .

As those young Nazis marched past, there were little rushes from the sidewalks, mostly of women and girls. All their arms were outstretched in salute to the flags. There were cries, the shrill cries of girls' voices, *Heil Hitler!* There were not many men about, I noticed.

Later that morning, along the whole length of Unter den Linden, loudspeakers were placed, and guarded by the Green Police. Through them at eleven o'clock came enormous, far-reaching, reverberating voices, as though giants were shouting across deep valleys. They proclaimed the glory of the German people. They reminded the German people of their God-ordained destiny. They hailed the nobility of their chosen leader. Presently they repeated the oath to Hitler as it was spoken slowly by the section leaders of the National Socialists, of whom there were a million in Germany, assembled at the same hour for this purpose. I listened to those words roaring down the street through the microphones:

"I swear unbreakable troth to Adolf Hitler and unbounded obedience to him and his appointed leaders."

Tremendous shouts of, *"Heil Hitler!"* thundered out. They were followed by a ruffle of drums and a fanfare of trumpets.

It was rather awe-inspiring. I felt the touch of a cold finger down my spine, as I do always at such moments of ceremony—the funeral of a king or hero, the passing of some spiritual force. These voices and that oath were the proclamation of a national loyalty to one man invested with enormous power over a great people, and the affirmation of a national faith in the virtue and strength of one race, which was German. It was not without significance to the rest of the world. Those magnified, enormous voices were perhaps calling out the destiny of Europe.

But one thing perplexed me. It was really astonishing. For some reason I was almost alone in Unter den Linden with those thunderous words coming out of space. There was no crowd here—no more than a few groups of people, lost in the length of the avenue. The vast population of Berlin had not turned out to hear the oath of allegiance, unless they had gone elsewhere—though Unter den Linden is very central.

All day, and late into the night, there was endless oratory through loudspeakers—in streets, in restaurants, in picture palaces and public gardens. Hitler's propagandists had imitated the methods of Moscow in using this way of mass suggestion. I thought they were overdoing it. Certain words and phrases were dinned into the ears of the people. "The German Folk" ... "Our Leader" ... "The German Destiny" ... "Comradeship" ... "Unity" ... "Service" ... "Hitler! ... Hitler! ... Hitler!" I tired of them in a day. Did they still fail to stun German senses after a year of repetition? Was any thrill left in them?

I went that evening into a big café, one of those enormous places where the German middle class gathers to keep warm, and drink some kind of liquid, and talk with their friends and families. At nine o'clock or so the inevitable loudspeaker was turned on.

It was an historic hour. It was the fourteenth anniversary of Hitler's campaign. It was he—*Der Führer*—who was about to speak from that tavern in Munich where he was assembled with his old comrades who had fought with him and helped him to power.

When his voice came through I sat up, alert and eager to

hear its timbre and its words. It was the voice of a man who held the fate of a nation in his hand, whose lightest word would be obeyed as a sacred command. He was the mesmerist who had put a spell upon the German people so that they followed him blindly. That very morning they had sworn unbounded obedience to him and "unbreakable troth." Peace or war in Europe depended utterly upon his conscience, his policy, and his command. He could lead Germany along the way of civilised ideals, or back to brutality. It was worth listening to Hitler, I thought.

But—and that was curious—nobody else seemed to think so in this café. The place was typical, I am sure, of thousands of others in Berlin. The people here were of the usual kind, middle-class business men with their friends and women folk, commercial travellers, shop assistants, clerks, insurance agents. No one except myself sat up with an alert interest. Most of those people, if they listened, looked dazed and stupefied by too much of that kind of thing. A group sitting near me, rather higher in class, I thought, than most of the others, went on talking in low voices, though one of them—a distinguished-looking man of middle age—seemed to listen with half an ear and not like what he heard.

Others didn't listen. A young man continued to write a long letter. A young woman powdered her nose and used her lipstick with the aid of a tiny mirror in her handbag. She was not listening to the voice of Hitler. Only one little comic-looking man, with a high collar and a tie which slipped up to his ears, stood to attention when, through the loudspeaker, came the solemn hymn of victory, *"Heil Dir Im Siegeskranz,"* by which Hitler himself was heralded.

"This," I thought, "is all very extraordinary. Has Hitler lost his popularity? Have I been all wrong in thinking that he has the majority of the nation behind him? Has all this propaganda bluffed the world and left these Germans cold?"

I listened to Hitler's words, blurred through the microphone so that I could not catch many of them. He was paying a tribute to his dear comrades—men like Roehm, Heines, Goering—men who had proved their loyalty, their comradeship, their courage.

He could not have reached power, he said, without them. He was deeply, and profoundly, and eternally grateful for their loyalty, their comradeship, their courage. His brave Storm Troopers had led the way to Victory. Their comradeship, their loyalty, their courage. . . .

His voice roared through the loudspeaker, deep sometimes, harsh sometimes, shrill sometimes. He spoke of the German destiny which had not yet been fulfilled. They must build for the future. The foundations only had been laid. A heavy responsibility lay upon his brave Storm Troopers. The future depended upon their loyalty, their comradeship, their courage. . . .

It was a day in February of 1934. It was four months from a day in June when many of the men to whom he had paid this tribute, to whom he professed eternal gratitude, for whose loyalty, comradeship, and courage his voice broke into emotion, were shot by his orders like mad dogs. That was not yet on the programme.

4

I went about Berlin keeping my eyes and my ears open, talking to many people of different classes, trying to penetrate somewhat into the hidden spirit of this Nazi revolution. It was not easy to get a clear line of conviction. There were many inconsistencies and many mysteries. There had been a Jewish persecution carried out in the early days of Hitler's triumph with great brutality, according to many accounts by credible witnesses. Jewish intellectuals were still being dismissed from their posts. But the stores of Tietz and Wertheim were open, and many of their assistants were Jews. I saw Jews moving about their business unmolested, though with uneasy eyes.

Hitler proclaimed his desire for peace. He offered friendship to France, and any form of disarmament to the lowest level, if France would agree to German equality.

Goering, even, denied that he had any belief in war or any intention of preparing for war. Had he not been in the last war? he asked. Did people think he was a madman? (It did

not occur to him that the answer would be "Yes"!) Was it not
ridiculous? he asked.

Baldur von Schirach, a young man of twenty-eight in command of the Hitler Jugend, declined to admit that the youth
of Germany had any warlike spirit or purpose because they
marched about in uniform, like boy scouts. It was to build a
new world of comradeship and not to destroy the world that
they submitted to a little discipline and showed their ardour
for service.

But it was curious that whenever I picked up a German
magazine it was stuffed with pictures of soldiers in steel helmets
and pictures of the World War. There seemed to be a new and
morbid interest in the life of trenches and dugouts, in great
guns and aërial bombs and all the machinery of death.

In the very centre of Unter den Linden there was, during
my visit to Berlin, an exhibition called *Der Front*. All day long
German boys had their noses glued to the windowpanes.
German students with their girls paid a mark to go inside.
Now and again a middle-aged German and his wife stared at
the windows, hesitated for a moment, and then went in. It was
a war exhibition, devoted to the instruments of slaughter—
trench mortars, machine guns, aërial torpedoes, large-sized
shells, lurid pictures of battle by sea, land and air. A guide
showed a young German girl how to work a machine gun.
She was very much amused by this demonstration. "*Ausgeseich-
net!*" she exclaimed, as though a machine gun were a charming
piece of mechanism which might be nice in the home.

Why all this revival of interest in things which the rest of
the world—England, anyhow—was trying to forget?

I asked the question of a young Nazi, who was highly intelligent and very sincere, I thought.

"It's difficult to explain," he answered. "But it's not at all
what foreigners think. You see, in England and France you
were proud of your soldiers after the war. It was your victory.
You put up war memorials. You had your two minutes' silence.
You had your poppy day. But in Germany it was all too painful
at first, and our returning soldiers were insulted by Communists and Social Democrats. They had their badges torn from

their shoulders, and their Iron Crosses were grabbed. No one remembered the heroism of the German troops and all their victories and sufferings. Now at last, under Hitler, we wish to remember. We're proud to remember the courage of our fathers and all they went through in those frightful years. It's a revival of German pride in heroic achievement, but not a revival of the war spirit, or the wish for another war, which we all know would be the end of European civilisation. You won't find a single Nazi who has war in his mind—except perhaps as a menace of war against Germany itself. I assure you that is true."

He believed it was true.

An American lady who had long been married to a German came to tea with me at the Fürstenhof. We talked freely about the German situation and mentality, until I noticed that several young waiters were listening with their ears cocked.

"Most people in England, and everybody in France," I told her, "believe Germany is preparing for a new war."

She was astounded and shocked.

"But that is impossible! It's ridiculous! Why should they believe such an absurdity?"

I gave her some of the reasons. Every news reel in every cinema showed German youth drilling, marching, parading. There was a conviction that Germany was re-arming secretly and that every German was a soldier. Hitler's book *Mein Kampf* was not exactly reassuring. All that stuff about absorbing the other Nordic peoples and extending the German Kultur over Holland, Denmark, Sweden, parts of Hungary, Austria, and Czecho-Slovakia was alarming. The Hitler régime had begun with brutality against the Jews. The spirit of the bully was exalted by the Nazi creed. Men like Rosenberg, with his wild, mystical nonsense about the Germanic race and the old paganism, were preaching a cult against intellectualism and proclaiming the coming reign of instinct and biological force. It was a denial of all civilised ideals. It was deliberately a harkback to barbarism. There was a book by a man named Banse, a professor with an official appointment as a university instructor. It was written in the spirit of blood lust. It exalted

war. It called upon the German people to smash France and
England in the fulfilment of a divine destiny. There was a lot
of rubbish like that.

The lady who had lived many years of married life in Germany listened to my words attentively. She was very much
surprised.

"My German friends laugh at Rosenberg's nonsense," she
said. "Do you think they take it seriously? As for that man
Banse, I have never heard of him, and I doubt whether the
people I know have ever heard of him. As for all this marching
and drilling, it means nothing as far as war is concerned.
Germans like it, just as the English like football and cricket.
They love to go marching along, singing songs and feeling fit.
It gives them a sense of *Kamaradschaft*, which is a great need in
the minds of young Germans. I know so many of these young
Nazis. They talk very freely to me, because I am the wife of a
German and therefore, in their minds, German. They never
talk of wanting war. On the contrary, they hate the idea of it.
If ever they speak of war it is because they have a fear that
France and her allies will force it upon them and march
through Germany. Naturally they feel that they must defend
the Fatherland. Wouldn't any other nation feel the same?
Wouldn't England, if it were threatened with invasion?"

It was then that I became aware of several young waiters of
the Fürstenhof listening with their ears cocked.

"We had better get into a quiet corner," I suggested. "We
are having an audience."

We retired and continued our talk. She was a very knowledgeable lady. She knew Herr Hitler and admired him.

"He is all for peace," she assured me. "Foreigners don't believe in his sincerity. But I'm certain that he wants to make a
friendship with France. It is his strongest wish. And you must
admit that he has said so publicly several times. Why doesn't
France accept the offer?"

I found others in Berlin who believed in Hitler's sincerity—
some of them English people who were in close touch with him.
They sized him up as a simple-minded man, fanatical, of
course, and with the obstinacy of a fanatic, but sentimental,

emotional, and honest. His head, they said, had not been turned by power. On the contrary, he had abandoned some of his wild ideas and the verbal fury of the demagogue. He was becoming a statesman. He was anxious to preserve peace in Europe. His claim for equality in arms down to any level or up to any level was, after all, just. Its justice had been admitted —and then repudiated—by England and France. He was a very pleasant person to meet—perfectly modest and unassuming —rather gentle even. They liked him. . . . It was before the thirtieth of June, when he was not so gentle with those who had been his comrades.

5

During my visit there was a place in Berlin where one could hear many interesting things about the Nazi régime and its personalities and secrets. It is a restaurant called Die Taverne, at the corner of the Kurfürstenstrasse—the rendezvous of foreign correspondents, young Nazis of the official class, young leaders of the Storm Troops, actors, dancers, singers, and habitués of the old night life of Berlin, now closed, or cleaned up, in the first fervour of Nazi idealism. I went there to meet some friends and to listen to the latest interpretation of affairs.

It is a house of low rooms, and wooden benches, and long tables. When I entered first, at eleven o'clock in the evening, an orchestra was playing light music loudly, but it was not so loud as the voices of the company, divided into groups according to their social set or profession or nationality. The rooms were thick with smoke, and the reek of wine, beer and coffee. It was difficult to hear oneself talk. That didn't matter much. But it was more difficult to hear other people talk, and I wanted to hear. There was good talk in progress at the table where a seat was found for me. The men and women around me—all correspondents of foreign newspapers—seemed to know the inside secrets of this new régime and all the men who were pulling the strings. They were talking freely, I found, as critics and sceptics of the Nazi creed, careless of being overheard by any spies and informers, or by two young Germans who were at Nazi headquarters.

"Fried sausages?" asked an intellectual lady on the opposite side of the table.

Fried sausages seemed to me a good idea at that time of night.

I was sorry the orchestra was making such a hideous din with the latest atrocity of American jazz. But I strained my ears to hear a monologue by a man who, as I knew, was a distinguished correspondent in Berlin.

"Underneath all this pretence of unity," he said, "there's a lot of discontent and friction. The left wing of Hitler's brave boys are beginning to get fractious. They want to know when the Socialist part of the National Socialist programme is going to be fulfilled. There's not a sign of it yet. The banks still control the financial situation under that subtle-minded old gentleman Dr. Schacht. Weren't they to be nationalised according to the programme? Big industry still carries on—not too well—wasn't something going to happen to that? There was to be a levelling of classes, but the old social distinctions still go on, and Socialism is a long way off. It rather looks, think some of Hitler's young braves, as if the beloved leader has been nobbled by the old crowd. He doesn't seem anxious to carry out his own programme. They knew, of course, that he got his funds from Mr. Thyssen, the Steel King. Mr. Thyssen is still calling the tune. Where, then, are the ideals of the State which was to be built up by the ardent spirit of youth? Echo answers where? ... *Herr Ober! Noch ein Bier, bitte!*"

Some time after midnight a very tall, heavily built man came into the restaurant. He was greeted with enthusiasm by groups of friends. I thought he looked remarkably like the late Lord Birkenhead in his genial moods. He had a hand for everybody. He raised it to salute young men and women too far to reach. He moved about from one group to another, restlessly, good-humouredly. He was Hitler's bosom friend, as I knew. When Hitler is tired of good works and noble oratory this big man with big hands sits down to a piano and plays to the *Fürher*, soothing him with light music, or selections from Wagner, played magnificently by those big hands.

He came to sit by my side for a few minutes and put his hand on my shoulder.

"I want to talk to you!" he said. "I've been away in Munich with Hitler. We must certainly have a good talk."

I regretted that he was lured away by a group of young friends who desired conversation with him. With them he stayed only two minutes. It was necessary to shake hands with other groups.

"There's a lot to be said for this Nazi organisation," said a man at my side. "They have done a good deal already to lessen unemployment. It may be uneconomical—these public works —but it puts wages into the pockets of four million men. It takes despair out of their hearts. England might learn a lesson from it. Those Labour Camps are admirable. Better than letting young fellows lounge about and go bad."

"What about all this militarism?" I asked.

The man at my side shrugged his shoulders.

"German youth likes it. They're not panting for a new war. All the same——"

He was silent for a moment and then lowered his voice:

"The rank and file have no sinister intentions. They're just simple lads with a certain idealism, easily led. The trouble is in their leadership. Some of their chiefs are thugs and bandits. One hears horrible stories. It's a danger when a great nation like this is led by a group of low-class characters."

"How about Hitler?" I asked.

"He's loyal to his lieutenants. It was through them he came to power. I believe personally he is a man of good character. In his house of scandal—one hears all the rumours—no one flings mud at him."

I stayed until the small hours in the Taverne.

6

One of the leaders of the Hitler Jugend came to see me at the hotel. He was one of the lieutenants of Baldur von Schirach, that young man who had absolute command over the mental and bodily training of ten million German boys. This visitor was also a young man, who spoke very perfect English with a slight American accent. Because he had spent some time in the United States he was able, he claimed, to look at the Nazi ideals with a certain coolness of judgment hardly possible to other young Germans. Nevertheless, he was an ardent Nazi. He saw the one undeniable thing, he said. He saw that Hitler had rescued German youth from despair.

"Two years ago," he said, "there was no hope in Germany. Unemployment was eating into the hearts of the young men. What was the good of getting a degree at a university if there was no vacant post and no chance of livelihood? They took to tramping about the country like gipsies, doing odd jobs now and then—wearing out their hearts and their boots. It was the same in all classes. The young working men could not get jobs. What was the use of their strength and skill? They had no hope in the future. Then the whole nation felt humiliated by the attitude of foreign powers. The reparation payments were an intolerable tribute. Every nation was armed, while Germany was unarmed. Hitler changed all that spirit of defeatism. He gave German youth hope and faith in the future and restored their self-respect."

"But this blind obedience to one man," I said, "this worship of race, this national discipline which insists that everyone shall act and obey according to the dictates of Herr Hitler and General Goering, how do you defend that? Where, for instance, is liberty?"

The young Nazi—perfectly candid and straight looking—smiled at that question.

"Isn't liberty rather a catchword? Have any people, even in England and the United States, ever had liberty to attack their form of government, or to conspire against the State, or to make a propaganda in obscenity? One must have discipline, especially in a country like Germany, where there were so many parties armed against each other. Now we are united in one loyalty. It's the most marvellous achievement. Think how Germany was divided. For the first time it's really one nation."

We reached the inevitable subject—the danger that all this discipline and training would lead to a new war.

"Why all this military parade?" I asked. "Why all this beating of drums and waving of flags? Why is youth disciplined by drill sergeants?"

He shook his head.

"It's self-discipline. It isn't military any more than the spirit of your boy scouts."

"Boy scouts don't practise bombing exercises," I told him. "They are not educated in racial fanaticism. They aren't taught that war is glorious and necessary for manly virtues."

My young visitor stared at me and thought within himself.

"I can quite understand that people regard us with suspicion," he said. "But, honestly, our foreign critics misjudge our motives and ideas. So far from being a danger to other people, we are convinced that we ourselves are in danger, unarmed, and surrounded by armed nations hostile to our race. Haven't we some justification for that belief? And surely we ought to warn our youth that one day they may be attacked and that their duty is to defend the Fatherland. We believe, certainly, that no nation can be great or strong unless its young men are ready to fight and die for it. Doesn't England believe that too?—in spite of refusals to fight for King and Country by young Pacifists at Oxford and Cambridge."

We talked for two hours. I was much impressed by this young man's intelligence and sincerity and charming courtesy of manner. We discussed the economic situation, and the work of the labour camps, and the Socialistic ideals—rather romantic—of many young Nazis. But it was the question of the war spirit which nagged at him.

"Will you let me send you some of the magazines written for the Hitler Youth?" he asked. "You will see that Baldur von Schirach is not a propagandist of blood and slaughter. And I think you will admit that these little magazines are not for foreign propaganda. They are written for the boys to read in their camps and homes."

The magazines arrived, and I read them.

They were as he said. I could find no incitement to war,

no glorification of war, apart from the need of courage and sacrifice in case of attack. There was an article by Baldur von Schirach ridiculing the view of foreigners that the Nazi uniform and training were for war purposes.

Why do we wear these same clothes [he asked]? Why do we all enrol in this one organisation? We do this, my comrades, and all of you know it, because we look upon this uniform as the garb of comradeship. We do not want to conquer the world, but rather our own Fatherland. We don't want to be masters of other nations. We want to master ourselves. We say Peace, and we mean Peace. But real peace can only exist under the condition of equal rights and security. Adolf Hitler has announced that Germany is willing to disarm down to the last machine gun, if others do the same. The safest assurance of peace can only be found in a state of equal disarmament. Germany will have to insist upon this equality which does justice to her honour. As far as security is concerned, we should like to ask who needs security more than we? France, for instance, is secure, according to the statement of her minister, Daladier. . . . Our hopes for peace in Europe and the world, are set on the youth of all nations. As far as the German youth are concerned, we are willing to coöperate. Can we do more?

I was impressed by that article. I could not believe that it had been written for foreign propaganda. It was in a little magazine called *Wille und Macht*, the chief publication of the Nazi Youth. These words were sane, reasonable and just. If all German youth were thinking, or taught to think, like that there could be no quarrel with them. And yet it was perplexing. The speeches of their leaders were sometimes in glorification of the war spirit. Von Papen had jeered at young men who wished to die in their beds.

I came to believe that the younger Nazis, the mass of these German boys, did not hanker after war, but were drilling and marching because they believed that Germany would be attacked. But that was not very reassuring. It left one apprehensive. It would be so easy for their leaders to make use of all this discipline, this vitality of youth, this passionate enthusiasm for the German race, this dynamic force of youth, and switch it, by a single speech, a single act, into war fever. Millions of

young men, assured that Germany was in danger, or that their
frontiers were threatened, would march towards the fields of
death with a sense of sacrifice in their hearts and old songs on
their lips. It was all very dangerous, even though one believed
they said Peace and meant Peace. But one could not blame
them for vitality, loyalty and discipline.

7

I had a disquieting conversation in Berlin with a French
business man who had been there long enough to study the
psychology of the Nazi mind and the underlying meaning of
Hitler's régime. Although a business man, he had the philo-
sophic mind and was in touch with political circles.

"Tell me," I asked him, "how do you analyse this situation?"
He looked at his wrist watch.

"I have half an hour," he said. "Do you care to listen to the
result of my studies for the past six months?"

"I am a good listener," I told him.

"Let me divide my inquiries and conclusions," he said,
"into eight chapters. . . . Chapter One . . ."

The gist of Chapter One in this historical survey was that
thirty-five per cent of the German people were ready to die
for Hitler.

"And that," said my friend, "is a lot in a people of sixty
million and more."

They were willing to die for Hitler because he promised
them all the things they most desired—employment of youth,
freedom from foreign restraint, pride of race, hero worship—
with Hitler as hero.

"The mass of people outside that thirty-five per cent," said
my friend, "are indifferent, and waiting to see what is going
to happen, hoping for the best but fearing the worst. Then
there is a minority, but an important and large minority, of
bitter critics who think that Hitler is a low-class adventurer
surrounded by men of evil character, bent upon the destruction
of property, religion, and the old tradition of German character.
They hate him because he is so powerful against the Junker

spirit. They hate him because he threatens the industrialists. They hate him for a hundred different reasons, some of them intelligent and some of them passionate.

"Chapter Two. Germany re-arms. It's half accomplished. There is no doubt of that. I have the facts. Thousands of new men have been taken on by Krupps and other armament factories. Their imports of steel and iron have been enormously increased. What are they making? Safety razors? Steel nibs? They are making guns and rifles and every kind of weapon. In two years they will have re-armed. We must regard it as a *fait accompli*. We cannot stop it now. What then is France—and I speak from my own point of view—what then are we French people going to do about it?"

I was interested to know, and he outlined his idea in Chapter Three.

"We must accept the *fait accompli* and exert control. France, England, Italy, Czecho-Slovakia, Poland, and other countries, must—or should, if they have any sense—agree to act in case of German aggression. That is the only policy. There is no alternative by which European civilisation may be saved. A preventive war is not possible. The people wouldn't stand for it. It is out of the picture. Let us, then, proceed to Chapter Four. That must penetrate more deeply into German psychology. Why, for instance, is Germany a danger to the European system? Why should we be afraid of granting her equality, even without control? . . . Chapter Four . . ."

Chapter Four was vastly interesting and so were Chapters Five, Six, Seven and Eight.

This French business man had been reading a lot of German literature. He had soaked himself in the German *Mythus* as interpreted by Alfred Rosenberg and others. It was a hark back to paganism and the German tribal system. That system was essentially different from the European and Christian culture as developed by the Romans and by the Catholic Church. It did not recognise a nation. It did not acknowledge the value of constitutional government under a monarchy supported by a Parliament and by free discussion. It did not even acknowledge the limitation of frontiers. It was racial and tribal. The

Germanic tribes would be governed by chieftains under one supreme chief whose word would be law and whose person would be half divine, like one of the old pagan deities, half god and half warrior. The tribal system would extend beyond the frontiers of nations. Blood would call to blood. There would be a loose confederation of the Germanic race with its roots deep in the primæval forests. Scandinavians, groups in Poland, Hungary and Russia, would come within the tribal confederation. They too belonged to the German forest with its deep roots in the pagan past. The old gods were not dead. They were only sleeping. They had been dispossessed by the Christian myth, weakening, hostile to instinct and nature, devitalising, dehumanising. Strength, courage, vitality would be the virtues of manhood again, instead of introspection, intellectualism and morbid consciousness. The pagan gods, the pagan spirit, would stride back into life.

"That is the stuff they write," said this Frenchman, "and that's the stuff they are teaching to young minds in Germany. We do not take it seriously enough. In my judgment it is very serious. It's a challenge to European civilisation and Christianity. We are apt to dismiss it and say it is just the ravings of a few lunatics. But it is a definite philosophy which is held by men who have the destiny of a nation in their hands. It is the education being given to the minds of the young people, plastic in the hands of those who mould them. One cannot understand what has happened in Germany—Hitler's advent—the spread of the Nazi cult—the attack on Jews and Catholics and the Protestant dogma—without taking all this into account. It is not an accessory of the Nazi faith. It is fundamental. It is the mainspring of German energy. It is the reason why we cannot regard them as equals and partners in European progress."

It was a disturbing conversation. Yet I must in fairness admit that afterwards I talked with many Germans who ridiculed, or pooh-poohed, that philosophy of paganism, and shrugged their shoulders at the name of Alfred Rosenberg.

In Berlin I came to one, and only one, definite conclusion about German mentality. It was in agreement with the analysis of my French friend regarding the percentage of Germans who were ready to die for Hitler, but my conclusion was in different terms. It seemed to me from personal observation, and the accounts of other observers, that one might draw a line according to the age of the population. Those below the age of forty were attracted by the Nazi ideal. Those above the age of forty were deeply sceptical or utterly hostile. Broadly, that I think was true, apart from small minorities who still believed, under forty years of age, in Communism or Liberalism, or other forms of thought disallowed by young men in brown shirts.

8

Berlin is not Germany. I was glad to go into the smaller towns and villages on the motor journey which I have interrupted in this narrative. It was four months after that visit to Berlin that I passed with my fellow travellers through the Austrian and German customs and drove into Bavaria.

We stopped for a time in Garmisch, partly because of pleasant recollections there. My wife—have I said that the laughing lady was my wife?—wished to show the artist the old houses in the Frühlingstrasse, with its distant view of the Glaxenstein and the Zugspitz. We wanted to sit once again outside the Gasthof of the Drei Mohren, where every day on a summer holiday we had taken our coffee. We wanted to recapture something of the spell which Garmisch had put on our imagination.

It is always difficult to recapture impressions like that. There is always something missing. My wife missed a rapid little stream which we had had to cross on the way to the Frühlingstrasse. It had dried up. There was no sunshine lying on the walls of these seventeenth-century houses with their elaborate paintings of German knights, and ladies, and garlanded maidens, and festooned flowers, under deep eaves and old roofs supported on carved poles. There were lowering clouds in the sky, and there was a thunderous feeling in the air. Garmisch did not look so well that day.

The landlord of the Drei Mohren recognised the lady and was delighted to see English visitors. In his garden was a party of young officers of Hitler's Storm Troops—about fifteen of them

—who had arrived in lorries. They sat at a long table drinking beer and enjoying themselves, without rowdiness. They were very smart in their uniforms, and only hostile eyes would think they looked a brutal crowd. At our table we agreed that they were well mannered and nice-looking. They greeted the landlord and each other with the words *"Heil Hitler!"* spoken as though it were a joyous message.

"Of course, the Bavarians aren't Prussians," said the artist, as though that explained their genial appearance.

That was perfectly true, but I remembered that the Bavarian regiments had fought longest and hardest against the British all through the war on the Western Front. There was nothing soft about them—nothing that might be called lamblike. But the Bavarians, and especially the peasants, seem a good-natured people, and friendly, even to the English who fought with them. At Garmisch once a year one sees them in a holiday mood when thousands of peasants make their way from surrounding villages for what is known as the Hochzeit. We were there on one of those days and saw all those peasants in their national costumes, of which they are proud. They are still worn as a workaday dress, and not as an advertisement for tourists. But on the day of the Hochzeit they were in their very best clothes—the men in short jackets of many colours, over embroidered shirts and leather shorts with tassels; the women in lace caps, white bodices above their corsets, and full petticoats with fancy pinafores.

A big crowd in costumes like that—looking as though they were the company of an old-fashioned opera—had gathered in the high street to watch a country wedding, which is the chief ceremony of the Hochzeit. Presently there was the sound of a German band doing some heavy trombone work, and the best of a big bass drum. Some of the burghers, wreathed in brass, made tremendous music down the street. They were followed by small boys and girls like Hansel and Gretel, who strewed flowers along the way. The parents of the bride and bridegroom arrived on a cart, looking very solemn and important and self-conscious in their gala clothes. Then came the bride and bridegroom in another farm cart loaded with their household furniture. The bride wore a little crown on her braided hair. She sat there holding the hand of a young man with roguish eyes. Behind them, on a dray, came an enormous double bed, at which the crowd roared with laughter. Then followed a procession on foot of family friends and relatives, led by the oldest peasants of the district—a husband and wife—so old that they were bent nearly double as they hobbled on, hand in hand, and the old man's beard was like that of Rip van Winkle.

They went to the public gardens down by the river Loisach, which flowed merrily through, and the rest of the day was given over to dancing and beer drinking. The young men and women sat at long benches, facing each other, and many a boy, in a green hat with a feather stuck behind, had his arm round a girl's waist, but when he snuggled closer and tried to get a kiss, his face was smartly slapped by a girl who knew the limit of propriety in Garmisch.

The bride and bridegroom led the dance on a high platform. They were joined by other couples. The women twirled round to the brazen music—twirled like teetotums, until their petticoats billowed out and their long white drawers were revealed to an admiring crowd. The platform was cleared for men only. They danced like Morris dancers in England, but with a lot of knee and thigh slapping, until, as a *tour de force*, the bigger men turned the smaller men upside down and smacked their backsides with resounding whacks. It was very German.

I sat down on a bench crowded with Bavarian youths and drank beer with them. They were very friendly. I couldn't bring myself to hate them as a menace to civilisation. I could not bring myself to believe that they were a brutal and brutalised crowd, lusting to make war on their neighbours. They were *gemütlich*. These boys were the sons of the men who fought in Flanders with a courage and stubborn pride which lasted for four and a half years of enormous sacrifice.

9

Leaving Garmisch, we motored through a valley between the Bavarian Alps, until we began to leave the mountainous country and came into a landscape like the unspoiled parts of Surrey, with good meadow land, and fine trees, and hedges tangled with wild flowers. Near the little town of Weilheim there was a lake where a crowd of young Bavarians were sunbathing. There were no Nazis in uniform. The sign of the Swastika was not stencilled on brown arms. They had left off politics with their clothes, and it occurred to me that a touch of nudism might be useful in getting rid of so many coloured shirts in Europe. It might do away with the wearing of political symbols and the badges of the bully spirit. One sunbrowned skin is much like another, and, as Carlyle once proclaimed, all men are equal when they are stripped of clothes.

On our way to Munich we passed the Starnbergersee, another lake, which is the week-end paradise of the Müncheners. Little white yachts were sailing there. Boys, stripped to the waist and bronzed to the colour of red Indians, paddled their canoes. High divers were exhibiting their prowess. A swarm of young people who had been serving in shops and offices were bathing and sprawling in the sun in their week-end return to nature. They were beyond the reach of loudspeakers reminding them of German destiny, the purity of the German race, the nobility of Herr Hitler. For a little while, here in this water and on these wooded islands, there were no collecting boxes for the Nazi organisation.

We were twenty-five kilometres from Munich. The roads were crowded with cyclists, all pedalling furiously in the hot sun to get back to supper after a day's outing. Fat women in white shirts and shorts perspired over their handle-bars. Girls with straw-coloured hair and limbs that would not have shocked a Greek sculptor kept pace with their boy friends. There were motorcycles with pillion riders, but very few cars. As we neared Munich I was reminded of Wimbledon Common on a Bank Holiday. Here were picnic parties on the edge of the Wald. Photographers were snapping family groups. But, unlike Wimbledon Common on a Bank Holiday, there was no litter of paper bags and orange peel. The Germans are a neat and tidy people.

When we entered Munich—the headquarters of Hitler in his first campaign—we were not sure of the street in which we should find the hotel we had chosen for our stay. A young motorcyclist was ahead of us and saw our hesitation. He inquired of Gaston where we wanted to go. It was unfortunate that at that precise moment something went a little wrong with the car and we stopped dead. Gaston was embarrassed. He urged the young motorcyclist to continue his way.

"Danke schön! Danke schön!" shouted Gaston, waving on our self-appointed guide.

But the young man, having begun a good deed, was resolved not to leave us in the lurch. He cycled round us until we could start again and then acted as pilot. It was extraordinarily civil of him. We were strangers and meant nothing to him. I wondered if an English motorcyclist would take so much trouble over a car full of Germans, doubtful of their way at Hyde Park Corner. I decided that it wasn't likely.

We stayed at the Grünewald, a pleasant and modest hotel in a good position. It was not without a wrench that we had decided against the Vier Jahreszeiten—the Four Seasons—where my wife and I had stayed several times. The head waiter there was a great friend of ours. He greeted us always with delight. But times had changed, and German money is a bad bargain on the English exchange, unless one is provided with *Reisemarks* to be cashed at a bank each day with many formalities and pencil scribblings on passports, and a waste of time, as we found on this journey.

Outwardly Munich was unchanged by the Nazi revolution, as it had been unchanged by many centuries of German history. We found the old landmarks—the tall towers of the Frauenkirche which have looked over Munich for seven hundred years, the great Rathaus where crowds gather to watch the procession of kings and knights and princesses round the clock which plays little tinkling tunes like a musical box. It plays the tunes now at one o'clock instead of midday, because the crowds do not interfere so much with business in the lunch hour. We walked along the Neuehäuserstrasse with its old gilded houses, the highway of the beer taverns. They were all there, those famous taverns, the Augustiner, the Löwenbrau, the Rathauskeller and many others. We knew them all. We had sat down in them to gargantuan meals, each dish being enough to feed a family. We had drunk many glasses of *dunkles* and *helles* in them, that beer which is the nearest thing to the nectar of the gods on a hot day after a visit to the *Alte Pinako-thek* and the *Neue Pinakothek*, where there is the noblest collection of German art.

"I must have a look at those pictures again," said the artist.

He had a look at another work of art, more recent than the pictures by Pacher and other great masters. It was the War Memorial in Munich, in the public gardens.

It is an open tomb, to which one goes down by steps. In the centre of this walled space lies the figure of a German soldier in bronze, dead, as I saw so many dead in the fields of Flanders. All around are bas reliefs of other Bavarian soldiers, serving their guns, throwing bombs, defending the front-line trenches. Their names, thousands of them, are carved on the walls. Our artist had fought against them. One of their shells had smashed his arm. He stood bareheaded, and his soul paid tribute to the men who had suffered the things he had suffered, done their duty as he had done it, and stuck it out in that hell of the Western front until they found a bit of shell with their name on it and then had rest. Among the wreaths was one from the West Ham Football Club.

Was it all going to happen again twenty years after? In France they thought so. In England many friends of mine thought so. Would all this youth of Germany, the marching battalions in Berlin, those peasant boys of Garmisch, trudge up the same old roads to the same old battlefields, to die under storms of high explosives and the sweep of machine-gun fire, like their fathers and elder brothers in the same old quarrel with France? No, I could not believe that. I do not believe it.

10

Munich is a noble old city, laid out on spacious lines. As the capital of Bavaria it has a certain grandeur and stateliness, but its burghers built their own houses for comfort and took pride in making them beautiful. It is a garden city, and the *Englischergarten* especially is as good a park as one may find in any big city, including London, where the parks are famous. Nature has been allowed its playground here, and the gardeners have left fair spaces for a little wildness beyond the trim lawns and flower beds. There are charming paths through little woodlands, and the ground billows here and there, rising to a hill crowned by a temple from which one can look over Munich with its domes and spires and palaces, set on fire when the sun is sinking.

It is the capital of Catholic Bavaria, crowded with great churches where there are still many worshippers. Monks walk through the streets in their habits and sandals. Nuns in many different costumes guide their schoolchildren on afternoon walks. It is impossible to believe that Alfred Rosenberg and his pagan cult will ever prevail over the Catholic faith of these people in Munich.

There is one man in their city who is strong in defence of that faith. Sunday after Sunday he stands in his pulpit and denounces the absurdity and wickedness of those who would bring back the old pagan gods and attempt to undermine the foundations of Christianity. He has crowded congregations to hear him, and under his pulpit are secret police, making notes of his sermons with sinister intent. Orders were issued to arrest this man—Cardinal Faulhaber—who is alone in his audacity of criticism in a régime which forbids free speech if it is hostile to the Nazi creed. There was a prison waiting for him, though all Bavaria would have been stirred with anger if any hand were laid upon him. The news of his impending arrest reached Adolf Hitler in Berlin, and, unlike some of his lieutenants— Captain Roehm among them—he was aghast at the thought of such a thing. He gave orders for an aëroplane to be made ready. He flew that night to Munich. "Are you mad?" he shouted angrily. "What is this I hear about the arrest of Cardinal Faulhaber? I forbid you to lay a finger on him." (I had this story from a man who knew, and who knows, most things that happen in Germany, not often published.)

Cardinal Faulhaber had made one of his addresses on the afternoon I arrived in Munich. He was angry because his procession on Corpus Christi had been restricted to a small area. He was angry because the Catholic boys were forbidden to parade with their badges and banners. He addressed them from the front of his cathedral.

"Your flags have been forbidden," he said, "but you have come without them. We have lost our liberty, but you have not lost your faith."

I asked an important officer of the Nazi headquarters staff if it were true that orders had been issued that the Town Hall should not be decorated on this feast day, although ninety per cent of the citizens are Catholics.

"No doubt it is true," he said. "We have no objection to the Catholics having full right of worship and all liberty. But their priests and cardinals are playing politics. That we do not allow. The Pope is not the ruler of Germany. Let him mind his own business, which is religious and not political."

He belonged to the "No Popery" cast of mind.

II

I called at the Brown House in Munich. It is, as most people know, the headquarters of the Nazi organisation in Bavaria. It was here that Captain Roehm—accused by Hitler of the vilest immorality, arrested by Hitler himself, and shot by his orders—had his office. It was here that many of those young men, shot like dogs on the Thirtieth of June—they had been Hitler's comrades in the early days—did their business as administrators of all public offices and works in Bavaria, when not rushing about the country in powerful cars, or giving parties at the expense of people who had put their pennies into the collecting boxes, according to the charges brought against them after their deaths by the man who owed his power to them.

The Brown House was guarded by Storm Troopers in steel hats with rifles. No one challenged me when I entered the hall which was stacked with banners bearing the Sign of the Crooked Cross. A young Nazi sat at a desk there, and I asked for a certain officer to whom I had an introduction. He directed me to a house on the opposite side of the road, but before I went there I looked at some works in progress round the Brown House itself. They were surrounded by hoardings, but I could see through some gaps to an open space—houses had been knocked down to make it—in which were some curious dome-like shapes of concrete. They were the domes of an underground building capable of holding forty thousand people—a great crowd. It would be used as a gas and bombproof shelter in case of aërial attack. All over Germany there are other shelters of that kind, built, or being built, with furious haste.

The officer to whom I had an introduction was in his room, and I was asked to go up. He rose from his desk as I entered, and I saw a young man with fair hair, singularly and even arrestingly handsome. He was extremely polite, and desired to know what information I wanted.

I wanted an immense amount of information. I wanted to know a thousand unexplained things about this Nazi organisation and its philosophy and mentality. I wanted to know whether it was succeeding in creating a better kind of life in Germany, whether Hitler was secure in his power, whether another revolution was likely to happen, whether Germany was advancing to economic ruin, and other little questions of that kind. But I could not ask too much. I contented myself with asking less—much less—and in all fairness I must say that this handsome young man answered me with great patience and apparent candour.

There was only one subject which he refused to discuss. When I asked about the economic state of Germany he made a grimace.

"I am no economist," he answered. "Let's talk of something else."

I understood from the face he made that he didn't think much of the economic state of Germany.

I tackled him about the belief of France that Germany was preparing a new war, and he laughed at what he considered the absurdity of such a notion.

"Germany doesn't want to attack anybody," he answered.

"Hitler knows what war means. He was blind for half a year. He went through the horrors. He knows, as we all know, that another war would end European civilisation. He is ardent for peace. I assure you—and I know what is in his mind."

He looked at me with very blue and very luminous eyes.

"We have no quarrel with France," he continued. "After all, they are Franks, at least in the north. They are our kinsfolk —to some extent. In any case, we don't want to interfere with anything they do. We only regret that they allow so many coloured people in France. That seems to us a grave mistake from their own point of view and ours."

We got onto the race question, and he gave his views, which were not quite so extreme as those of Alfred Rosenberg.

"We want to keep our race as it is. It isn't pure. We quite agree that it's mixed, but we don't want it to be more mixed. We want to keep it uncontaminated by Jewish and other alien blood as far as possible. Is there anything very wicked about that?"

"Why this hatred against the Jews?" I asked. "They have brought a lot of genius into Germany. You owe to them much of your music and art and wealth."

"They are, after all, aliens," he said. "There are six hundred and fifty thousand Jews in a nation of sixty million. They held the key positions. They controlled the bar, the medical schools, and the business world. They were not German in their instincts and loyalties. We wanted to get control of our own nation."

"Your methods were pretty brutal," I said.

He agreed.

"There were beatings and brutalities in the first few days. It was done by younger men who thought they were doing something fine. We regret all that, and it has been stopped. If you go around Munich you will find the Jews going about their business unmolested. As a matter of fact, we don't expel any Jew if he can prove that he is doing service for Germany. All the same, we must admit that the Jewish boycott is serious."

He meant the boycott of German goods by the Jewish world outside.

He began to talk about Germany's international position.

"Some people think that we made a mistake in withdrawing from the League of Nations, especially if we are sincere about peace. But we withdrew because of endless discussion which was leading nowhere, and because our claim to equality, at whatever level of disarmament, was first accepted and then evaded. We thought it best to get into direct touch with France and other nations, using more direct methods. At Geneva it was all words without acts. Every delegate talks to the gallery. There is no reason why there should not be a friendly relationship between France and Germany. The younger groups in France have no hatred of Germany. They are perfectly reasonable and no longer cling to the heritage of hate. We understand French mentality. It's natural and inevitable that they should be obsessed with the fear of invasion, after being twice invaded within living memory. But we want them to believe in our sincerity when we offer a pact of peace. It is sincere, from Hitler downwards. There would be great enthusiasm in Germany if we could arrange a friendly understanding."

I spoke frankly. I told him the causes of French fears. They were convinced that Germany was re-arming and that the spirit of Germany under Hitler was aggressive and warlike.

"No," he said. "That's untrue! Anybody who stays long enough in Germany to get at the truth must admit, if he is honest, that we have no aggressive plans or purpose. We are arming for self-defence."

"Against whom?" I asked. "Who is likely to attack you?"

He looked at me again with those very blue and very luminous eyes.

"We may be invaded. We know that there is real danger. Germany is a corridor between France and Russia. If Russia has a war with Japan other nations will be involved. France may want to march through Germany."

It seemed to me a fantastic idea, but this young man believed it. Other men I met believed it.

He spoke later about the internal situation of Germany.

"The older people find it difficult to accept the Nazi régime. The young look forward to building a new world. The old folk want to get back to the past. That is very natural. It's difficult—it's impossible—for people of middle age and onwards to re-adapt themselves to new conditions and put their imaginations forward to a new state of things. They don't like new states of things. They're traditional. They're afraid of change. They believe in the *status quo ante*. There is, of course, a good deal of socialistic theory in the ideals of National Socialism. That was the original programme of Hitler. Needless to say, Big Industry doesn't favour those ideas. There is a silent hostility to anything smelling of Socialism. Nevertheless—and one wants to be fair—many employers are coöperating well. They are keeping on men if it means less profit. Of course, our economic position—well, I have already said I am not an economist! —is not settled. We are in a state of transition from one system to another, and it comes at a time when the world crisis doesn't help. Our internal difficulties are very great. Everyone understands that. We can't stand alone. That's evident. We must trade with the rest of the world. We must sell things to them. But all that is for the future. Meanwhile we are trying to reduce unemployment by public works, and by an intelligent control of industry. We haven't done too badly."

He claimed some rather fine achievements.

"We're breaking down caste," he said. "At least, we're trying to break it down. We get young fellows of all classes into the labour camps, and that makes for comradeship between them. We insist that all work is equal in value if it is done with a spirit of service for the Fatherland. It doesn't matter whether a fellow is a bricklayer, or a machine minder, or a university student, or professor, or scientist; his job is ennobled by the spirit with which it's done, and there is no distinction of merit. Of course we're only at the beginning. It's a great adventure, and youth is inexperienced and makes many mistakes. Some of the key positions are in the wrong hands. There are square pegs in round holes."

He spoke a sentence—I found it in my notes—which did not strike me very forcibly at the time but now has a sinister significance.

"*Hitler*," he said, "*is going to reorganise the leadership*."

Those words were spoken in the month in which the day fell when the leadership was "reorganised"—the Thirtieth of June.

12

It was this young man in an office opposite the Brown House who passed the word along that I wanted to visit some of the labour camps, and put me in touch with one of the leaders of that service, the *Arbeitdienst,* as it is called.

He called round in the afternoon and clicked heels. He was in Nazi uniform, with the badge of the Labour Service on his cap, designed by himself, as he told us afterwards.

He was a high officer in the service—an *Oberfeldmeister.* He was also a German baron with a noble name—a man of middle age, but very young-looking and even boyish in his manners. He spoke most excellent English, having been a prisoner in England during part of the war, and a visitor to the United States, where his sister is a well-known artist.

My wife and friends were anxious to see the labour camps, but I was doubtful whether they would be allowed to join me. I was especially doubtful whether a lady would be permitted in the camps for men, but the *Oberfeldmeister* saw no objection whatever and invited us all. On the way out by motorcar he told us that he was very keen about this work and had to inspect all the labour camps in Bavaria. There were, he said, twelve hundred camps in the whole of Germany, with an average of two hundred young men in each camp; that is to say, two hundred and forty thousand men in all. They were all volunteers, with the exception of the university students, who had made a law unto themselves that no one could take a degree without serving six months on the "Labour Front." They made roads, cut down timber, drained marshes, cultivated allotments, and did other work of a useful kind not in conflict with work which was being done by the ordinary ranks of labour.

"They get valuable training and good discipline," said the *Oberfeldmeister.* "There is a competition among employers for their service afterwards, and we have no difficulty in getting jobs for them The experiment has a real moral value. These boys get well fed, physically fit, and full of spirit Instead of lounging about waiting for jobs which may be long in coming, they have a good time in these camps, where they are not worked too hard, and where they get lectures on all sorts of subjects and plenty of interest. They are of all classes, and you will be surprised to see how caste has been entirely broken down. There is an excellent comradeship between the university students and the boys who come from peasant families and factory populations. It's one of the best things ever done in Germany. We really can claim a good deal of success."

We motored to a place called Förstenried, about ten miles outside Munich, into the heart of a fir forest. A good new road through the forest led to the camp.

"It was made by our lads," said the *Oberfeldmeister*. "It will be very useful for the woodcutters and the clearing of timber."

We arrived in the early afternoon during "rest time" and heard with surprise that all the young men had to lie down on their beds for an hour and a half after their morning's work and meal. Most of them were lying down when we arrived and entered their wooden huts. There were about sixteen to twenty in each room, and they lay on their bunks one above the other, reading, or talking, or sleeping.

A word of command was called out by the superintendent of the camp, and instantly all the young men tumbled out of bed and stood to attention. The *Oberfeldmeister* greeted the officer with the usual salute and the "*Heil Hitler!*"

The camp officer gave us the programme of the day. The young men get up at five-thirty. They have six hours of work, for which they are paid twenty-five pfennig. They have five meals a day, of good but simple food. They can go out from six to nine and have a free time from Saturday afternoon to Sunday night. They have lantern lectures, a cinema, and other means of entertainment and instruction. They go to bed at ten o'clock.

"May I talk with them?" I asked.

Both officers were pleased for me to talk with them, and while my wife and friends were chatting with the officers I had an amusing time with the volunteers of labour.

They surrounded me and answered my questions with the greatest good-humour. In a few minutes they were all laughing heartily. I asked them if they had enough to eat, and they shoved forward one of their comrades and said he always over-ate himself. I asked if they were bored with this kind of life, and they were much amused. So far from being bored, they said, they found it almost too exciting! It was a gipsy life. They felt very fit. There were always things to do. It was a great game. They were very keen on it. Of course, they got as tired as dogs and were glad of a good sleep and this rest time. They turned the tables on me and asked who I was and why I was interested in them. Was I by any chance a newspaper reporter? I told them I was a writer of books.

"Novels?" asked one of them.

When I admitted this weakness there was a roar of laughter. Evidently they thought a novelist was a very funny fellow.

"I may write a novel about you," I warned them, and the laughter rose again.

"But that is impossible!" said one of the young men. "No novel has been written without a love story, and in this camp there are no women."

That remark was greeted with hilarious applause.

"*Gott sei Dank!*" said one of the young men fervently.

We had a good time together. They were like a crowd of English schoolboys, though some of them were odd types. They came from all parts of Germany, they told me. Some of them were students, others mechanics, others country fellows from the farming districts.

The camp commandant was eager to impart further information to me and interrupted a more amusing conversation.

"They get free medical attention," he said. "Every second day a doctor comes and looks them over. We have a sick ward for any of them who feel unwell. But there is very little of that. There are only two beds in the ward, and they are not often used."

I saw the sick ward, very neat and comfortable, and then I left the officers again to talk to a young man who attracted my attention. He was sitting alone in the courtyard, stripped to the waist and dressed in nothing but a pair of shorts. He was busy polishing a pair of top boots, and he was a fine figure of youth, very good-looking and with a touch of the aristocrat in his appearance, half naked as he was.

"How goes it?" I asked.

He looked up and smiled.

"Fine!"

"Do you like this kind of life?"

"It's not too bad!"

He told me he was a university student, waiting to take his degree. He thought it a trifle hard that he should have to wait until he had done his six months' service on the Labour Front. It was rather a waste of time, he thought, from the point of view of studies and the career he wanted to follow. Still, it was amusing. The work wasn't too hard, and it was a good healthy way of life, with plenty of fresh air and exercise. Six months would soon pass.

"How do you get on with the older men?" I asked.

He laughed.

"They're good chaps! All classes, but with a spirit of comradeship. There are some other students here, and naturally we drift together now and then for talks about things which interest us. It's not a bad existence."

The *Oberfeldmeister* joined me again.

"I'm glad you're talking to these lads," he said. "They're a fine crowd, don't you think? Some of them were in good jobs, but left them in order that married men might fill their places in a time of unemployment. That's practical idealism!"

"How much does all this cost?" I asked.

The *Oberfeldmeister* reckoned it up. Counting food, lodging, clothes, and boots, he thought that each lad cost two marks a day.

My two friends, the artist and the novelist, were both much impressed.

"I'd like to see this sort of thing in England among the unemployed," said the artist. "I can't think why we don't do it. It's a cure for demoralisation."

He was already on the best of terms with the *Oberfeldmeister*. They were both interested in art. And the novelist had made the surprising discovery that this German officer, so boyish-looking and so hearty, was a devotee of an English poet who is read only by very high souls in England—Alice Meynell.

We went to see another camp near the village of Gauting. The camp commandant was an ex-police officer with a rasping voice and a severe sense of discipline which made all his young men jump at his word of command. The bully type, I thought. But I revised that opinion after a short acquaintance. He had humorous and kindly eyes. He was very appreciative of our lady's little jokes. He was obviously popular with his young men, although he put them through their paces like an army drill sergeant. He was a passionate gardener and loved his flowers. No man can be a bully who loves a garden. He was also a lover of pigs and proud of the camp pigsty.

"The pig," said my wife in German, "is a noble animal."

She detests pigs, but the camp commandant agreed with enthusiasm.

"*Ach, ja! Wirklich! Man kann davon nicht genug sagen.*"

One of the boys brought up a white kitten to show us, and another exhibited a tiny fallow deer, only a week old.

I chatted with a number of these labour volunteers. They were all cheerful, satisfied with their food and general conditions, enthusiastic even about this open-air life.

"It makes one strong," said one of them, showing his muscles. "Before I came I was nothing to look at."

Some of them knew a little English, learnt in school. They were proud to speak a few words of it. One of them spoke remarkably well, although he had never been to England.

"What do you think of the Nazi régime?" I asked, indiscreetly perhaps.

"Good!" they said. "It's a régime of youth. It belongs to us. And Hitler is a great leader. He has saved Germany from despair."

I did not press them more on that subject, but it was obvious

LABOUR CAMP, MUNICH

that any volunteer to a labour camp must be enthusiastic for Hitler and the Nazis.

My wife was interested in the appearance of one of the volunteers. He looked very young—no more than a schoolboy.

"Why is that boy here?" she asked. "Is he strong enough for field work?"

The commandant called him up and gave him a slight tap on the shoulder in a fatherly way.

"What's your age, my lad?"

The boy sprang to attention.

"Seventeen."

"Do you find this life too hard?"

The boy grinned.

"I like it."

"Well, go and lie down again."

The camp commandant turned to my wife.

"We don't often take them as young as that," he explained. "But there were special reasons in this case The boy's parents were unable to keep him. We don't work him hard. When he first came he was a half-starved chap. Now he's filling out a bit."

We were taken to the group headquarters and had further explanations about the *Arbeitdienst*. Our *Oberfeldmeister* spent most of his time in giving lectures on history and social subjects in the various camps. Of course the camps were all provided with radio. Their minds were kept active.

I had a few mental reservations about that activity of mind and the kind of lecture which might be given in these camps, Was the philosophy of Alfred Rosenberg expounded? Were the boys taught that the intellect was inferior to instinct? Were they impressed with the tribal spirit and the cult of paganism?

It was my wife who asked about religion, and it was the *Oberfeldmeister* who answered.

"We don't give any religious instruction, but every boy is perfectly free to have his own religious beliefs and to go to any church he likes—if he likes. We leave all that to his home influence. Any other system would be impossible in one of these camps, where the boys come from different parts of Germany and have different forms of belief—Catholic and Protestant."

We invited the *Oberfeldmeister* to dinner, and he came with a portfolio under his arm. He was an amateur artist and was willing to show his work if our artist would do the same. The *Oberfeldmeister's* work was more than that of an amateur. It was remarkably good, with a fine sense of design and colour.

Over dinner, and afterwards, he talked freely: first of his experiences as an English prisoner in Yorkshire, and then of the Nazi philosophy and organisation. He was critical of its leadership. He did not believe that youth had had the experience to lead a great nation. There were too many young and inexperienced men running the show, he thought. What does a boy of twenty, or even twenty-eight, know of statesmanship or life? In another twenty years he may begin to know a little.

It was late in the evening when I induced him to talk about the chance of another war.

"Germany won't make it," he said. "The Nazis are not out for war."

"Then why this wish to re-arm, and all this drilling and marching?" I asked.

"We believe," he said, "that Germany may be attacked and made the battleground of another war. We are not easy in our minds about Russia and France. We cannot leave ourselves defenceless."

He spoke, I am certain, with sincerity. He impressed us as a man of simple honesty, without guile and without fanaticism. He was charming, friendly, and sympathetic. He was a lover of beauty and had the soul of an artist. . . . I do not know whether he is still alive.

13

From the younger leaders of the Nazis in Munich I heard the best side of the Nazi faith. Among them in the labour camps I saw the spirit of service, the enthusiasm for the building of a new Germany, and the vitality of German youth. I liked these young men. They were not of a brutal type. They seemed to me friendly, intelligent, and good-humoured, though doubtless they could be made brutal and cruel—as most men may be—by a propaganda of hatred against those who might be charged with treachery to National Socialism, or with heresy against the Gospel according to Adolf Hitler. I was impressed by the work of the *Arbeitdienst* or Labour Front. I agreed with my artist friend that it would be good if a similar idea could be adopted in England. But there was a darker side to the picture, as I well knew. Above this mass of enthusiastic boys were evil-minded men with sinister designs and a streak of madness.

That side of things was stressed by an English friend of mine in Germany whose business interests brought him into close touch now and then with many classes and many aspects of German life and opinion.

"Underneath all this façade of hopefulness and this blare of propaganda," he said, "the painful truth is that Germany is advancing towards another crash. Everybody knows it, and there is a fear in their minds of severe hardships ahead. They are buying up clothes, foodstuffs, boots, and other things necessary to life. They are convinced—as I am—that they will be on rations before the autumn. Hitler's intention is to prohibit imports as far as possible. As a matter of fact, it's forced upon him. There's no money in the till—no real money. Foreign traders won't give credit any more because they don't get paid in their own currency. The Jewish boycott is much more formidable than Germans acknowledge. They are stopping the sale of German goods all over the world, and especially in the United States. There's a tremendous decline in the export of everything produced in German factories. The London Jews have cut out Germany with the knife of vengeance—Shylock's knife."

"The Germans have asked for it!" I remarked.

My friend nodded.

"Exactly. The amazing stupidity of German mentality is shown by the fact that Hitler and his propaganda merchants are attacking the three most powerful institutions in the world."

"What are those?"

"The Catholic Church, International Jewry, Freemasonry.

Then they're surprised that they have innumerable enemies abroad!"

"What about the younger leaders?" I inquired. "They seem keen fellows."

My friend shrugged his shoulders.

"Some of them show their keenness by driving around in high-powered cars and throwing their weight about. In any case, what do they know about the administration of a great nation? Damn all! They come to Munich, for example, from all parts of Germany—Berlin, Hamburg, and other cities, where they have a pull with the powers that be. They have taken over all public offices formerly administered by men who knew their jobs. They have no experience whatever in the civil service. Is it any wonder that they are making a great mess of it? Their idea of public service is to keep on spending money, and they do that remarkably well. You know that Munich has some pretty good art galleries——"

"World famous!" I agreed.

"Well, these young gentlemen are not satisfied. They're building a new palace of German art in the *Englischergarten*. Bigger and better, is their motto. Unfortunately, they didn't consult the engineers before laying the foundations. Every time they put in a pole it floats away. That is very characteristic of their goings-on. Great enthusiasm and no efficiency."

My friend agreed that the labour camps were run on good lines, but they did not affect the general condition of affairs.

"People of the middle classes and business folk generally," he said, "are utterly fed up with the régime. They have no faith whatever in the future under Hitler. They are convinced that it will lead only to further revolution and all kinds of horror. They see—my own German friends—that Hitler is simply pandering to mass emotion which doesn't get him anywhere. Women worship him. Young boys are ready to die for him; but the bulk of level-headed Germans think that he is a simple fool, who mouths a lot of high-sounding stuff which gave him a power quite beyond his intellectual grasp. And isn't that true? How can a great nation like this prosper under a gang of leaders, some of whom have very evil minds, while others are just soldiers of fortune, or plausible propagandists? It's too preposterous. It is, indeed, an infernal tragedy."

"What's going to happen?" I asked.

He had the gloomiest views of what was going to happen.

"Germany has exhausted her reserves of wealth. There will be an almighty smash. Hitler will be tempted to make some dramatic gesture abroad in order to distract attention from economic failure. They are already telling the people that they're in danger of attack and must prepare for a defensive war. We all know those defensive wars! One happened in Belgium. The Nazi leaders—most of them—have gone back to the mentality of 1914. They believe that they've got the other nations frightened. Meanwhile even little schoolboys are being taught rifle shooting—an hour and a half a week—and learning the mechanism of machine guns. A nice education for the young mind!"

He was inclined to believe that there might be an internal revolution.

"There's no real unity," he said. "Bavaria has no use for Prussia. The old divisions of opinion are only suppressed and driven underground. Lots of these Nazis are Socialists and Communists, impatient with Hitler because he doesn't go fast enough towards the socialistic state. On the other hand are the old Nationalists and Monarchists, biding their time. The older folk in all parts of Germany have no faith in the new régime, and detest it thoroughly. Only Hitler's personal prestige keeps the show together."

In Munich the young airmen were out in the streets, collecting for the progress of "civil aviation" in Germany, and holding up the passers-by with insistent but good-natured demand. Although I was, I imagine, obviously English in a German crowd, they advanced upon me at every street corner, and being a weak man on any flag day, I yielded and put something in one of the boxes, being duly decorated with a small metal aëroplane which made me immune from further solicitation.

Gaston, our driver, refused until the eleventh hour, when two young airmen advanced upon him and shook their boxes under his nose.

"No! No!" he said. "I am a Frenchman."

This was not strictly true according to racial heritage, but true regarding French citizenship.

"That's all right!" said one of the aviators, still very friendly. "This is for civil aviation."

Gaston protested again with his good-humoured laugh.

"No! No! I don't believe a word of that! It's so easy to make civil aviation into military aviation. If I give you any money it will go into the bombing of French cities and the killing of French people."

This was regarded as a very great joke by the two young men. They assured Gaston that there was no danger of any such thing. The French people could sleep quietly in their beds. Germany had no idea of attacking France. It might happen the other way round, they thought.

"In any case," said Gaston, "I won't give you fifty pfennigs. It's a question of conscience."

"In that case we will not insist! *Heil Hitler!*"

There was no ill-feeling on either side. They parted with friendly salutes and more laughter.

"All the same," said Gaston gravely, "I would not decorate myself with the model of a German aëroplane."

I felt guilty with that bit of metal on my coat lapel.

14

There was no sign of trouble, no sense of impending strife, in the countryside beyond Munich. Outwardly, at least, here were peace and contentment. It was full summer, and the wheat was growing tall, and the pasture lands were green and rich. We passed many peasants leading their cows and had friendly greetings from them. Our car seemed to be the only one on the roads, and they stared after us, guessing that we were foreigners. It was parklike scenery, with dark woods framing the fields. Little old villages came into view, all with colour-washed walls and green shutters, very neat and clean, very German.

We found our way to Augsburg, a fine old city, strangely Flemish in appearance, with many mediæval houses which might have been in Bruges or Ghent, because of their stepped roofs and gilded fronts. There were faded frescoes on many walls. It was the home town of the Fuggers, the predecessors of the Rothschilds, who were the bankers of many states in Europe. Their house still stands, and in the square opposite the cathedral is a statue to Hans Fugger—Promoter of Science. The cathedral is of the Baroque style, overloaded with rich ornament, but impressive as one stands looking up the high nave, decorated that day with silver birches, cut down and placed against the tall columns.

The people of Augsburg were going about their business without any look of apprehension as to political troubles or a coming crash. They looked prosperous, although, when I inquired, I heard that the metal and cotton textiles produced in their factories were not finding good markets and that business was very bad. It did not affect the spirits of the children. They went laughing down the streets on their way from school with their neat little satchels.

In some of the shop windows we noticed a display of wooden spoons and heard a story about them. It was reported to Adolf Hitler that the wood carvers in the Black Forest were much distressed by lack of tourists. No one bought their wooden spoons. Hitler sent out word that he would be glad if German people would eat their soup out of wooden spoons, for the sake of those Black Forest peasants. In a few days three hundred and fifty thousand wooden spoons were sold. *Heil Hitler!*

We did not linger long in Augsburg, though a month there would be very pleasant. We went on to Ulm and halted on the Adolf Hitler Platz.

It is a very ancient city. The Romans were there, and left their traces among the Swabian tribes who dwelt there. The Frank came down the Danube and settled there. All through German history it has played a great part as a centre of light and learning through centuries of conflict. The monks built their churches and abbeys in the city. German art produced its masters here. The Münster of Ulm is one of the glories of Gothic Germany, with three spires pointing to heaven, and a high nave supported by flying buttresses, high above the old city with its narrow streets, its wooden houses, richly carved, its towers and walls and ramparts above the Danube—and another river, the Blau—working water wheels and wandering under old bridges in the streets. There is a magnificent Rathaus, built in the Flemish style, like the houses in Augsburg, and many old palaces hidden behind high walls. It was a city of princes, rich merchants, bishops, monks, painters, iron workers and great craftsmen. The old German spirit dwelt there before the coming of Adolf Hitler.

In the Gasthaus zum Schwartzen Adler—the Black Eagle— we sat down at a long table in an old timbered room. Our host was very busy, expecting a big company, and we had already seen that the city was decorated for the arrival of welcome guests. Across the narrow streets were long streamers announcing this event:

The New Germany greets the Old Pioneers!
Citizens of Ulm, hang out your banners!

The banners were hung out. The Swastika flag was a flaming scarlet all down the streets.

Ten thousand of the Old Pioneer regiments of Württemberg who had fought in the Great War were coming to Ulm to be received with honour by the municipality.

I had a talk with the landlord as he pulled corks out of bottles and kept an eye on his staff. He was a very genial man and ready for conversation.

"You are in a very ancient city," he told me. "Ulm has a long history. It has been a fortress for two thousand years. Many battles have been fought round about our walls. One of them was with Napoleon's army. You are now in real Germany. This is not Bavaria. We are Württembergers."

His wife objected to our conversation. She was getting flustered by the first arrivals of the great company.

"You talk too much, my man," she said.

I was sorry about that, because he was a man of knowledge as well as a good drawer of corks.

"Women do not understand the intellectual qualities," said

mine host. "But in any case I am keeping you from your *Mittagessen.*"

He wished me a good appetite.

The Old Pioneers arrived in lorries. They invaded the Black Eagle, and we sat among a crowd of middle-aged, grizzled, square-shouldered men who, I thought, took their pleasure sadly. At least, they were not gay and not at all in festive mood. But they were a good type. I stared at them with interest and a touch of emotion, because of old memories. These were the men who had fought us for four and a half years. They were the men who had been in trenches opposite ours at Ypres and on the Somme. They had been in the hell of Verdun. Twenty years had passed since then. They had become grey-headed and almost elderly. They looked careworn, as though life in the past twenty years, after release from trenches and dugouts, had not been easy for them. And I knew it had not been easy. They had been through the time of inflation. They were still in the time of unemployment. They had gone through years of anxiety, hardship and revolution. Perhaps they did not believe much in the Nazi régime and the new adventure of German youth. They ate their food silently or talked quietly among themselves, and then lined up outside and marched off somewhere—perhaps to the Rathaus—with a band leading them and playing heavy trombone stuff.

In Ulm there was another banner across the streets, and its words were repeated across country roads and at the entrance of villages:

The German People
Must Become
A Nation of Flyers.

In the market place, on a wooden pedestal, was an enormous aërial torpedo, made of tin, and painted red and white, like the colours of the Swastika flag.

I read the legend printed on the pedestal in big letters. It was:

One People,
One Danger,
One Defence.

It did not look very much, in the face of that aërial torpedo, as though this German aviation, for which the collecting boxes were busy, was going to be of a very civil nature. But in the minds of the people, as I knew by talking to them, there was a real fear—kept constantly over them by intensive propaganda —that Germany was in danger of attack from the air. That was the meaning of a feverish building of bombproof shelters in all their big cities. Their children were learning to dress themselves in gas masks. In the schools there was instruction on gas drill. In their imagination the sky was crowded with hostile planes coming from France—or Russia!

15

We went on our way to Stuttgart, through little low hills and a pastoral countryside. We passed through many old villages again with good old names for ancient inns—the Golden Ox, the Red Hussar, the Ear of Wheat, the Good Comrades. It was a land of orchards, promising a great harvest of apples and all good fruit. From almost every house in every village floated the long red-and-white banner with the symbol of the Swastika, black in a white circle. Even here in rural Germany, so deep in quietude, so aloof from the passion of great cities, so much as God may have meant men to live, as tillers of the good earth, with skill of craftsmanship and a sense of beauty, the slogans of propaganda floated across the roads to be read by peasant eyes:

Who Helps the German Air Force
Helps Germany.

If You Reverence Your Mother
Then Prove It by Joining
The Welfare League.

The German Folk Must Be
Air-minded!

The German folk, as we passed them through Württemberg, were bending over their fields, carting their hay, spraying their fruit trees, leading their oxen. They did not seem at all interested in this air propaganda. They were servants of the soil. It was the earth which needed them. But in many of the village squares were those frightful models of aërial torpedoes, mounted on pedestals, and painted red and white.

As we drew near to Stuttgart German youth was on the march, and busy with other forms of activity. A lorry-load of Nazis passed us. A battalion of the Hitler Youth came along the road. Nazi officers, saluted by outstretched arms, dashed by in motorcars. In Stuttgart there were Nazis everywhere in their light brown uniforms, and a column of Reichswehr troops, in steel helmets and field kit, marched grimly down the street, as though ready for immediate war or immediate revolution.

We were in a good position to watch life in Stuttgart as we put up at the Railway Hotel and looked down from our windows to a big square, in which, all day long and late into the night, there was much coming and going. It does not sound attractive —a railway hotel. One thinks of such places in England, ugly and surrounded by ugliness, without a touch of grace. But in Stuttgart the railway station itself is a magnificent building, recently finished; and the hotel has every comfort, with elegance as well as efficiency.

Stuttgart itself is like that—a good, solid, burgherly town, with fine shops and streets, modern and businesslike, but not without beauty and charm. The older city still retains its character, and there is a fine old market with timbered houses, and a Gothic cathedral exquisitely carved, and a noble Rathaus where the city elders administered the social services with a civic pride, until their places were taken a year ago by ardent young men in brown uniforms, who thought they knew much more about social service and ideals than these old baldheads, pushed out without ceremony in the name of Hitler.

There is a new Schloss and an old Schloss in which the kings of Württemberg once lived. The old Schloss was partly burned down three years ago, and many priceless treasures were destroyed, but it is still a great mass of mediæval masonry with many rooms, holding the armour and furnishings and tapestries of the kings and princes of Württemberg. Some of them were famous knights before German kingship became fat and bloated. Some of them were great rulers, devoted to art and crafts and the welfare of their people. Some of them were great black-guards, murderous, lecherous and drunken. Some of them loved music, and scholarship, and gentleness, and peace, in days when German life was coarse and the Four Horsemen rode by, backwards and forwards, with grins on their skulls as German villages were burning and the crows were busy above dead bodies.

It was in the old Schloss—as old as the twelfth century— that I was put in charge of a picture-postcard stall, to the amusement and amazement of a group of Germans. The guard-ian was anxious to show me a book. It contained a collection of pictures of the old part of the Castle, burnt in 1932. But he had left it in a distant place, and it might take a little time to find. Would I be so good as to look after his picture postcards for a while?

So I stood at the receipt of custom, prepared to sell my post-cards to any tourist, and hoping they wouldn't ask for change. A small crowd had gathered. They stared at three strange-looking Englishmen who seemed in charge of the ancient Schloss in the absence of its guardian. "Fine picture postcards!" I said. But they only grinned.

16

We had a great loss in Stuttgart. We lost our lady companion who had come out when I was abed in Sion. Now she had to go back to other duties, and we were sorry. I went with her to the station sometime after midnight. There were still crowds in the square—a mass of young girls who seemed to be assem-bling for some expedition by train. They were singing songs and laughing under our bedroom windows. It was not until two in the morning that the whole party—two thousand of them —surged into the railway station and left the silence of night behind them.

It was not a long quietude. Before six o'clock next morning life was astir again in Stuttgart. New crowds arrived. They were the old soldiers whom we had seen in Ulm. Lorries were waiting for them, and a detachment of Nazis formed a guard of honour. There was also a company of Reichswehr troops in their inevitable steel helmets. A band played them out of the square.

Later in the morning there was a great affair outside the Neue Schloss, where thousands of young athletes had assembled for a prize-giving. They were all in gymnasium kit and looked good specimens of young manhood. Most of them were certainly Nordic, with fair hair and colouring. The Green Police—the smartest body of men in Germany—kept the crowd in line. There was a great exhibition of Nazi banners, and bands were playing, and cheers were rising. Young Germany under Hitler seemed to be enjoying itself, careless of the loss of gold reserves, the prospect of rations in the autumn, the prophecies and rumours of impending trouble. These boys with bronzed limbs and sun-bleached hair had a look of faith in the future. There was nothing downcast about them.

Three English travellers in Stuttgart were a little dejected. We had lost our lady. The end of the journey would not be so gay without her.

"Let's have a drink!" said the artist.

We had a drink in the garden of a restaurant looking onto the square. Then we wandered round the old market with its timbered houses, and I had a talk with one of the market women.

She was a middle-aged woman with pleasant eyes, and after selling me some strawberries was very willing to talk to a stranger in her city.

"You're English, aren't you?" she asked.

"Yes, I'm English."

"Englishmen are very polite," she told me, and I liked the compliment.

I thanked her and inquired as to the state of things in Stuttgart.

She laughed and then gave a deep sigh, with her hand on her bosom.

"It is hard for working women, especially if their men have been out of a job for three years like my husband."

"Bad luck!" I said.

"He's in work again now," she told me, "but wages aren't enough to keep the household going. He gets seventy-five pfennigs an hour and works for forty-eight hours a week. But there are many taxes. Any man in a job has to pay ten per cent of his wage for the unemployed. Then there are other taxes. Rent is costly, and there's electricity, gas and so on. Our family, with my man's wages and mine, make seven marks a week for each person, after reckoning taxes and rent. That's not enough for comfort. There's no chance of saving a bit, or putting by for a rainy day—if anyone goes sick. One has to think of clothes and boots, and, now and then, a doctor's bill."

There were some nicely dressed girls coming through the market. I called her attention to them.

"Everybody seems well dressed," I said.

She laughed, and then lowered her voice until some of the girls had passed.

"Germans make a good show in the streets," she said. "But go into their homes. You will find a lot of poverty. Everybody has to stint. Every pfennig has to be counted. Every rag of underclothing has to be patched up. Food has to be served out carefully by spoonfuls. The father of a family grows white at the thought of his rent and taxes."

She hastened to defend her own courage.

"I'm not complaining about myself! There are many worse off. And I will say that I agree with Hitler about women not taking men's jobs. There has been too much of that."

"So you're all for Hitler and the Nazis," I suggested.

She looked at me with honest, smiling eyes.

"Did I say that?"

She lowered her voice again.

"I'm not sure about this Nazi government. The boys and girls go marching about with flags. Well, if it keeps them happy, that's good! But it doesn't bring in bread and butter. And we working people have collecting boxes under our noses every day of the week and put in a few coins, but where does all the money go? Some people think it goes to buy nice uniforms and big motorcars for the smart young officers. That's not quite right! Then there's this collection for the Air Force——"

"Yes," I said, and showed the metal aëroplane on the lapel of my coat.

"It might be dangerous," she said. "What are they for, all those aëroplanes? That's what I ask myself sometimes. What do we want them for? What is the meaning of all this propaganda about a danger creeping close to us?"

"That's what I've been asking," I told her.

She breathed hard, with her hand to her bosom.

"If war comes again I shall die! I know the meaning of war. I was in Strasbourg when it happened. My husband was in a Württemberg regiment. His letters told me all about the horrors. And now he's anxious and says it may happen again. No one wants war, I'm certain of that. Germany suffered too much to want another war. But it may happen. Wars happen without people wanting them. That's why I'm getting worried. I hope it won't come!"

"One must go on hoping."

She agreed.

"It's only hope that keeps one alive."

"*Ach Gott! Ohne Hoffnung kann man nicht leben!*"

I saw that for a moment tears had come into her eyes. She blinked them away and spoke a few words which touched me.

"I do not complain for myself. I am only afraid for the young people who don't understand. And it is no use talking unless one tells the truth."

I knew that she was telling me the truth, as far as she could see it in her brave simple soul. I am sure the things she told me —these hopes and these fears—were in the minds of many millions of German women of her class and age.

"*Glückliche Reise!*" she said when I told her that I was leaving Stuttgart.

I wished her luck.

17

I wandered about the streets of Stuttgart and fell into conversation with shopkeepers and others, who were willing to talk in return for my purchase of a guidebook, or a piece of soap, or a packet of chocolate. There was one man who talked to me for quite a long time and answered any questions I liked to ask him. He was a middle-aged man, thoughtful-looking, who lived inside a small newspaper shop. All the time we talked, his customers came up for the latest editions or illustrated magazines.

"What is this danger which the German people fear?" I asked him.

He looked startled for a moment and said: "What danger?"

I quoted the words on the pedestal of one of those aërial torpedoes which stood very prominently in the main square of Stuttgart.

> *One People,*
> *One Danger,*
> *One Defence.*

He understood the meaning of my question.

"That is a slogan from a speech by General Goering," he answered. "There is a danger, after all!"

"In what way?" I asked. "I don't see any danger threatening Germany at the present time."

He stared into my eyes.

"It is drawing near," he said. "At least there is a chance of it. If Russia is attacked by Japan, and France goes to the aid of Russia, Germany may be involved. Germany may become a corridor through which France would march. We are afraid that France would attack us in that event. Such accidents may happen!"

It was the same theory I had heard in the Brown House at Munich. It was the same idea expressed by the *Oberfeldmeister* in charge of the labour camps. I had heard it from other Germans. It was obviously part of German propaganda which had sunk into many minds.

"It's fantastic!" I told him. "There's no sanity in such ideas."

He served one of his customers with an evening paper, and then resumed his talk with me. My last remark had surprised

"Heil Hitler"
Stuttgart 2ⁿᵈ June 34

"HEIL HITLER," STUTTGART

him. He admitted that he did not believe such a thing would happen, although it was not beyond the bounds of possibility.

"Perhaps we are too much afraid," he said. "Everybody is afraid! That is the curse of Europe—this fear upon us. It is fostered by newspapers and politicians. Germany, among all nations, does not want to attack anyone. That is beyond all argument. And it seems to me incredible that French people— peasants and shopkeepers—should believe that Germany wants to fight France. That is a mad idea. You have only to talk to these young Nazis. They don't want war."

Two more customers arrived. They were Americans and wanted the New York *Times*. They didn't get it.

"Hell!" said the American, lapsing into his own language after speaking quite good German.

The man in the newspaper shop watched them depart.

"You foreigners," he said, "think that all this youthful marching about means war. But that is not in the German spirit. It is for the sake of national discipline and self-defence. Every country must have strength to defend itself. England thinks so, unless I am mistaken. It's necessary for national confidence. I say so, although I knew the last war and am not entirely favourable to the present state of things in Germany. I'm too old to share the enthusiasm and confidence of youth."

"What about business?" I asked. He was one of those men whom it was worth while questioning. He had honest eyes; he spoke the mind not only of himself but of his class—the middle class and middle age of the German people.

"Things are serious," he answered. "The economic state of the country is bad. We have very small gold reserves. Our cover for note issue is dwindling. Soon we shall have no more. Then I don't know what will happen. It will not be pleasant, whatever happens."

"Do you think it will be the end of the Nazi dream?" I asked. "Has Hitler failed?"

It was perhaps an unfair question to ask of a man standing outside his shop door in a street of Stuttgart. At least it was a dangerous question.

He answered without hesitation or fear.

"The Hitler régime is better than what happened before. One can at least say that of it. Nothing could be worse. That is why young Germany rallied up to Hitler and his campaign. He gave them a promise of hope and work. They had been demoralised by despair—as we all were. He made them great promises. He pledged himself to relieve unemployment. And he called upon their courage to rise again. Those were good words in young ears. What boy could resist them? And, after all, he has done something for the unemployed. There are four million less in Germany."

Another customer appeared—a young girl wanting a fashion paper, which he was able to provide.

"Of course," he said, "these young Nazis are inexperienced. They make mistakes. They will make many more. But they're keen, and the old men did not do well. You may do better. There is always that hope. It is a great adventure. We can only wait and see what will happen."

There were other people to serve, and I lingered to have a last word with this man, so intelligent, so friendly to the younger crowd. He turned to me with emotion in his eyes.

"If only we could be happy! Germany has suffered such agonies—more than any other nation—for twenty years. Haven't we suffered enough?"

Germany has suffered enough. That is true. But I could not comfort this man with the hope that Germany's sufferings were at an end. I was rather afraid that they would have many new agonies to go through, because of their financial state, and something wrong with their leadership, and something dark in the mentality of men who had the destiny of the nation in their hands. But I had no premonition of what would happen on the Thirtieth of June, not far away.

The manager of the hotel where we stayed had something to say about the international situation. He was contemptuous of French fears.

"Does France really think we are preparing to attack?" he asked. "That is ridiculous. How are we going to attack anyone? With what weapon? This table knife? The next war will be in the air. France could bomb us to death. That is why we are preparing for defence. That is why we have built a gas-proof shelter for two thousand people underneath the railway station."

Groups of young athletes came through Stuttgart singing old marching songs. There were lorry-loads of boys belonging to the Hitler Jugend, shouting and cheering as they passed. Nazi officers paced by, receiving salutes from the Storm Troopers, who were getting ready for a big parade. Here, in Stuttgart, one realised that Nazi youth was in the ascendant, very busy, very confident, very loyal in their hero worship of Hitler and his appointed lieutenants.

It was three weeks before the Thirtieth of June.

18

We departed from Stuttgart and went again into the heart of rural Germany, in the state of Baden. At Vailingen there was an immense old castle dominating the village. We passed through Boblingen, Jillingen, Muhlbacher and Pforzheim. It was a Sunday morning. In all the villages there were groups of athletes assembled outside the churches. At Durlach there was a parade of Nazi girls, in brown shirts like their brothers. Flags were flying, drums beating, young feet marching—until we entered Karlsruhe, where there was no vitality at all, but a very somnolent atmosphere.

Someone has told me that Mark Twain wrote some good stuff about the sleepiness of Karlsruhe. The dogs, he said, were too tired to yawn.

After we had wandered round a little in this residential town, with a pink palace built by one of its princes in the most atrocious style, and with fat statues of fat dukes in the open places, and with a kind of pyramid, in which one of them was buried, blocking the main street, we were overcome by a lassitude which took the strength out of our limbs.

"This," said my artist friend, "is not the City of Dreadful Night, but the City of Dreadful Afternoons."

We stayed at the Germania, which we were informed was the best hotel in Karlsruhe. In the hall the head porter was snoozing, and awakened with amazement to see three English visitors who asked for rooms. He gave me a room like a drawing room in Clapham Park in the days of Thackeray. It was immense. Its furniture was Early Victorian. It had faded wall papers. It had chandeliers and tinkling ornaments. In the corridors were faded photographs of German princes and officers belonging to the Hanover regiment. In one of them was a portrait of an American with fluffy whiskers and a bowler hat. His name was written underneath. It was Poultney Bigelow, whose name I remember vaguely as a friend of the Kaiser when I was a small boy. My father knew him. There was a faint smell of plush, mahogany and horsehair sofas pervading this hotel. I saw—I am almost certain I saw—the long-forgotten antimacassar. I certainly saw what-nots and waxen flowers.

At the desk the hall porter asked us to fill up the forms stating our nationality and date of birth and other particulars.

I took the opportunity of asking him a question.

"Did Queen Victoria ever stay here?"

"Many times," he answered. "She came very often to Karlsruhe."

I knew it. I was certain of it. And Karlsruhe has remained unchanged since her visits. The Nazi spirit has stopped short at its gates, intimidated by this mausoleum. No Brown Shirt appeared in its streets. No exalted youth marched in the park past that pink palace. It was a sanctuary into which no passion came. I do not believe that Adolf Hitler is worshipped in Karlsruhe.

There was one man taking tea on the terrace who even went so far as to denounce Hitlerism and all its works, thereby putting his life into my hands even now, if I were to identify him.

"It's a form of madness," he said. "These low-class people ought to be booted out of Germany. These boys who go marching about ought to be whipped. They think they can govern a great country like this! What do they know, these boys? What experience have they had? What is the measure of their conceit which makes them believe that they can do better than their elders? Are they doing better? Certainly not! Strip all this propaganda of its romanticism and one finds a Germany steadily on the way to ruin and, in my opinion, ripening for revolution. The leaders will quarrel among themselves. The younger men will be disappointed and disillusioned when they find that the new world they were going to build is a bankrupt world, breaking into anarchy. These boys have pushed the old people out. One is nothing if one is middle-aged. We dare not complain or open our mouths. There is no liberty of speech. One is sent to prison if one expresses any idea hostile to Adolf Hitler! There will certainly be war within ten years. What else can happen when children of two are taught to march?"

I was staggered that any German should say these things. But then I remembered that I was in Karlsruhe, where dwelt the spirit of a peaceful past, and where no doubt the old traditions of monarchy were hostile to upstarts like Hitler, and to dreams of National Socialism by young men in brown shirts who pushed their elders out of their places and swaggered down the streets of other German towns—until something happened on the Thirtieth of June.

19

From Karlsruhe we drove in the direction of the Saar, through a lovely pastoral country with coloured fields like a patchwork quilt. Cloud shadows lay across the tall growing wheat. Sturdy oxen tramped along the roads, dragging timber from the pine forests which we saw beyond the fields. German peasants stooped over the old earth, not thinking, I imagine, of politics, but intent upon producing the food which Germany will need this winter. We passed a gang of road makers stripped to the waist, and at Huttenheim and other villages the slogan of the *Arbeitdienst* was hung across the streets.

To Create Work
Is a National Duty

We had a talk with one of the officers of the *Arbeitdienst* or Labour Front. It was at Germersheim, where we came to the Rhine and a bridge of boats. All traffic was stopped because of some breakdown, and the Nazi officer sat straddled across his motorcycle waiting for this repair to be done. A group of young men stood about until they could cross with farm carts and lorries.

There was a pessimist among them who said: "This will take two hours."

There was an optimist who said: "We shall get across in ten minutes."

A smart young fellow fell into conversation and said: "I knew you were English because of your collar. You fasten it in front with two little buttons and a bit of whalebone."

The Nazi officer talked about his job. He was an inspector of camps like our friend in Munich, whom he happened to know.

"There are many labour camps along the Rhine," he told us. "They are all doing well. The fact is that it's better to train young men in that sort of way than to let them get demoralised. They are very keen and don't object to the necessary amount of discipline which is not too hard. Of course, they're all volunteers, except the students, who must do six months' work before they're through with their universities."

The optimist was right. We crossed the bridge of boats after a wait of ten minutes, and I looked down on the Rhine again and thought of its age-long history and its meaning to the German folk. Their romantic memories are crowded along this river. It has been the highway of their race and civilisation. The German tribes forced their way along its banks. Their knights and princes built their castles on hills above it. The old German legends arose out of its water. A thousand battles have been fought to cross it, and I saw, with my own eyes, a foreign army on its banks. I saw, one day, an English soldier draw a chalk line in the middle of one of its bridges. It was the Hohenzollern bridge at Cologne. An English sentry stood on guard there. Millions of men had died to get as far as the Rhine, and when they were there, nothing much was gained, and the world we had known was in ruins. It was only sixteen years ago!

We travelled through old Germany. Here again were fairy-tale villages in which the brothers Grimm may have found their stories. These old timbered houses, these ancient inns—

the Young Stag, the Cool Jug, the Wheatsheaf—had watched five centuries of history pass in Bellheim and Albersweiler and Offenbach.

They were pleased to see us in Pirmassens, a straggling town on a high hill, where they make boots and shoes which find a ready market, so that there were no unemployed in their factories. I often wonder now why they were so pleased to see us in Pirmassens. We were three Englishmen and one Russian. We were not in the first flush of youth which is always attractive. We did not distribute largesse. But they made a fuss of us in the hotel.

The little maid was the first to show her friendliness. She hovered around, asking questions and answering them, laughing at the small jests of the artist, excited by the romantic appearance of the novelist, even taking a kindly interest in me. The host came up beaming, hoping that we had good appetites, and that we should enjoy his simple food.

Gaston sat at a table with some citizens of Pirmassens. One of them was an old gentleman with a face like the prophet Saul. He was an art photographer, eighty-one years old and very poor. Pirmassens was not a great place, it seems, for art photography, being more interested in boots and shoes.

"What do you think of Hitler?" asked Gaston, talking to a commercial traveller at his table, as afterwards he told us.

The commercial traveller thought a lot of Hitler.

"His ideas will prevail through Europe," he asserted.

Others at the table were not so enthusiastic. A very amusing argument ensued between Gaston and his new friends. At our table we could hear gusts of laughter and excited voices. They were not hostile to a Russian who told them he was a Frenchman. They were eager to explain things to him. He was very good-natured in listening to their explanations.

We had an ovation when we left. Our hostess came out into the street with her husband. She was a buxom woman, and good-humour danced in her eyes. She was very anxious to know whether we had been well satisfied with our meal. She hoped that we should have a fortunate journey. She shook hands with each one of us as though we were parting after a long stay in Pirmassens. The host was equally warm in his farewell. Other people gathered to watch three Englishmen and one Russian, with friendly smiles. When we drove away the little maid and her mistress were waving hands at the window. We had made a very good impression.

Strange! I could not help wondering again if three Germans would have received such kindness, such friendliness, such a warm welcome, and a warm farewell, in any English village or manufacturing town. The answer is hardly doubtful. In nine places out of ten they would have been given scant courtesy.

"These Germans are a friendly folk," said the artist. "Since we entered this country we haven't had an uncivil word, or a single black look. They seem to like us. And one can't help liking them."

We were leaving Germany. We went through more villages, skirted more forests, and then, down a long dusty road, saw a pole barring our way. On one side of the pole was a German policeman. On the other side a French soldier. There was an examination of passports, an inquiry into what money we had. The pole was lifted. We passed through. We were out of the German Reich. This Saar into which we came was beyond the dictatorship of Adolf Hitler.

We came away from Germany with mixed impressions. It was difficult to sum them up in our own minds. We had been impressed by the vitality, the enthusiasm, and the discipline of German youth. There was something splendid about it. It was dynamic. It was a thrust forward of youth in a great adventure.

I looked back for a few moments at the way we had come. There, beyond that pole, was a great nation of sixty million people, with a great record of civilisation behind them, with noble cities, glorious cathedrals, innumerable villages, whose builders and craftsmen had had a sense of beauty, in a lovely country with giant mountains, broad rivers, peaceful valleys, fertile fields. Out of their blood had come many heroes, saints, scholars, painters, poets, the makers of music whose songs are in the heart of the world. "A great people and a kindly folk," as my friend had called them. Yet there are minds among them touched by some dark strain, called back to the primitive and pagan spirit, bewitched in this modern world by age-old legends which had their roots in dark forests and tribal cults. From all I had heard and seen, they were still divided between hope and fear.

German youth hoped. They were exultant, ardent. They believed that under the leadership of Adolf Hitler they would be the builders of a new Germany with a better kind of life for all of them. They were intolerant as youth is always intolerant. They were self-confident. They were self-disciplined. They were ready for any kind of service or sacrifice for this one man—Hitler, the builder's labourer—who was their hero and ruler. Were they not ready to die for him? Had he not given youth its chance and power?

But the elder Germans, the middle-aged men, the thoughtful people, who were able to think outside the framework of the Nazi faith, were nervous and alarmed. They did not believe much in flaming youth. They shrugged their shoulders at all this mystical stuff. They were, as good Catholics or good Protestants, deeply perturbed by the call back to paganism and the challenge to Christian faith. They were shocked and mortified by the speech and writings of these new rulers, who put instinct before intelligence and proclaimed their hostility to intellectualism—a denial, surely, of all civilised progress and ideals, a hark back to barbarism. They had no faith in these new men who had seized the power of the German Reich and controlled its machine. Their ears were stunned by propaganda blared at them through loudspeakers. German Destiny! The German Folk! Hitler! . . . Hitler! . . . Hitler! Business was going bad. Exports were dwindling. The gold reserve was exhausted. What was going to happen? Some people said they would be on rations before the winter. *Ach Gott!* Again? After all their misery in the time of inflation? Was this the new world promised by young men in brown shirts?

A new war was threatened. In every town there was a drive for the German air defence. In every village stood the model of an aërial torpedo. Was the river of blood going to flow again, after they had lost their sons—two sons, three sons, five sons—less than twenty years ago? Was the promise of a new world made by Adolf Hitler to be born in blood?

Hitler was a simple man, they said. An honest man! A great leader! But there were men about him not of exalted character —to say the least. And this simple man, this honest man, had established a régime in which free speech was stifled and no man could express a word of criticism without danger of death. That youth marching, waving flags, beating drums, blowing bugles, what were they doing, after all, for Germany? "It doesn't bring bread and butter," said the market woman in Stuttgart. "People of the middle class and business folk are utterly fed up with the new régime," said my friend in Munich. "Strip all this propaganda of its romanticism," said the man in Karlsruhe, "and one finds that Germany is steadily on the way to ruin and ripening for revolution."

I looked back for a few moments along the way we had come —back to Germany—and I had a vision of all these divided opinions, this exultancy of youth, and fear of middle age; this picture of peaceful, industrious, orderly people, peasants in their fields, life in the villages, the woodcutters and the harvesters, and that other picture of a nation hard pressed by economic failure, heavily taxed by its new rulers, uneasy, alarmed, not knowing what would happen three months ahead.

"We must wait and see what is going to happen," said my bookstall friend in Stuttgart who believed in the Nazi youth but had his doubts.

It was only three weeks they had to wait for one thing that happened, on the Thirtieth of June.

It happened when Adolf Hitler and Dr. Goebbels, his chief of propaganda, flew from Berlin to Munich, and when their Black Shirts shot a number of men like mad dogs. They were men like Roehm, Ernst, Heines, who had been Hitler's closest comrades and had helped him to power. They were men who had been his subordinate leaders. Roehm, most powerful among them, was Chief of Staff of the Brown Army.

In Berlin General Goering had been at work. He had not worn mittens, he said. There had been a plot against the

Leader. The plotters were dead. General Schleicher was dead, and his wife was dead, flinging herself across the body of her husband when the Black Shirts fired at him.

General Goering summoned the foreign press representatives. He told them of the plot and the shootings. There was no pity in his voice, as there had been no mercy in his act.

No one knew exactly how many had been killed—these leaders of the National Socialists, who had been the heroes of the nation a week before, or, if ugly rumours had reached the ears of certain groups, had been defended by Hitler himself with the suppression of all criticism by the Chief of Propaganda.

No evidence was given of the plot or plots. No list of names was published. The bodies of the dead men were cremated. Dead men tell no tales. It was Hitler's word against them.

I listened to Hitler's speech in the Reichstag as it came over the wireless to a little old house in England. His voice was harsh and hysterical at times.

"I gave the order to shoot!" he screamed. "Only ruthlessness and bloody intervention could have averted revolution.

"For twenty-four hours I myself was the Supreme Court for the German people. . . ."

He gave the numbers of those who had been shot as seventy-seven. As the days passed grave doubts were cast on those figures. New names of the dead crept out. Some of them had been known as men of noble character, like Dr. Klausener, mourned by the Catholics in Germany "because of his glowing love of Church and Fatherland"; and like Adalbert Probst, leader of the Catholic Youth organisation.

The body of Dr. Klausener was refused Christian burial, like all those killed in cold blood. His friends and relatives told of the tragic hour in which they stood before a little heap of ashes, "which is all that has been left for us."

What was that plot which Hitler said had threatened revolution, and his own assassination, and the lives of tens of thousands of Germans, and a bloody terror? The rank and file were unaware of it. Was it possible, or credible, that any leaders should have dared to proclaim a revolution against Adolf Hitler, who was the nation's hero, or at least the hero of his Storm Troopers and all German youth? Unless they had been stricken by raving madness such a plot was doomed to instant failure. Was it credible or possible that men of different shades of opinion— Von Papen, the old-fashioned Nationalist—General Schleicher, a soldier of the old school—Dr. Klausener, a Catholic leader— General Roehm, the Chief of Staff of the Brown Army—should have been plotting together? Was it to be a revolution of the Right or a revolution of the Left? If so, why were men of the Right conspiring with men of the Left? Who were on the Left? That man Roehm—a soldier of fortune, a man of deep depravity, if one may believe the accusations against him, a lover of banquets and vicious pleasures? Or Heines or Ernst, his lieutenants and comrades? One cannot believe that they were fanatics of socialism and democracy.

There must have been some kind of plot at headquarters— the dissatisfaction and treachery of men who wanted to grasp more power for themselves. But there is no evidence yet—there is only Hitler's word—that they were going to order out the rank and file and storm the government buildings. It is as deep a mystery as the Reichstag fire. None of the stories, or theories, of newspaper correspondents in Berlin are able to give even a plausible account of what happened behind the scenes on that night of the Thirtieth of June. No theory can fit up its jig-saw puzzle of murder and death.

In any case, and whatever evidence may be presented later, if ever in history, there will be no alteration in the verdict of civilized minds. This killing of seventy-seven men—or many more—without giving them a chance of defence was a return to the darkest period of mediævalism. It does not come within the code of civilised peoples. Could it happen in England or in France? If it could happen, even in England and France, would it not be a proof that all the human struggle for justice, for law, and for decency has utterly broken down? Those men, however guilty, might have been arrested and tried. There was no need to shoot them like dogs in the night. There were no armed forces in the streets, no sign in all Germany of any uprising. The alleged plotters had gone quietly to bed.

The greatest mystery of all is the part played by Adolf Hitler himself—that simple man, that honest man. Why should he give orders suddenly to shoot down the men who had been his closest comrades, and about whom, only a few months before, he had spoken with emotion and gratitude in a beer house at Munich? He knew their character before he had them killed. He might have dismissed Roehm from his post. His word was law. He might have dismissed Heines and Ernst, if he disapproved of their morals. Above all, why should he disband the army of Storm Troops which he had raised, and fall back upon the Reichswehr and his private bodyguard of Black Shirts, as though he feared the youth of Germany who had sworn allegiance to him, and who had, as I know, loyalty in their hearts? That is the great mystery, not yet solved.

Cheers rose up to Hitler in the Reichstag when he made his speech accepting responsibility for these deeds. Men there may have been uneasy about their own lives if they failed to cheer. There were not cheering crowds in the streets as Hitler passed. What crowds were there stared at him silently. To foreign observers it seemed as though Adolf Hitler had smashed something which, like Humpty Dumpty, could never be put together again by all the King's horses or all the King's men. Had he not smashed a dream—the dream of German youth? Had he not smashed the illusion of the Nazi enthusiasm for the building of a new world? Had he not smashed the faith and the hero worship? Had he not broken his own spell over the mind of those young men who had been ready to die for him, or to beat Jews for him, or to starve for him, or to dig for him? They had been sent for a month's holiday, during which time they were not allowed to wear their uniform. Some of them were to be allowed back on the streets, but the Brown Shirt army was to be much reduced, and the Reichswehr was the force by which Hitler would rule.

The world outside Germany was shocked and stunned. There was no insincerity in the expressions of horror which came from French, or English, or American minds. Hitler will find it difficult to regain the respect which was given to him, as a simple man, an honest man, even by his enemies. "When," said a distinguished French writer, "he comes to any international assembly such as the League of Nations, to which he wishes to return, he will be received by a great silence, *and all eyes will stare at his hands*."

On a Sunday in August of this year the German people were asked to vote for Hitler as President of the German Reich after the death of Hindenburg. The voting was preceded by a stupendous orgy of propaganda in every city and hamlet of Germany, urging the people to say *Ja* in favour of Adolf Hitler. Four millions said *Nein*, and that is a minority not without significance considering the courage needed to register an adverse vote. But a vast majority voted *Ja*, and Hitler became President and supreme chief of the German Folk by that answer of the nation. Those middle-aged Germans, doubtful of Nazi rule, apprehensive of the future, did not dare to express their fears by voting against the Leader. After all, what was the alternative, except anarchy and civil war and new horrors? The young Nazis, whose enthusiasm may have been checked and bewildered by the events of the last day in June, reaffirmed their faith in Hitler after the appeals made to them through every loudspeaker and by every leader, including the son of Hindenburg. And there is something in German mentality, something in this loyalty to Hitler, which is not to be understood by other peoples. The German mind works differently. It is not subject to the same impulses and instincts. A German lady, whose brother I know, and who is, I am told, charming, artistic, and intellectual, wrote to a friend in America after the black business in June. "Hitler has killed his friends for the sake of Germany," she wrote. "Isn't he wonderful?" It seems that the German people in the mass have even greater faith in Hitler because of his ruthlessness in destroying men— once his comrades—whom he accused of treachery to his own authority.

There are mysteries in the German mind we cannot fathom or understand. It is because of those mysteries that other peoples are uneasy and afraid.

IX

The Saar before the Plebiscite

WE CAME INTO THE SAARGEBIET three weeks before Hitler had "reorganised" the leadership of the Storm Troops, and six months before the date fixed for the plebiscite by which the inhabitants of the Saar would be called upon to vote for the form of government they desired. They could vote for union with France or union with Germany or for their own autonomous state.

On the very day we arrived the High Commissioner, Mr. Knox, who was responsible for good order in the Saar, according to the dictates of the Treaty of Versailles, was in Geneva stating his case for a strengthening of the police forces by men recruited from foreign sources. There had been a great deal of unrest and many violent incidents since the triumph of the Nazis in Germany. Many of the younger men, and perhaps even the majority of the inhabitants, were in sympathy with Adolf Hitler and had formed secret organisations in the Saar for propaganda purposes. Any individuals who expressed their dislike of *Der Führer* and his methods were apt to get a beating, or worse than that, from the Nazis in their midst. Their names were entered on black lists for future treatment, should the Saar go back to Germany, as certainly it would, in the opinion of most of its inhabitants, after the plebiscite fixed for January of 1935. Mr. Knox was worried by this state of affairs, which was getting out of hand.

Two things took me by surprise when I motored to Saar-brücken from the German frontier. The first was the extent of the Saargebiet, and the second was the overwhelming exhibition of Nazi flags in the towns and villages. Regarding the second point, it came to me as a surprise that under the rules of the international régime the Swastika flag should be allowed at all.

I had been to Saarbrücken once before. It was shortly after the establishment of international rule under French domination. But in a railway train one does not see much of the countryside, and on this motor journey I was startled by the aspect and area of the country which had been taken away from Germany.

I had always thought of the Saar as being a small district, entirely given over to coal mining. It was partly because of its rich mines that old Clemenceau had demanded its possession on behalf of France, as a recompense for the destruction of the mines in northern France during the war—though he had other motives of a political and geographical kind.

But we found ourselves travelling through pastoral and wooded country, with considerable hills on the horizon. Many watercourses, including those of the Blies, the Nied, and the Prims, cut their way through the mountains. Magnificent fir and beech forests clothed the slopes, and through their clearings we had a view of valleys crowded with villages and farmsteads, very German in their character. I thought of the coal-mining country in England, which creates a black devastation in and round its area, and where the towns are dreadful in their squalid ugliness. Here, around one of the most important coal areas of Europe, nature still remained undefiled. Beauty had not been blasted off the earth, and in the fields which spread a patchwork quilt across the countryside there was an industrious peasantry at work. Even the cows were clean.

The area of the Saargebiet is about the size of Greater London. Its population is something like 830,000 people, most of whom, barring a very small minority, are of German stock. They have their own dialect, I am told, but we heard nothing but German in the villages and in the city of Saarbrücken itself. To say the least of it, old Clemenceau's reckoning of one hun-

Saarbrücken
4th June 1934

?

1935

SAARBRÜCKEN, 1935—?

dred and fifty thousand French inhabitants of the Saar was an
inaccuracy. The truth would have given him, perhaps, a tenth
of that number—but then, statesmen and diplomats are not
good at arithmetic, especially when they are sitting at a table
trying to grab other people's territory.

President Wilson, who sat at the same table, had spoken fine
things about the self-determination of peoples, and not handing
them about like chattels for the spoils of war, but he had weakened under "the Tiger's" persistent claims, and seemed to be
convinced that there was some justice in the argument about
compensation in the Saar for French losses in the coal-mining
areas of Picardy. It was not known then that the mines of the
Lens coal fields would be quickly reconstructed on the most
modern methods, and that France would use the coal of the
Saar, not for her own industries but—more than fifty per cent
—for selling coal in other people's markets.

However, these little calculations are not easy to make round
a table where the whole map of Europe was being altered by the
victors in a great war. France obtained control of the Saar
mines for fifteen years. After that period—as President Wilson
insisted—the people would have their plebiscite to decide their
future destiny. Meanwhile an international commission would
look after them.

The High Commissioner had comfortable quarters, as I
found when I presented my card. In fact, he had taken possession, for dignity's sake, and perhaps a little comfort also, of the
fine Schloss on the hill above the city. Other big buildings were
commandeered as government offices.

In our first tour of the town we were astonished, as I have
said, by the prodigal display of Nazi flags. Almost every shop
was flying the scarlet banner with the Swastika in a white circle.
It was afterwards explained to me that this flag, after the advent of Hitler, had been regarded as the national colours, which
are permitted to be flown in the Saargebiet.

Other things astonished us, after a brief acquaintance with
life in the Saar. Everything was bought and sold in French currency. That monetary system had been established in the time
of German inflation, when the value of the mark withered

away to nothing. The miners had asked to be paid in francs. Afterwards the franc became the unit of exchange. But the franc in France does not go as far as the franc in the Saar. That district is, I believe, the most favoured spot in Europe for making a little money go a long way. There are few taxes. The inhabitants are immune from French and German taxation, and their own is light. There are no customs for foreign goods. I found that I could buy Virginia cigarettes cheaper in the Saar than in the King's Road, Chelsea.

At a first glimpse—and a last glimpse—the people looked prosperous and cheerful. There was no sign of oppression by foreign powers. Not a single French flag flew in the Saar. No French troops were visible. The police belonged to the Saar itself and were Germans.

2

On our first evening we went to the smartest café in Saarbrücken, as a good vantage point for studying life in this city. It was quite a gay place, more animated than the cafés or cabarets of Lyons, which we had found so empty, or those of Munich, which we had found so dull. The Saar, in which every German heart is supposed to be bleeding because of its exile from the Fatherland, and from the tender care of Adolf Hitler, was putting a brave face on this inward suffering, at least in the Café Keffer.

They had a big orchestra of young Italian women, who played well and looked nice. The girl who played the "traps" had a comical way with her and seemed to get a lot of private fun out of banging the big drum, crashing the cymbals, and rattling the triangle. The girl who played the first violin carried on a conversation with her eyes across the bow. These alluring young women were much appreciated by the youth of Saarbrücken, some of whom were very smart. I noticed three people who sat at the next table to us. One of them was a tall girl with very dark hair and an aristocratic type of face. She wore a white coat, cut like a fencing doublet, and a white frock excellently shaped. Many of the other visitors to the café were not typical of a mining city, as one knows mining cities in England and

Wales. They were distinctly well-to-do. There seems to be a Smart Set in Saarbrücken.

In the city, as in the countryside, all these people were German. There was no getting away from that. They spoke German, their names were German, their look was German. And I must say they looked remarkably free from the cares and anxieties which I had found in many minds across the line, where German people live under the dictatorship of a man who is ruthless in his killing when killing seems good. Unfortunately, however, the deeper one inquires into the appearance of human cheerfulness, the more one finds that there is, as the Americans say, "a nigger in the woodpile." There are many niggers in the woodpile of the Saar. I heard all about them from a French official who has been in this district for a long time and knows everything which goes on below the surface.

"It's a delicate situation," he told me. "This place is seething with political passion. You mustn't be deceived by the show of Swastika flags. Lots of those have been hung up under compulsion. Every day there are cases of private vengeance and bullying by Nazi groups. There have been many ugly incidents of violence."

"But, surely," I said, "all these people want union with Germany? Why should there be any need of compulsion?"

My French friend explained, and anything he explains is stated in such moderate terms, with such fairness and thoughtfulness, that one is convinced of its accuracy.

"You see, ever since the war this Saargebiet has been cut off from the pressure of events in Germany. The old parties still remain, and the Nazi steam roller has not gone over them. There are still Communists, Socialists, and the Centre Party, which is, of course, Catholic. They are just as divided now in political opinion as Germany used to be before the coming of Adolf Hitler. And some of these groups are anxious about what will happen if they return to Germany. They may be put into concentration camps. Worse things than that may happen to individuals on the blacklist. The Socialist Trade Unions, for instance, have had their funds confiscated in Berlin, and that is annoying to men who have subscribed year after year and now

find this money taken away from them. You can easily understand that, in a tough population like this—a lot of miners
among them—politics are likely to lead to fights and scuffles.
The High Commissioner hasn't enough force to prevent that
kind of thing very easily. During the plebiscite which has just
been fixed for next January, there may be grave trouble."

"What about the police?" I asked.

My French friend was not strong in his belief of police im-
partiality.

"Eighty per cent of them are Nazis," he answered. "And
anyhow, there are not enough of them to maintain order if there
is real trouble. That's the whole point. The High Commissioner
asked the League of Nations to increase the police by recruiting
from other countries, but that has been turned down. They
only agree to consider a strengthening of the force from within."

Those were the niggers in the woodpile, hidden beneath the
outward peace and prosperous appearance of life in the Saar.

I had conversations with some of the inhabitants. There was
a friendly young man in a bookshop, who put his customers on
one side to give me his views.

"We are all glad the date of the plebiscite is fixed," he told
me. "We haven't much longer to wait for liberation from this
intolerable and humiliating position—cut off from the German
Reich, and living in a kind of No Man's Land."

"Has it been very intolerable?"

"To the spirit," he answered. "To any German mind."

"Is there any doubt regarding the plebiscite?" I asked.

He laughed.

"None whatever! Ninety per cent of the Saar will vote for
reunion with Germany. Whatever their politics may be, they
are all Germans. We belong to Germany in blood and soul. We
can't be cut off from our roots. Besides, every young man here
is a Nazi and has sworn allegiance to Hitler. Look at all these
flags down the streets!"

"Yes, they look good," I said. "But perhaps some of them are
for safety's sake."

He smiled and shrugged his shoulders.

"I agree that it's safer to show them. But apart from all that they do reflect the mind of the people in the vast majority. We are loyal to the Fatherland. A man must go with his own folk, unless he's a traitor. People say we are less taxed than those in Germany. That's true. People say we have more liberty. Well, that may be true. But Germany is our mother. Do people kick their mothers to save a few shillings of pocket money? Are men base enough for that? Not in the Saar."

He was very emotional on the subject. He talked for a long time, ignoring his customers.

I talked with other people in other shops and at café tables.

One and all talked in the same strain. They had an absolute conviction that the plebiscite would show a majority of ninety per cent in favour of union with Germany. But I noticed that they stated this figure of ninety per cent with a kind of violence, or at least with a passionate emphasis, which made me suspect that they were not quite sure and were concealing hidden doubts by this reiteration. If they were so certain of that majority, where was the need of so much propaganda from Nazi Germany and of so many emissaries from Hitler's intelligence service, according to information I received?

Nevertheless, I was convinced, on the whole, that the plebiscite would show a vast majority in favour of reunion with Germany. It might not be ninety per cent. It might be only eighty-nine per cent. It seemed a waste of time to go on making inquiries on a point like that, when all the answers were identical.

But I had a different kind of answer in a small shop where I bought some cheap article and entered into conversation with the man behind the counter.

"I suppose there's no doubt about the plebiscite?" I remarked. "The Saar will go back to Germany. The majority will be— ninety per cent, won't it?"

I was startled by the sharpness of the answer.

"Why do you say that?"

"Everybody tells me so," I answered mildly.

He was a middle-aged man with a thin, haggard face and moody eyes which suddenly flared with an inward flame.

"They tell you lies!" he said harshly. "Why should we vote to go back to Germany and put our neck in chains? Why should we give up our liberty to live under the rule of cut-throats and bullies—those Nazi Storm Troopers? Germany is not civilised. Under Hitler it has gone back to barbarism. Here at least we are free from that disgusting philosophy of paganism and race madness. We are Germans, that is true. But we are not the Germans of Adolf Hitler. We did not fight in the war for that end. We fought to defend the Fatherland and its traditions of Kultur. They have been killed by young louts. If we go back to Germany, we go back to a government of bandits and murderers. We who do not agree with them will be shot like dogs. And there are many in the Saar who do not agree with them. We have our own ideas of liberty and justice. Our intelligence is not enslaved by Nazi propaganda. We are still—some of us—untouched by that madness."

He spoke with extraordinary intensity and passion, until presently some customers came into his shop. Even then he was ready to go on talking; but I was alarmed. I was alarmed for this man's sake. There, I thought to myself, is a man of courage, and there also is a man who will be a dead man before I come to the Saar again. It was not safe to talk like that in Saarbrücken.

This conversation took place before the Thirtieth of June. I could not help wondering afterwards what reaction those shootings of Hitler's subordinate leaders will have in the Saar. It will not increase the confidence of men who belong to different political views—the Socialists, the Catholic Centre party, to say nothing of the Communists, who are fairly strong, I am told, in the mines. They know now that Adolf Hitler is not so gentle in his methods as was formerly supposed. They know now that Hitler's Black Shirts have a habit of shooting those they dislike. The Catholics will think of Dr. Klausener, a devoted servant to Church and Fatherland, to whose friends and relatives there came one day a little heap of ashes. It may make a difference to the majority, which will vote for union with Germany in the plebiscite of the Saar.

X

The Dilemma of Hungary

AFTER MY VISIT TO VIENNA in the early part of the year, I went to Budapesth. It was at a time when the political situation of Hungary was difficult, owing to the events in Austria and Italy's support of Austrian independence. Ever since the war, which had mutilated Hungary in a most shameless and senseless way, putting more than two millions of her people under alien rule, the Hungarians had looked to Germany as their only and natural ally, from whose future power and friendship they might expect a revision of the Treaty of Trianon —the dominating motive of all their policy and of all their hope. Now the Nazi régime in Germany had aroused a hostility in Europe which had resulted in new combinations among the other powers, and stiffened resistance to any peaceful and agreed revision of frontiers. Italy, under Mussolini, was scheming for alliances which would counterbalance other European blocs and bring Austria into its sphere of influence. Hungary was part of this scheme. Mussolini was in favour—he had often said so—of treaty revision. He was ready to give Hungary better markets for her produce—desperately needed. The Hungarians were faced with the dilemma of choosing between Germany and Italy, for their present advantage and future hope. Was it possible to make use of Italy while still keeping in close and friendly touch with the new rulers of Germany? A very difficult game!

In the train from Vienna I had a talk on these subjects with a very distinguished-looking man. He wore a tall white cap and was dressed completely in white, being the cook in the *wagon restaurant*. He accosted me in a friendly way as I passed his kitchen.

"English?"

I nodded.

"I was in England before the war," he said. "I knew London better than Budapesth."

He still remembered the English language, remarkably well.

"How are things in Hungary?" I asked.

He thought things in Hungary were not going well. The farming folk were suffering a good deal, owing to the fall in prices and the lack of markets. The political situation didn't seem to him good.

"Hungary is surrounded by nations who play politics and kill trade. One of these days, I suppose, if they go on with this insanity, there will be a new war."

"What do the ordinary people think?" I asked him. "The newspapers say the Hungarians want a king back."

The man in the white cap laughed.

"The newspapers say a lot of stuff which isn't true. They use their imagination. It is a great gift of theirs! No doubt there are Hungarians who want a king again, but the peasants and shopkeepers are more interested in raising prices. It is the same with Treaty revision. They were passionate about it fifteen years ago. Now they are patient. They know that if revision were forced now there would be another war—and that's the last thing they want. They want peace and a decent chance of prosperity."

I talked for some time outside his kitchen. He was a thoughtful fellow, with the intelligence of the common man, which is often so much higher, I find, than that of his leaders, because it is unprejudiced by the lust for power and personal ambition, and abstract theories and hatreds and megalomania.

"You will be late for dinner," he reminded me presently.

I was glad to see Budapesth again and to look across the Danube. There are really two cities here, linked by chain bridges, across that broad and noble river, down which all history has flowed in endless tides of human tribes coming westwards into the heart of Europe. On the right bank is Buda. On the left bank is Pesth.

That evening, after unpacking my clothes in a room of the Duna Palota which was once the Ritz, I looked across to Buda, rising steeply from gardens and terraces, with a thousand twinkling lights where the old houses are massed. The church of St. Stephen, where the crown of Hungary is kept for a king who is long in coming—there is a young man named Otto whose head it would fit—cut the sky with its thin spire; the skyline which was streaked with an orange bar below flame-tipped clouds, was fretted with the roofs of the old palaces and public buildings. Down in the Danube many lights were reflected. The shadows of the bridges were black across it. There was a touch of magic in this scene as the sun went down across the hills.

By day, when the sun is shining, one does not lose the sense of beauty. Budapesth is marvellously placed for spectacular effect, and some of its buildings—among them the Houses of Parliament—along the river frontage give it a nobility which is unfortunately not extended to the streets behind, which are mean and commonplace.

I smoked some cigarettes in the elegant lounge of the Duna Palota and watched the social life which makes this a rendezvous of pleasure. A fat Nubian with a large smile served me with Turkish coffee. His zouave jacket and baggy red trousers were familiar to me, and by some miracle of memory he remembered my face, or pretended to.

"It is a little time since you come here," he remarked. "You had many friends."

It was twelve years or so since I had been there. At the time there was an international commission on the Danube, including a British gunboat with some very sprightly young officers who did themselves well at the Duna Palota, and danced with the loveliest ladies. The hotel lounge had been filled with a strange company. There were international sharks who had come to make business out of a defeated nation. Russian exiles who had retreated with Wrangel to Constantinople sat brooding over the past and wondering what dark adventures waited for them in the unknown future. Little adventuresses, once spies, perhaps, had found their way to Budapesth, as a place where they might begin new chapters of their strange eventful history. Hungarian officers who had been exiled during the Bolshevik régime of Béla Kun were giving dinner parties to any foreigners who would listen to the grievances of Hungary.

I had made many friends, as the Nubian reminded me. The Hungarians have a genius for hospitality and propaganda. They surround an Englishman with their most intelligent and attractive ladies for propaganda purposes, so that it is natural, as well as just, to recognise instantly the claim of such a nation to treaty revision. I met one Englishman in Budapesth who confided to me that the only meal he had ever paid for in that city, where he had spent a year, was breakfast. I had had the same generous entertainment. There was a little countess who led me about like a lamb, pouring propaganda into my ears. It was very pleasant.

2

There was no sign of poverty in the Duna Palota. A Hungarian officer of high rank and large stomach sat drinking liqueurs, and smoking cigars, and watching the ladies. One or two of them were worth watching. There was an English girl in a frock of silver thread cut low at the back. She was conscious that her beauty was admired. Beyond the lounge a band was playing—American jazz, of course—and several couples were dancing. It was a pleasant picture of *la vie de luxe*.

But a hundred yards outside the Duna Palota there was the other side of the picture in Hungarian life. I saw it next morning when I went for a stroll along the way by the Danube. A peasant woman was crossing the road. She hesitated for a moment, I noticed. Something about her—perhaps the pallor of her skin— made me look at her, just as she swayed and fell with a crash in the middle of the road.

There were people about, but no one ran to this woman's aid. On a seat near by was an elderly man who looked like an army pensioner. He turned his head to look at the prostrate woman but did not move. They seemed to be leaving this affair to me, and I went over to the woman and tried to lift her up. A young soldier came to my assistance and helped me to carry her to one of the seats in the embankment garden. Then he strode away hurriedly. The peasant girl—she was quite young—lay as though dead. I wondered what on earth I should do. I could not walk away from a dead or dying woman.

I went up to ladies who were passing and asked them if they understood German. They did, and I begged for their help.

"This woman is very ill. Can you do anything?"

They were very doubtful whether they could do anything. They had to look after their own children, they said. But one of them bent over the peasant girl, who stirred and whimpered and presently sat up, looking bewildered, and wiping the dirt off her face. After a little while she began to talk, and one of the ladies told me what she was saying.

She had walked in from the country, a long way and without food. Her husband was an agricultural labourer out of work. They were starving and could get no food for their little girl. This woman had trudged across the hills to Budapesth, hoping to find someone who would take care of the child—some home, perhaps, for hungry children.

"There are many like that," said the Hungarian lady. "There are thousands of unemployed peasants over there in the country. It is a bad time for agriculture, they say. But what can one do?"

She passed on with her friend, leaving the woman to wipe the dirt off her face, and the cold sweat which made her skin wet.

There were thousands like that beyond the hills of Buda; although it is strange that men and women should be hungry in the midst of a grain-growing country with bountiful harvests. How do things happen like that? How is it that the old system of life, by which there used to be food for those who grew it, has broken down? Does it not look like the breakdown of human intelligence and a lurch towards calamity?

I asked that question, "How does it happen?" in a house on the hills of Buda where I took lunch with a Hungarian husband and wife. It was the lady who answered first.

"It's the injustice of life. We are, of course, all mad. There is no sanity in the world. I am giving up hope in humanity."

She laughed, but there was no mirth in her eyes, which were very sad.

Her husband, who is a great scholar, answered in a matter-of-fact way, without irony—though he is ironical—and without despair—though he, too, has very little faith in the intelligence of those who rule the world.

"Hungary has been going through a bad time. It is due a good deal to the world depression which has brought down the prices of agriculture. Our trade has been strangled by political hatreds, and all the customs barriers between the Danubian states. The sufferings of the peasants have been increased by an old-fashioned land system. There are three million agricultural labourers without any land of their own. Many of them—poor wretches!—have been turned off the farms because of the poverty of the landowners who can't get a price for their products. There is no dole for them. They depend for life on local charity, which is not sufficient, owing to bad times. The government has tried to do something about it. Some time ago they passed measures of land reform which made about ten per cent of the soil available for small holdings, but it hasn't been a great success. The small holders—ex-officers and others—who bought their farms ten years ago, are now mostly ruined. It's a tragic story, but things are getting better now. Hungary is finding new markets. Italy has been taking more grain. I think we have got beyond the worst times."

We sat over coffee, talking of the international situation. This Hungarian scholar had been very ill. He had been nursed back to life by this lady with the sad eyes which flashed now and then with passion. Both of them had been through a bad time, and, as Hungarians, had a sense of bitterness because of the mutilation and spiritual agony of their nation.

"Liberty," said my host presently, "is no longer in fashion! Youth has gone Fascist in the greater part of Europe. Intolerance is the order of the day. Dictatorship is the only way of rule."

"How long will that last?" I asked.

My friend raised his thin hands.

"Who knows? There is only one answer to dictatorship. That is revolution, and that is never pleasant. There will be a frightful uprising one day—peasant revolts—barricades in great cities —a new reign of terror. But it won't happen yet."

My hostess was restless. She went to the window several times and then moved about the room. Suddenly she turned to me and spoke with anguish.

"We are all drifting towards war again! I dare not think of it—after all we have suffered. I try to prevent myself from thinking by reading all day long."

"She devours English novels!" said her husband, looking towards her with a smile.

When I took my leave it was this lady who led me down to the garden gate and held my hand very tightly for a moment when I said good-bye.

"Life is terrible!" she said, in a low voice. "Everybody is talking of another war—twenty years after that last one which ruined us all. It's as though we were all doomed by some frightful destiny. What is the meaning of it all—this life?"

I could not find any comfortable answer.

She told me of her own private griefs, and I could only say: "I'm sorry!"—which are poor words.

Abruptly she dismissed her sorrows and spoke as though all were well in the world.

"You go straight down this path to the chain bridge. It's a lovely view, isn't it? And lovely weather for the time of year!"

I went down the steep path. It was, as she said, a lovely view across the Danube. But a shadow came between me and the sunlight on this hill beyond Buda. So many people were talking about a new war. I had heard such talk lately in railway trains, in restaurants, at café tables, in Paris, Berlin, Vienna, London. The fear was in many minds all over Europe. It was in my own mind, though I refused to believe it.

"Oh, God!" I cried on the hills beyond Buda.

3

I sat one day in the drawing room of another Hungarian friend, whose pretty wife poured out tea for me. We had been talking, just chit-chat for a time. I watched the faces of these two people. It is difficult to tell the Hungarian type, I thought. This lady might have been a Parisian. This man—a writer— might have been Spanish. They had both been very helpful to me, but suddenly, when the conversation turned on politics, the husband looked at me with angry eyes, as though I were responsible for unpleasant things.

"It's all the fault of England and France!" he said. "They cut us to pieces by their infamous Peace Treaties. Now Austria is being made the cat's-paw of Italy. It's the puppet of the great powers—all pulling against each other, all intriguing, and play-ing a game of poker with the lives of the peoples at stake. Hungary is involved. Hungary is one of the pieces on the board."

"Don't get so excited!" said his wife. "Let me give you some more tea."

The Hungarian laughed, and the anger went out of his eyes, but he went on speaking with bitterness.

"Mussolini is utterly cynical. Do you think he cares anything about the happiness of Austria or the prosperity of Hungary? Not a little bit! He is quite unscrupulous. He was once a Social Democrat, and only swung to the Right when he was dismissed from the editorship of *Avanti*. But it was he who pulled the strings for the attack on the Social Democrats in Vienna. What hope is there for Europe when such things are done and when such men are directing its destiny? I feel afraid sometimes. I feel that something terrible is going to happen to civilisation."

In that charmingly furnished apartment—it might have been a flat in Knightsbridge—there was a sudden silence be-tween us. The finger of fear had touched us again.

My host—that Spanish-looking man—broke the silence by an uneasy laugh.

"Perhaps I exaggerate! I've been working too hard. Some-times one gets apprehensive."

The lady shifted the conversation to a less sinister subject.

"Foreign newspapers write too much about the return of the Habsburgs. They forget, or don't know, that Horthy and Gombös, who rule Hungary, are not in favour of monarchy. We are ruled by Protestants, although sixty per cent of the people are Catholics. It's more likely that Dollfuss is in favour of a king in Austria. He is a Catholic. He has a kind of mysticism."

"All that is unimportant!" said her husband with a touch of impatience.

It seemed to me interesting. The return of the Habsburgs to Hungary and Austria would not be a minor episode in history. And I was told by other people, contradicting the white-capped cook, that the majority of the peasants and the old aristocracy still hunger for a king of their own. In Budapesth I talked with people who believe that this part of their hopes may not be far away, though not immediate in fulfilment. But the Hungarian mind is difficult to interpret on this subject. Many Hungarians are hostile, as far as I could make out, to the return of Otto as Emperor of Austria. They remember that Francis Joseph ruled Hungary from Vienna and came rarely to Budapesth. But if the young Otto would be King of Hungary, elected by the people according to ancient tradition, they would swear allegiance to him. Hungary never confiscated the royal estates. The boy Otto was educated by Hungarians. The Crown of St. Stephen is waiting for him, unless the Great Powers would declare war if he came. They won't risk that, knowing their helplessness, unless something "slips" in the present structure of Europe. My friend the cook in the *wagon restaurant* was right, I think, when he said that the peasants would prefer a rise in agricultural prices.

Hungary does not want union with Austria at the present time.

"Two beggars don't make one rich man," said one of my friends in Hungary, and the phrase has stuck in my mind.

In Budapesth I found a prevailing belief that Austria is bound to go Nazi—though that was before the Thirtieth of June, when the killing of Nazi leaders shocked many of Hitler's most ardent sympathisers, and before the Nazi rising in Austria on July 25th, which ended in utter failure. They were convinced that German influence would be strong in the long run, in spite of Italian support and money. That pull of race and markets is, they said, strong in the instincts of the country people outside Vienna. Sooner or later the *Anschluss* with Germany is, they thought, inevitable. Some of the Hungarians don't like the idea of that. It is not too much to say that some of them—perhaps the most intelligent—are afraid of it. They are afraid that a united German race, reaching to the frontier of Hungary, might overflow into Hungary itself, where there are blocks of German folk on the other side of the Danube only a few miles from Budapesth.

Hungary is anxious. It is watching with nervous eyes the game which is being played by the great powers with Austria as king's pawn on the chessboard. There are possibilities of grave danger in that duel of wits, with Mussolini looking over the shoulder of Dollfuss. "What about Czecho-Slovakia?" ask my Hungarian friends. That new conglomerate nation, steered by the nimble mind of Dr. Beneš, has enormous numbers of Hungarian folk within its frontiers—and it is not comradely. It is scared of Germany, and is working overtime, they say, in the munition factories. Its long-range guns could fling shells into Budapesth. For a long time it has refused to extend any reciprocity to Hungarian products, unless all claims to treaty revision are withdrawn; and the government of Hungary refuses utterly to yield that condition.

I had a long interview with one of the members of the government, the man most responsible, under the Regent Horthy and the Prime Minister Gombös, for Hungarian diplomacy. His charming courtesy and suave smiling face were of pre-war heritage. His silver hair seemed to belong to the portrait of a diplomat of the old school.

"Our trade treaty with Czecho-Slovakia was repealed in 1928," he told me. "We had to seek new markets in Germany and Austria at a time when the price of wheat, upon which our population lives, had dropped from twenty pengoes to eight. We have been through hard times. It has been terrible for the farming folk. Fortunately we have found new markets. Italy is taking Hungarian grain. Germany is buying from us. We have new hope in the economic field."

He spoke with candour about the necessity of retaining German friendship while accepting the overtures of Italy.

"Hungary," he said, "is faced with that dilemma. We are at the crossroads of history. We must watch events very closely. We must act very cautiously."

I wondered if this old gentleman knew the minds of his own people as well as the white-capped cook in the *wagon restaurant* on the way from Vienna. It would be good if the rulers of the world would talk more with their cooks.

4

Perhaps they have been talking with their peasants. It is one of the paradoxes of the time that Hungary is inclined to be more liberal now that the other nations are in the grip of dictatorships, or Fascist discipline, which denies liberty of opinion. Hungary still carries on with a Parliament—as old as ours—and there is even some kind of opposition, although within very mild limits. Most of the members are elected by open voting, which means that the electors have to vote—or find it advisable to vote—as their landlords or the government agents desire. But the present Prime Minister, General Gombös, has pledged himself to introduce the secret ballot before the next election, two years hence. It is a bold pledge. There are many Hungarians, I was told, who doubt whether he can take that risk.

Outwardly the dictatorship of Admiral Horthy is of a mild kind, after post-war episodes—which were not mild. The people have grown used to it, and the government has relaxed its discipline over ordinary life. People talk more freely in Budapesth than in Vienna and Berlin. In this city the restaurants and cabarets may keep open all night—personally that doesn't fill my mind with envy—and have a freedom not allowed in London.

Not that Hungary is exactly the land of liberty! There is no censorship of the press, but there is suppression of newspapers if they go beyond the limit. The social structure of the country is still undemocratic, though I hesitate to use the word "feudal" after a rebuke from a distinguished Hungarian for whose intelligence I have a high respect. There is no great Hungarian middle class, the merchants and bankers being mostly Jews and Germans. The bureaucracy has become a kind of petty nobility.

It was Count Teleki—Teleki Paul, as he is called—who objected to that word "feudal" which I attached to Hungary.

"I really don't think it is right," he said, "to describe Hungary as feudal. I quite agree that the distribution of land is not exactly democratic. But many of these big properties are not in the hands of people descended from feudal families—as far as the word 'feudal' can be used at all in Hungary, where we never had a feudal system like that of Western Europe. Many of the big estates are in the hands of the descendants of foreign families who served in the armies or supported the political interests of Austria and its rulers. Now many are in the hands of new owners, and especially of Jews, who bought them. The aristocracy in the country is eighty per cent impoverished, and it is surely not their power which keeps up the system. The banks are certainly a much greater power."

I took tea with Count Teleki one afternoon in Budapesth. He talked of the economic stagnation of the Danubian states, due to customs barriers and political jealousies. He saw no immediate possibility of treaty revision which would give back to Hungary the minorities now under alien rule. He has a kind of dream—he laughed when he talked to me about it—of a loose federation in which the present states would be broken up into smaller groups, according to race and affinity, with a certain autonomy but under a central leadership. Who would be leader? A King? An Emperor? A President? Could there be any common loyalty and discipline among all these peoples of the Danube, with different interests and languages and traditions? It would be a difficult affair to arrange, he acknowledged. Yet, unless there is some kind of federation, no progress towards prosperity can really be made. Now, always, there is the danger of explosive forces—the abominable prospect of war, created by political and economic rivalries.

After our conversation he led me to the door of his apartment in Budapesth, and his parting words ended with a laugh.

"I am not even yet ready to admit," he said, "that human nature is incurable of its stupidities!"

That seemed to me a valiant optimism. I still cling to the same faith—or at least to the same hope. For if we surrender that, there is nothing left but despair.

I had other conversations in Budapesth. I could fill many pages with them. But Hungary is too remote from the centre of the European drama to excite interest in its national problems and difficulties, though it is one of the pieces on the diplomatic chessboard. Its position between the Slav world and the Germanic world makes it a kind of buffer state. With Germany on the one side and Italy on the other, it must play for safety. Its interests are deeply involved in the Austrian problem. But I was assured of one thing. Hungary is for peace—as long as possible. It is ready to wait for the fulfilment of hopes. Its economic situation makes it ready to enter into any kind of commercial federation which would break down the hostilities of other Danubian states. There are a few Hungarian Fascists who may make trouble later on. One day her peasants will demand more land. One day, perhaps, but not yet, a king will put the crown of St. Stephen on his head. Meanwhile, Hungary watches and waits—with courteous words to Hitler on Monday, and cordial words to Mussolini on Tuesday—conscious that all Europe is seething and that her own fate is in the cauldron.

XI

The Road of Remembrance

ON OUR WAY BACK TO PARIS—Journey's End was near—we went from Saarbrücken to Metz. There was no visible frontier between the Saar and France. No guards were on the road, and no customs officers. But abruptly the character of the villages and people changed. The names over the shops were French. The tricolour floated over the *Mairies*. There were long stretches of open country without hedges. The villages looked squalid and untidy, after German neatness and their pride in old houses, freshly painted. But Metz itself is a fine city with a Gothic cathedral and many old houses and walls and towers. We lingered there a little, watching the life of the town. It seemed quiet and dull. French soldiers of the garrison were playing billiards in the cafés, or sloping about the narrow streets, looking as though they had the *cafard*, which is another name for boredom.

The road to Paris led us past the old front line of two wars, still within living memory among old people of France, and the reason of their constant cry for "security." Past Moulins we came to Gravelotte, and open fields at which we stared, trying to remember things we had read in history. It was in these fields on the side of the road that the German Guards charged the French Chasseurs in 1870. The graves of French soldiers who had fallen there were scattered along the wayside. The earth was red where they had fallen, as though still stained by their blood.

Our artist remembered the names of many villages where German Uhlans had fought, and where these old cottages, still standnig, had been the billets of blond-bewhiskered soldiers of Von Moltke. Rézonville was one of them. Along its straggling street the German cavalry had tethered their horses. Mars-le-Tour was another name which awakened these memories. There had been some stiff fighting there. Frenchmen in old red trousers and képis had lain dead in the village street. There was a memorial to them on the side of the road.

And then, other memories, more recent, less than twenty years old, crowded upon us. We were following the roads behind the old front line of the last war as it was fought in France. The trees along the road were very young, we noticed. They were not more than sixteen years old. Here and there, in chalk quarries and sunken roads, we came across old gun emplacements and dugouts. Then we came into a town called Verdun, where most of the roofs were new, although, to our surprise, there were houses which must have been there before this name was another word for death, for colossal sacrifice, for human heroism tried to its uttermost, for the tears and agony of France.

Now Verdun is a rendezvous for tourists, who go to see the battlefields, though there is little to see of the horror that happened there. In front of the restaurants and cafés were notice boards:

Tour of the Front.
Visit to Forts Vaux and Douamont.
The Trench of Bayonets.
The Cemeteries of the Dead.

"Revolting!" said the artist who had been wounded in the war. "They've made a peepshow of it all."

The novelist laughed bitterly at the mockery of life.

Here at Verdun a million men had died—French and Germans. Now there was talk of another war. Now tourists came to get a thrill out of this zone of death, delighted if they could pick up a shell cap or a German bullet.

We had lunch—a bad lunch—in a restaurant prepared for a crowd of such tourists. But we were the only visitors, and the proprietor and his wife complained that their business had gone bad.

"Even the Germans don't come now," they said, with deep melancholy.

"Did they come?" I asked.

"More Germans than any others."

"God!" said the artist. "What a nerve!"

We had just been in Germany. We had liked the German folk. But now that we were back in France, the French point of view took possession of our minds again irresistibly. It was astounding that the Germans should come to Verdun in great numbers, to wander about the battlefields where so many French had died because of them.

That thought was in my mind when I stood in front of the war memorial dedicated to the French soldiers who had fallen at Verdun. The number of their dead was given—400,000. I ought to have known that number. But for a moment when I read those figures I thought they must mean casualties.

"Four hundred thousand dead," said the guardian of the memorial. "A million dead on both sides."

"You have many visitors?" I asked.

"Of all nationalities," answered the guardian. "But more Germans than other people."

Something in my expression, something perhaps that I said, caused the guardian to utter a rebuke which abashed me. He was an old soldier of the war. He had been at Verdun before he became the guardian of this memorial to his dead comrades.

"Why should they not come?" he asked. "They lost their men here as we did; their fathers—or their sons. It is their right to come. I prefer them to other tourists who come without the same reason. I have more sympathy with them. The German soldiers who fought against us in the war are now good comrades."

I was silent for a few moments. Those words were noble. I felt humiliated by the foolish thoughts that had been in my mind.

"The Germans are well received in Verdun," said the man. "They behave very correctly. The German is, after all, a human being."

"True!" I said. "True! And you are not afraid that they are preparing another war? So many French people are afraid of that."

The guardian of the war memorial stared into my eyes.

"I do not share that fear," he said. "The Germans know that another war would be the end of civilisation. They don't want it. Those who come here tell me so. All of them. And I believe it. As for France, we older men are hostile to all ideas of another war. France is for peace. Is not this memorial a lesson to us? Do we want to lose more blood? Every intelligent man in France —every woman—is dedicated to peace."

He was thoughtful for a few moments. He seemed to be thinking of the mind of France as he knew it.

"There are things happening in the minds of the young people," he said, "which I do not understand. I am not sure of some of our young men. They are behaving foolishly. They are impatient with our government. They are arming themselves for some conflict. It is this Stavisky affair which has upset everybody; and youth is impatient with the older men. They think they know best. There may be trouble in France. That is regrettable. Nevertheless, we do not wish for war."

He was anxious to talk further. He had not many visitors— none of those Germans who, he said, were well received in Verdun. He was pleased to explain his ideas to an Englishman; and I was glad to have them. This war veteran of France was a philosopher, I found, without prejudice against his former enemies, and with a belief that humanity was endowed with sufficient reason to avoid another war.

"I'm glad to hear you say these things," I told him. "I leave you with renewed hope."

We saluted each other on the steps of that memorial to four hundred thousand dead—those soldiers of France whom I had seen so often in the years of war along the roads which led to the front line. I had seen them in their trenches from Arras to Rheims. I knew their valour.

In this town of Verdun I met a Frenchman who had known our own men in that war, and still remembered them with a sense of comradeship—rare in France, as I have found.

"Your Tommies," he said, "were magnificent. But they would not take care of themselves. They treated war as a sport —and it is not a sport! I remember them at Kemmel. It was a most unpleasant place. It was very much shelled. But your soldiers would not keep their heads down. They preferred walking in the open to going along the communication trenches. They were very rash, those young men!"

He referred to the belief in France that another war was coming.

"I do not believe that!" he said. "Every *ancien combattant de guerre* in France is on the side of peace. The idea of another war fills us with horror and despair."

"And youth?" I asked. "What of the younger men?"

He raised his hands and laughed.

"They are ridiculous, those boys! I have no patience with the Jeunesses Patriotes and the young imbeciles who call themselves Royalists. But they are mostly in Paris. They do not represent French opinion. They are without importance, although they make a lot of noise and keep the police in a state of exasperation."

We drove on, still following the road behind the old line of battle, and through the villages which had been very close to the furnace fires for more than four years—Clermont, St. Menehould on the Aisne, where the "Old Contemptibles" had first arrived. It was all very peaceful, and the fields of wheat had far horizons, and the roads were straight and long, and the sky of France was heaped with fleecy clouds. French peasants were cutting their hay, but the road seemed empty of all motor traffic, and there were stretches of country which seemed uninhabited, in contrast with Germany and many children in German villages.

2

We came to Châlons-sur-Marne and stayed there on our way to Paris. There were still people in Châlons who remembered the sound of German gunfire very close to them during the first battle of the Marne and the second. There were people who remembered those war days with all their terror more vividly than what happened last year or the year before. It was almost twenty years ago since the first days of war. The children who had been hurried away in perambulators were now grown up. Some of them were the mothers of babes. Women who had given their kisses to French soldiers on their way to death, whose beauty had been fresh in those days, were now middle-aged or elderly. There were no guns passing, no cavalry riding through, no ambulances bringing back wounded, year after year. Châlons was very quiet.

It was very dull.

"Heavens alive!" cried our novelist, "this must be the dullest little town in France. How are we going to amuse ourselves? There's nothing to see and nothing to do. It's almost as bad as Karlsruhe!"

In Châlons-sur-Marne there was nothing to see and nothing to do. After dinner at the Haute Mère Dieu we inspected the cafés and went into one which seemed to be frequented by French officers of the garrison. It was the Pot d'Etain—the tin Pot.

There were only a few officers and civilians inside. Opposite the table where we sat two of the officers were middle-aged men—one an army doctor in uniform. They both looked extremely, and even painfully, bored. It was obvious that they had exhausted all conversation, even about the Stavisky affair, which had been a boon to French conversationalists. They sat quite silent, smoking and drinking vermouth or some other liquid. They had the *cafard* in Châlons-sur-Marne to the nth degree.

At another table were six or seven younger officers. One of them was strikingly handsome, with a noble face. The others were good-looking boys, with their képis hung on the pegs above their chairs. Four of them were playing bridge. Two others were watching. Another was reading *L'Illustration*.

The artist pulled out a small-sized sketchbook and did a drawing of the handsome young man, who was unaware of the honour. The novelist was deep in thought and boredom.

On our left were two civilians, both of them young men, and one of them extraordinary. He had a thin, delicate-looking face and a tiny moustache. I had an idea he looked like D'Artagnan. But it was his eyes which were extraordinary. They were, if I may say so, explosive eyes. In repose they were melancholy and deerlike. But when he spoke and became excited, as he did quite frequently, a light suddenly flamed in them and became very intense, and then seemed to burst, like a flash of lightning.

I don't know how we came to get into conversation with him and his friend, but presently we joined their table. I think my English cigarettes were helpful. I think also that the artist's smashed arm brought the subject of conversation to interesting issues.

"It was not amusing, that war!" said the young man like D'Artagnan. "I was seventy-five per cent damaged. Wounded four times, and not lightly."

I was surprised that he was old enough to have been in the war, and he laughed when I told him so.

"I am older than I look. That is strange, because I am not of a placid disposition. My mind is always working like a dynamo with foolish thoughts."

"And your tongue is always wagging with foolish words," said his friend.

D'Artagnan agreed, with a sudden burst of laughter.

"That is true! Sacred Name! That is true! But, after all, our tongues were given us for speech."

His friend was of a more stolid type, and confided to me later in the evening that he was not a Frenchman by birth. He had been born in Roumania and was now a commercial traveller in Germany and France.

"What do you travel in?" I asked.

"Porcelain and drainpipes. I find the work very interesting."

The young man like D'Artagnan accepted my offer of a drink. He chose crême de menthe, which seemed to be bad for his nerves, as I told him.

"I like its colour," he said, holding up the glass. "And it burns in one's stomach very agreeably. There are more dangerous things in life. Politics are among them."

"How are they in Paris now?" I asked. "I am told that youth in France is going Fascist."

D'Artagnan, as I call him in my mind, was astounded at that remark. He laughed incredulously.

"Youth going Fascist in France? No! No! Who told you that?"

"Many people," I said. "Friends in Paris and elsewhere."

He laughed even more derisively and spoke to the young Roumanian.

"This gentleman says he was told that youth is going Fascist in France! Is it not unbelievable that people should say such things? Is it not amazing that people should give such a false interpretation of what is happening in France?"

He turned to me again.

"No, monsieur, what you have been told is false. It is a grotesque exaggeration. It is only a little, little, little minority" —he put his hand down below the café table to show how very little that minority was—"which believes in the idiotic principles of Fascism."

"All the same," said the Roumanian, "French youth demands a change in the system."

D'Artagnan's eyes had one of their explosive moments. The flame lighted, then grew in intensity, and burst.

"Youth!" he cried. "Youth! What is this youth? What experience has it? What knowledge? What wisdom? Youth is always unreasonable, intolerant, and ignorant, and false in its reasoning. I know, because I have been young and remember the great nonsense which I used to talk."

There was a slight movement at the bridge table. The handsome young officer had been called on the telephone. He asked one of his comrades to play his hand. When he disappeared to the telephone box, the other young officers laughed. I suspected that there was a girl at the other end of the telephone.

The Frenchman like D'Artagnan was speaking about democracy. He had the greatest contempt for democracy, though he was no Fascist.

"Humanity," he said, "is incurable! The mass of people everywhere are wholly unintelligent. They take no interest in politics or in any other subject of interest. The mob wants to eat, to sleep, to earn just enough for life, and a little more if possible. They are incapable of improving their minds. Wisdom does not come to them—in the mass, I mean. There are always exceptional individuals. There is always a minority with great intelligence."

"What astonishes me," I said, "is the amount of intelligence one meets almost everywhere. I sit down to a café table in France or Germany, or anywhere else, and there are nine chances to ten that I shall have a conversation with a most intelligent and reasonable individual. And yet all this intelligence in the world today does not seem able to make itself effective. It doesn't alter the economic conditions. It doesn't give the world peace. It seems to be thwarted and overpowered."

"How do you account for that?" asked the young Frenchman.

"I can't."

D'Artagnan folded his arms. He thought intently. I could see him thinking. Little blue veins appeared on his forehead, a little pulse beat above his left cheekbone. One could almost see his brain working.

The young officer returned from the telephone and resumed his hand at cards. Three minutes later a girl and a middle-aged woman—evidently her mother—came into the café and sat opposite the card players. The girl—a pretty creature—tried to attract the attention of the handsome young officer, but he had his back to her and was intent on his game.

D'Artagnan resumed his conversation after this intensive thought.

"It's like this: The individual is reasonable, up to a point— I will agree on that—until he gets a little power as a politician. He is not independent in that power. He is appointed by a committee. He says to himself, 'I must play up that committee for my wife's sake. She wants a better social position. She wants me to earn more money. I am myself ambitious.' He loses his individuality. He loses his reason. He is the creature of a committee—the slave of a party. There is no more intelligence in him. He has surrendered his mind, and character. That, I think, is how it goes. That is the nature of our politicians."

The pretty young woman was getting impatient. She was quarrelling a little with her mother in a low voice. She left her table suddenly and went across to the handsome young officer and put her hand on his shoulder. He was playing bridge. But he was also engaged in a love affair, it seemed. He apologised to his companions and went out of the café with the girl and her mother. Those left behind shook their heads and laughed. Their handsome comrade was hopelessly entangled. Sad! sad! they seemed to say by those expressive glances at each other.

My D'Artagnan leaned across the table, with his thin face supported in the cup of his long thin hands.

"Monsieur," he said, "there are three powers in the world—they are evil."

"Tell me," I asked.

He told me solemnly.

"Gold. Woman. Cruelty."

I begged him to omit woman, but he utterly refused.

"This situation in which we find ourselves," he said after an argument on that point, "what is its cause? The answer, monsieur, is beyond doubt. Corruption! We are all steeped in corruption. The world wallows in corruption. It has demoralised every nation."

"I am inclined to agree," said the Roumanian.

D'Artagnan burst out laughing.

"This gentleman is inclined to agree! It is the first time he has agreed with anything I say. I find that enormously amusing."

He laughed for half a minute and patted the Roumanian on the shoulder. Then suddenly, with an abrupt transition, he became grave again and addressed further remarks to me.

"In France," he said, "this corruption happened after the war. The war had lasted too long. It had caused too much suffering. It has been four and a half years of darkness and death. After the war those who survived wanted to enjoy life. I do not blame them. But they were determined to enjoy life at all costs. Demoralisation took possession of them and spread. Sacred Name! One remembers! The rich contractors! One remembers them! They battened on the devastated regions. They grew rich and fat on those contracts. They had motorcars, servants, women. They flung their money about. They wanted to be happy, those rich, fat men! . . . Now all that has crashed. What have they left? Nothing! It has gone, though God knows where. Where does money go? What is the meaning of gold? What is the mystery of wealth? Business has gone bad in France and everywhere else. People cannot sell the goods they produce. They talk of Japanese competition, but it is deeper than that. Something has broken in the exchange system of the world. Something has smashed the old structure of life. I endeavour now and then to penetrate those mysteries: not, I assure you, with any success! Sometimes I laugh when I am alone. It is so absurd to waste time thinking out impenetrable mysteries!"

He laughed, then, boyishly, at his own absurdity.

"Let's have something more to drink," he suggested. "This conversation is entertaining. My friend here sits like an owl, wondering what I shall say next!"

The Roumanian nodded.

"I can't keep pace with your conversational flights," he said good-naturedly.

"There is, of course," said the Frenchman, "one enemy of mankind who must be killed before he kills us."

"Who is that enemy?" I asked.

"Monsieur, I refer to the Machine, that infernal thing invented by man's genius, and now the destroyer of human labour and human values."

"It ought to be the servant of humanity," I answered.

"But it is not! It has mastered man. It has turned him away with idle hands and no wage. It is the demon who destroys the souls of the employers. They want more money. The machine becomes more efficient. Labour, the toiling classes, the young, strong men, are thrown out of work. It is destroying human skill and handicraft! It is breaking down the old balance of life. It must be controlled and mastered, or the machine will destroy the values and rewards of life."

The two middle-aged officers who had been so silent and bored could not overhear this conversation. It might have interested them. Now they put on their képis and left the café. As one of them passed I heard his deep sigh. There was no amusement for him in Châlons-sur-Marne.

"There are no leaders of nobility," said the young French-man. "They were all killed in the war. Our politicians are cor-rupt."

He struck his hand to his forehead.

"That reminds me. There is a most remarkable article in *Gringoire* this week. It is really worth while reading. It is an article about the President of the Republic. Its irony hurts one. I laughed until I was hurt. I must fetch it for you."

He left the table to search for that weekly paper, and when he'd gone we had a few words about him with the Roumanian.

"He is a Parisian type," said the young man. "He is very explosive."

"His eyes are explosive," I remarked. "I have never seen a man's thoughts burst through his eyes like that."

"He is a very fine type," said the Roumanian. "But he was badly wounded in the war. It has made him nervy and a little bitter."

The Parisian came back with *Gringoire*. He spread it out under my nose.

"Read that!" he cried. "Read it aloud. It is vastly amus-ing."

I read it aloud, word for word. It was an article called "The Man Who Weeps." It was written with a sharp and cruel wit. At every other sentence our D'Artagnan laughed loudly.

"What irony! What wit! What cruelty! What truth!"

When I had finished reading, he became grave again.

"Could you imagine such an article being written in an English paper about your King George?" he asked.

I could not imagine such a thing.

He nodded.

"It is the misfortune of France that such an article could be written about one of her Presidents. That shows the state into which we have fallen."

He discussed the Stavisky affair and the scandals it had re-vealed.

"It is very weakening to France," he said, "and now we shall need all our strength because of something which is going to happen."

He stared into my eyes, and all his mind and body and soul seemed to be in that intensive look.

"What's that?" I asked.

"War!" he said. "There will be war before ten years have passed."

"Ten years?" asked the Roumanian, as though doubting that figure.

The Frenchman turned on him sharply.

"Monsieur, I said *before* ten years!"

The Roumanian nodded.

The Frenchman turned to me again.

"There will be a revolution in France. We are preparing for it. All the parties are moving in that direction. The politicians will arrange a diversion to unite the French people. They will arrange a war for this diversion. Then all our pacifists, our *anciens combattants de guerre*, our Jeunesses Patriotes, our Left and our Right will unite, and join up, and put on uniforms, and march. They will all be ready to fight again because, as I have said, humanity is incurable."

He breathed very heavily. The little veins stood out on his forehead again. For one moment he seemed to suffocate.

"If that war comes—when it comes—it will be a chemical war, with gas and disease as the new weapons. Those things will be dropped from the air. It will be no use having a good body or a fine physique. The body will be choked and poisoned —the bodies of young men and children and women-folk. It is not an amusing thought, that! It is not a good thought to go to bed with—and now I must go to bed."

He seemed to be a little contrite at having talked so much.

He looked at me and laughed.

"If I were to express my ideas," he said, "in the pure style of Anatole France, I should be shut up in the madhouse of Charenton. I do not always speak like this! I go for weeks without talking. I am absorbed in silence and thought. Pardon me if I have wearied you."

I assured him that none of us was wearied. He had given us much interest in Châlons-sur-Marne.

We shook hands. I held his long thin hand for a moment. It

was very hot. I shall always remember him, with his D'Artagnan look and his explosive eyes.

The Roumanian said the last word:

"What the world wants," he said, "is a new prophet!"

3

There were fields of the cloth of gold beyond Châlons, and a straight road led through Montmirail and La Haute Epine. We came to Ferté-sous-Jouarre, and something called to me. That name? This village? Yes, I remembered, and there was an aid to memory, in a long tall column above a flight of steps by the road side. I read the words:

> *To the Glory of God*
> *And the Lasting Memory of*
> *3,888*
> *British Officers and Men*
> *Whose Graves are Unknown*
> *And Who Landed in France*
> *In the Month of August,*
> *1914.*

They were officers and men of the British Expeditionary Force —the old Regulars who had been rushed out in the first days of the war, and who had fought across the Aisne against the right flank of Von Kluck's army, which reeled back when Gallieni struck with the army of Paris. I had seen their bodies in the fields beyond Meaux. They lay among piles of German bodies, who were being burned by French peasants after the German retreat. They belonged to our Royal Fusiliers, the Warwicks, the Lancashires, and Northumberlands, the Guards, the Royal Scots, the Queens, and the Buffs. They were the men who had first landed at Boulogne, and marched through French villages, where the women flung their arms about them, and the old men danced round them, and children brought them apples and flowers. They were the young men who astonished the French people by their zeal for washing and shaving. They

were the men who first sang, "It's a long, long way to Tipper-
ary." They were the men who were first to die.

At the side of the memorial was a small box containing a
book, intended, I suppose, for the names of visitors—a quaint
idea. Does one leave visiting cards on the dead? It was the
novelist who observed this book and called me over to look at
it. Its pages were scribbled over with messages, not to the dead
but to the living.

The Dictatorship of the Proletariat will end all wars.

Down with War, which only enriches the Schneiders and the Krupps.

The Soviets will avenge the War!

There was only one greeting to the dead:

Un poilu de la Grande Guerre à ses camarades, les Tommies.

"Come away!" said the artist, gravely offended by the scribblings of Communists and pacifists. "That kind of stuff is like
the dirty words boys write on lavatory walls."

We came to Meaux, where there was a market in the Grande
Place. There was no market there when I first saw the town
in the early weeks of the war. The Four Horsemen of the Apoca-
lypse had ridden this way. The Germans had passed through
before their retreat. A few French inhabitants still remained
and told stories of terror. I remember some Alsatians who had
written German words over their doors to appease the enemy.
Gute Leute. It did not make them popular with their fellow citizens. Not far from Meaux at that time was the German line.
The noise of gunfire was very close. And Paris was very close.
I remember those days as though they were yesterday: the
emotion of them, the exhaustion of them, the intense and horrible drama of them, never eclipsed by four and a half years
more of war experience. Meaux! And now here I was again,
twenty years after.

Along the road outside the town was a statue to Gallieni. It was here that he directed the attack on the right wing of Von Kluck. It was here that he stood one day when the army of Paris was transported by taxicabs, commandeered for that purpose. The old taxi drivers were proud to do this job. They helped to save Paris, and France, that day.

Paris was only twenty-nine kilometres away when the French *Etat-Major* was in the village of Claye, through which we passed. We should have been anxious in England if the enemy had been only eighteen miles away from London.

We drove along those twenty-nine kilometres until we came to the Porte de Pantin, and the outskirts of Paris, by way of the cattle market and the quarter of La Villette.

It was Journey's End. Gaston, our driver, who had steered his wheel over three thousand kilometres, across many frontiers, was gay at the sight of Paris again, and told some of the stories he had forgotten to tell us, as he worked his way through the surging traffic.

"Paris, after all, is—Paris!" he remarked. "One feels at home here. Its people are intelligent, on the whole. One has many good conversations. It is, one may say with truth, the capital of civilisation."

The Stavisky case was still going on. The government of Doumergue was threatened by a combination of the Left. Paris was still obsessed by fear of Germany, not lessened by the massacre of Nazi leaders on the Thirtieth of June. We plunged into the life of Paris again, after a journey which had revealed to us the minds of many people and peoples. We had found that fear of the future was the dominant thought in this anxious Europe of 1934.

Epilogue

I HAVE COME BACK from this European journey with the unpleasant conviction that we are approaching and not withdrawing from a "crisis" in many countries. Politically and economically there is a state of distress which is getting worse instead of better. There is a hard winter ahead in Germany, who has exhausted her reserves as well as the patience of her creditors. Her financial position is desperate, and those German people who have gone through the valley of despair and hoped that at last, under Hitler, they could see the promised land flowing with milk and honey, are now told that once more they must steel themselves to hardship and short commons. Their export trade has dwindled, and they can no longer afford to buy the imports they need for industry and household use. Dr. Schacht, that master of debt repudiation, has notified the world that his country is not in a position to repay interest on loans, or must get new loans to do so. The lenders are not likely to loosen the purse strings after past experience, and are getting anxious, like the United States, about their own ability to make both ends meet. Those people whom I met in France, Switzerland, Austria, Italy, Germany and Hungary, did not exaggerate their anxieties or their distress. It is true that the standard of living among the working classes has risen during the past twenty years, and that they are no longer willing to suffer the grinding poverty and the filthy squalor of their former

330

conditions. But that does not ease the problem. It makes it more difficult to hold their patience in these days when, for reasons they fail to understand, and for which no explanation can be given by their leaders, they find that there is no market, or no good price, for the fruits of their labour, that taxation is increasing, and that industry is slowing down or at a standstill.

France is deeply anxious because of the loss of the tourist traffic, and the difficulty of selling goods on a gold standard to countries on a paper currency. Her silks are no longer bought by her old customers. Her wines are wasted. The French peasants, like the man I met on the roadside in Burgundy, stare at their vineyards with their ripening grapes and say, "Our labour is in vain." Their industrialists in Lyons are closing down factories. In Italy there is a horrible deficit on the budget, and business men cry out that they have been bled white by taxation beyond the limit of endurance. Free trips to Rome and back do not assure the prosperity of the people, and their Leader is faced with the necessity of reducing the wages of the working class and trying to secure the allegiance of Socialists—to whose ranks he once belonged before he denounced them as traitors —in order to gain their help in a new programme of economy and common sacrifice.

This economic distress—worsening as the weeks pass—is causing bewilderment in many minds and exasperation in many others. It is partly the cause of political passion. How can any people have faith in their government or in their political system when their leaders fail to find a solution—or even to propose one—for the setting right of this mad world, in which the strength of a man's right arm, or the cunning of the human brain, seems useless because so much labour is unwanted and the products of labour are unsold? A score of times I heard those words, "The world is mad," by common folk who are the victims of this madness. Surely, they said, the politicians might do something about it. But the politicians do nothing about it, except to increase this insanity by intensifying political and economic nationalism. The people themselves do nothing about it and go on voting for the leaders of the lunatic asylum in which we are all living. I think that woman in the kiosk by the lakeside of Geneva said the truest thing I heard on this journey when she told me that everybody wanted to pull the eider-down over his own head. Each nation sets up tariffs against its neighbour's goods but wants a free market for its own. Until we share the eiderdown we shall get no warmth.

There is one hope, and one hope only, in Europe today for a recovery of order and tranquillity. It is the intelligence of the common crowd. I returned from this European journey with renewed faith in the kindliness, the humour, and the shrewdness of the ordinary folk. Those qualities of mind and character are revealed, I think, in conversations recorded in this book. Those talks are uncoloured by my own ideas or temperament. They are exactly as I jotted them down immediately after hearing them. I had not picked out unusual types of people who stood aloof from their own crowd. These people with whom I chatted in market places and cafés spoke, I am sure, the thoughts and fears working in the minds of their fellow citizens. And everywhere I went I was convinced more and more of their desire for peace with their neighbours and a decent chance of livelihood. That is all they ask of life, and it does not seem too much, and yet they believe it to be so much too much that they despair of getting it.

That is the astounding and alarming phenomenon of life in Europe as I have seen it on this journey. There is no belief in the chance of peace, although all peoples desire it. Everywhere there is a sense of doom in the minds of men and women. They believe themselves to be driven by an inescapable destiny towards a new war, the approach of which they dread. There is nothing they can do about it, they think. There is no preventive of war, as there is no cure of cancer. "It happens without people wanting it," said the market woman in Stuttgart. Because there has always been war there must be another war—the next—which will, as most men agree, complete the ruin of the last to the ultimate scrap heap of human wreckage. That is the fear which is haunting and obsessing the mind of Europe today. It is very strong in France. It is equally strong in Germany. It is in many English minds. It is, as I have told, a conviction among the very men who are building the new palace of the League of

Nations. It is the commonplace of conversation—and the only doubt about this next war which is coming is the date of it—before ten years or after ten years. Yet nobody wants it. Everybody regards it with horror.

There is no faith in treaties, pacts, leagues, or any kind of document signed by the world's statesmen. Before the ink was dry on the Pact of Locarno French generals were building new defences along their frontier. Before the pens had been laid down after signing the Kellogg Pact for the outlawing of war, millions of shoulders were shrugged at this make-believe. The Four Power Pact of which Mussolini was the author was still-born. How, then, can the peoples believe in the pacts, or the statesmen who make them, or the possibilities of peace?

That old cardinal in Rome whom I interviewed put the scepticism of the world into one sentence: "Everybody is discussing disarmament while every nation is increasing its armaments—even England now!" He thought it was unwise and very dangerous. So do most men and women, but they go on voting for an increase of national defence because of this fear in their minds, and because no nation will remain unarmed while others are arming to the teeth. Each country is trying to attain greater security in the coming conflict, so increasing the fears of its neighbours, setting their nerves on edge and lessening the chance of peace. It is the vicious circle which is whirling us towards a new calamity.

Germany is picked upon as the mad dog of Europe. In England and France there is a deep conviction, not to be shaken, that Germany is preparing a war of vengeance and aggression. That war will come undoubtedly before ten years, or after ten years, if the statesmen of nations hostile to Germany see no other way of dealing with those people than defensive alliances, heavy armaments, and a continual denial of their claims to equality. France is making love to Soviet Russia as one means of help in the coming war. Soviet Russia is allowing France to make love to her because French armies may come to her aid in a war with Japan. Italy—afraid of Germany united to Austria with a frontier on the Brenner—is supporting Austrian independence with money, increasing an intolerable burden of taxation, and with promises of armed support. The munition factories in Czecho-Slovakia are working overtime. And Germany is rearming steadily and unchecked. Any fool can see the outcome of all that. Sparks will fly into the powder magazines before ten years, or after ten years, and though Germany may be smashed again and a new Treaty of Versailles may be signed again, it will not be a consolation to the last Frenchmen who walk across the fields of dead with Paris behind them in ruin, even though Berlin may be equally destroyed and the population of German cities massacred by aërial bombardment. Anything that may give a faint hope of avoiding this horror which looms very close to us should be tried by statesmen who are not utterly insane. There is one such hope, or at least one possibility. It is possible for France to make peace with Germany. That is an absolute conviction I brought back after conversations with German people.

It will be seen from what I have written in this book that I am not blind to the dangers which lurk in German mentality. I am perfectly aware that the Germans are arming, drilling, marching, and resolved that they will no longer be kept in a state of inferiority among nations. If Germany were invaded or menaced by encirclement to such a degree that she felt herself thwarted beyond all toleration, the nation would fight with desperate resolution. Those legions of young men under intensive propaganda are ready for any kind of sacrifice for their Fatherland. Their own fervour of national self-consciousness does not need any further propaganda. It is in their hearts— this sense of duty and sacrifice even to death.

All that is vastly dangerous in the European arena. Later on, the spirit of this German youth may be called upon by its leaders for a war of aggression, or vengeance, or any other kind of war, but at the present time the rank and file in Germany are not aggressive in their mood towards France. They believe that it is they who are in danger of invasion. They think, and perhaps with some truth, that it is they who have reason for most fear, not being armed as yet to anything like the level of France, and at the mercy of a combination of powers following the lead of France, and fully armed. France is haunted by the fear of a new war. So is Germany. Every German has that fear at the back of his mind, and it is because of this fear that they wish to re-arm.

I know nothing of what is working secretly in the minds of men like Hitler and Goering. Who knows? But the average German with whom I spoke has no quarrel with France and is willing and anxious to make a lasting peace with France. "After the Saar comes back to Germany," they say, "there is nothing we want from France except friendship." I believe they are sincere when they say those words, and they in turn believe utterly in the sincerity of Hitler when he offers France peace and friendship. He has done so four times publicly and with emphasis, but never once have his words been received in France without disbelief, cold irony, or studied insult. That seems to me a mistake from the French point of view. It is indeed more than a mistake. It is a tragedy. Because if there is any chance whatever of those two people burying the hatchet and working together in assured peace, the economic as well as the political anxieties of Europe would be relieved. Disarmament down to a low level would be possible. Taxation would be eased. Prosperity could revive. Fear would be lifted from the minds of other peoples. Without that fear sanity might come back to international affairs. Hitler may have dark reservations in his mind. I know nothing of that. I am assured by people who know him well that this chance of peace with France is a fixed idea in his mind, in spite of quotations dragged out of his old book, *Mein Kampf*. But supposing he wished to lead France into a trap by this offer of peace—even then, if I were a Frenchman, I would risk it rather than accept the certainty of another war. Because Hitler has, after all, to reckon with the mood and temper of his people. He must hold their support to keep his neck safe. And the German people are, I am certain, eager to be friends with France. It sounds strange and unbelievable. There are few English and fewer French who will believe it for a moment. And yet it is true, unless I am utterly deceived. I will go further and say that any offer of friendship from France, made generously, would be received in Germany with profound emotion and enthusiasm. That is an enormous chance for European peace, still open. The chance may not last for more than a year or two, if that, because the present tension cannot hold very long. Some accident may happen to put the fat in the fire. The Saar, for instance, is stuffed with explosives.

I feel bound to put forward this view, which I hold firmly, though, as I know, it will be criticised severely and disbelieved. But I am not sanguine enough to hope that France will answer German offers of friendship with anything but frigid refusal. There is hardly a man or woman in France who would give them the slightest consideration. One knows the reason why. Every day, almost, something is said or done in Germany which outrages the sensibilities of other nations. The treatment of the Jews is a hark-back to the black days of mediæval intolerance. It is senseless and mean and cruel. Germany owes an immense debt to the genius of the Jewish race, in science, in music, in art, and in trade. Because some Jews are corrupt and evil-minded there is no excuse for this attack against their race and liberties. There are corrupt and evil-minded people, God knows, in other strains of blood, including the blondest of the Germanic stock. As my business friend in Berlin told me, in his survey of the German situation, there is a dark strain of paganism, a sinister philosophy putting instinct above reason and brutality above tolerance among those who educate and dominate German youth. I am not ignorant of all that, nor unaware of its enormous menace to civilised ideals. But it is a mistake to suppose that all Germans read the works of Professor Banse—I haven't met one who did—or believe in the *Mythus* of Herr Rosenberg, or accept the Aryan nonsense by which Herr Hitler himself is touched. The English people would not like to be judged by the hot air of some of the politicians speaking during election fever. Not every Italian accepts blindly the orations of Mussolini. In Germany there are great numbers of men and women who smile at the absurdities of the Aryan myth and who are fairly sane in a mad world and a morbid nation. Anyhow, there they are, those Germans. One cannot exterminate them. With all their faults—we have our own—the mass of them are good-natured, kindly, decent living folk, very friendly to any stranger who comes among them. Is it impossible to live on good terms with them? I think not. I think indeed that they have an almost pathetic desire to be liked. A good deal of their present hysteria is due to having been treated like a pariah race by their ex-enemies. It is strange but true that they have an admiration for French culture and character, though there is no reciprocity in that regard. Let not Germany be judged entirely by the statesmen who are now her spokesmen. France is not to be judged as a nation by her deputies, elected as they are by a free vote of the people.

If then France will not make friends with Germany—and she won't—what other hope is there of peace in Europe? There is only one other, and that is not very strong. It is the detestation of war among those who remember the last—in all countries. As I left Bolzano those words rang in my ears: "If any officer comes to me and says you are wanted for a new war I shall shoot him dead on the spot. The last war was enough. What madman will make another?" That hatred of war, and the realisation of what the next war will be like, is in the minds and hearts of millions of men in all countries. They are, as I must admit, men of middle age or over middle age. It is possible that youth, too young to remember what happened twenty years ago, has not the same dread or the same hatred of another call to arms. There are some who would welcome it as an heroic adventure better than boredom, better than unemployment, better than this present distress. But the middle-aged men are not without influence. It is they who control the trade unions and the political groups in many countries. There will be civil war in some of those countries if the statesmen call upon them to advance to the same old battlefields, whatever the reason they give. That I think is certain. And civil war is not amusing.

One is uncertain of the younger men. Many have been on the side of intolerance and brutality in coloured shirts in many countries. They are impatient of parliamentarism and prefer sticks to the ballot box. Post-war youth, in which so many of us hoped, has failed to advance with flags flying to some better kind of order and to that Brave New World which was to be so much better than the mess which the older folk had made. But among this youth, here and there, are groups of serious young men who are not afraid to prefer peace to war and know that the next war, if it comes, will destroy all the heritage of civilisation as it still remains, insecurely. They are not afraid of fighting, but they are very much afraid of being dragged into the stupidity of a war made by politicians in a blue funk, or by dictators losing their prestige, or by newspapers beating up the passion of the mob. The mob is thinking rather hard. It is not so herd-like in its stampede. The intelligence of the individual counts for something.

Not for very much. I was not speaking insincerely, or merely for conversational purposes, when I expressed my astonishment to that young Frenchman in Châlons that all the intelligence in the world today does not seem to make itself effective and seems to be thwarted and overpowered. There is tremendous power in the hands of those who sit in the council chambers and the foreign offices. A whole nation may be cowed and coerced by a gang which seizes the machine guns and the ordnance depots. More dangerous than all, the intelligence of the average man and woman is sapped, twisted, impassioned irresistibly, by the constant presentation of doctored news and false views by the national press. People cannot know what is kept from them in the news columns. That is the plight of German minds reading only a dictated press. One has to base one's views on the facts which come to one. No man can think beyond the knowledge he acquires by reading and talking. He is bound to think falsely and draw wrong conclusions if he is duped day after day by a distorted presentation of what his neighbour nations are doing and saying. That is what is happening in most countries. The press is censored, doctored, and poisoned by political control. It is the most evil force in the modern world, keeping up the tension of fear between different nationalities, poking up passion, and sowing the seeds of hatred. On my journey I was struck by the number of people who denounced journalism. It is not a good introduction to present oneself as a journalist in foreign countries. Deputies and bankers are not more unpopular.

This year of 1934 will not shine brightly in the pages of history. It has been darkened by many black episodes, and the spirit of peoples is overcast by gloomy apprehensions. Looking back on this journey I made, I am unable to see much light ahead with any promise of happiness and peace for the European peoples. The darkness is relieved only by the astonishing patience, good-nature, decent character, industry, humour, and comradeship of ordinary folk in the mass who get on with the job of life as best they can in adverse conditions, and manage, by some miracle which is the commonplace of human nature, to get a little joy, a little laughter, on their way.

All these countries envy England. They are astonished by the stability, order and tranquillity of the English people.

They wonder how it is that England goes on without a sign of political passion and without any apparent menace to its old tradition and ancient loyalties. They would like to know the secret of our present recovery from economic disaster. They wonder if it will last. And certainly, when one comes back to England from the continent of Europe, one has a sense of returning to a country free from tyranny, civil strife, and dangerous forces at the flash-point of explosion. One can talk without looking over one's shoulder lest a spy should be about. One can hear a knock at the door without starting up and wondering if a gang of young louts is coming to beat one about the head because of a difference in political ideas. One can cultivate one's garden without the fear that the lads of the village are receiving new stores of high explosives for blowing up local trains. England is, at the moment, a good country in which to live if one is lucky enough to have a job and a living wage. But we are very close to those other countries across the Channel, and it is an illusion to think that we can remain aloof from their troubles and conflicts. At the moment our statesmen are arranging secret compacts or understandings—nothing written down, of course—which will involve us deeply in any future clash of forces. "The Rhine is our frontier," said Mr. Baldwin, and by those words he promised France the lives of our young men in another Franco-German War, though the young men whose bodies will be the target for the guns have not been consulted on the point.

We are drifting, lurching and hurrying towards a new war,

of uncertain date but of certain consequence to present statesmanship. There is only one consequence of the old game of
alliances and counter alliances, and competition in armaments,
and economic warfare, and international fear: It is war. It
must be war. And we all know that the next war will be fought
largely in the air, and that there is no adequate defence of
attack from the air. There is only the chance of retaliation. We
all know that civil populations—the women and children—
will be the first victims. We all know that science has prepared
some very pretty surprises for us in the way of death machines.
It won't matter very much to elderly folk who have had their
day, but it seems a pity that the children of life and the beauty
of youth should have to look forward to such unpleasant experience with an end to love and laughter. It seems a pity also
that all the hopes of the human race, all its ideals, all its struggles
for civilisation and happiness should be thrown on to the scrap
heap of the ruins which will be made.

The murderous spirit arising from racial and political passion
in Europe today shocked the world on October 9th of this year,
1934, when King Alexander of Jugo-Slavia and M. Barthou, the
Foreign Secretary of France, with other innocent victims who
happened to be in the line of fire, were killed by an assassin at
Marseilles. This horrible tragedy was more sinister than the
deed of a madman intent upon the murder of a crowned head
with that insane hatred which has so often caused the death of
kings and presidents. It was a political act of vengeance. It was
a racial vendetta instigated by a group of Croats against the
ruler of a state in which their people are a subordinate minority
whose leader had been slain in cold blood.

Pity and horror were not the only emotions which excited
world opinion when the news of this tragedy was flashed over
the wires. Fear, unreasoning and panic-stricken, leapt into many
minds. They thought for a day or two that this deed might
touch off all the explosive material stored beneath the surface
of European peace. Had not the murder of an archduke at
Sarajevo led to the World War in 1914? That was the first reaction on minds in which there is much fear but little knowledge
of what is happening behind the scenes. Other people, more

closely in touch with international rivalries, had another anxiety. What if the murderer, or murderers, were proved to be Italian? That would put all the fat in the fire after the insults exchanged by the press and radio stations of Italy and Jugo-Slavia and a growing hostility in recent months between those two peoples. It was a lesser evil when the assassin and his accomplices seemed to be of Croat origin.

A boy king was acclaimed in Belgrade. There is a new Secretary of Foreign Affairs in France. But the remembrance of fear remains. Some tragedy like this, some madman's act, some spark lighted by accident or wickedness, may set a blaze to Europe again. That at least is the fear which haunts millions of anxious minds aware now that there is no chance of disarmament among the nations, all competing to acquire new weapons of destruction. They are afraid almost to face the headlines of next day's papers lest some new alarm should be recorded. That is not a state of mind conducive to human happiness or to peace itself, because Fear is the foster father of War, and it is in that state of mind that European peoples are now living day by day.

Are we all mad? It looks like that. Sometimes I think so, until I remember my conversations with wayside acquaintances in many countries. They seemed so sane, so wise, so friendly, these common folk who do life's drudgery and have no power over their own destiny. Can't they make their intelligence effective somehow? Can't they break through this net which imprisons them in folly? There is a solution for all these dangers and abominations. It is for the nations of Europe and the world to set up an international code of law and to enforce its decisions against any criminal group of gunmen—any nation of gangsters —by common action against these law breakers. They should have a police force strong enough to maintain order and bring the bandit nation before the courts. This common defence of the law has been adopted in every civilised community. If a man is seen stabbing another the crowd rushes to intervene without enquiring into the causes. There is a policeman round the corner who says: "What's all this about?" and takes action in the name of the law. Is it impossible to adopt such a code for the defence of civilisation? I'm afraid so. But there is no other way of avoiding this anarchy of nations, this tribal warfare between peoples who dread its coming. What wrecks the chance of intelligent coöperation of all these nations who, if released from the fear of war, might advance together to a new era of human happiness? I remember again the words of a simple woman in Geneva: "Everybody wants to pull the eiderdown over his own head."

Date Due

		PRINTED	IN U. S. A.	